Dahlia Moore

Two Steps Forward, One Step Back:
Changing Women, Changing Society

ACADEMIC
STUDIES
PRESS

Dahlia Moore

. . . .

Two Step Forward, One Steps Back: Changing Women, Changing Society

. . . .

Boston
2013

Library of Congress Cataloging-in-Publication Data:
A catalog record for this title is available from the Library of Congress.

ISBN 978-1-934843-84-0 (hardback)

ISBN 9781-168113-02-3 (paperback)

Book design by Ivan Grave

Published by Academic Studies Press in 2012, paperback edition 2013.
28 Montfern Avenue
Brighton, MA 02135, USA
press@academicstudiespress.com
www.academicstudiespress.com

Contents

Introduction

All societies change constantly. In some societies, and in certain periods, change is rapid and profound, while in others, change is slow and superficial. One of the most significant changes that can be seen in many of the Western societies relates to gender issues: freedom, equality and the status of women. The focus in this book is on Jewish Israeli society, in which the status of women has improved in recent decades, but not to the same extent as that of women in most Western societies. Many and diverse factors, as well as inhibiting forces, impede change in Israel, and yield a rather slow rate of improvement in the status of women in the political, economic, social and even familial spheres. Some of these inhibiting factors are common to other societies (such as patriarchal ideologies and traditional division of labor); others are unique to Israeli society (like the role of the military), and their impact is compared.

Organized attempts to change women's status in Israel began in the mid-1980s, with the appearance of the Women's Lobby. Almost thirty years after feminist activism started out in Israel, changes in women's status are noticeable, but women are still far from equal. Their political representation is limited both at the national level (in the Israeli parliament, the Knesset, only 18% of all Knesset members are women) and at the municipal level (only four women serve as mayors); they are economically inferior to men—they still earn less than men, are over-represented in female-typed occupations (such as teaching, nursing and secretarial work), and advance at a slower pace with fewer of them attaining high managerial positions; they have no official status in any of the religious institutions (though the law was changed and municipal religious councils can nowadays include women); women in military service are still limited in the jobs they can perform, their advancement is limited, and they still serve mostly in non-combatant positions; their standing according to family law (which is religious law in Israel) is still inferior to men's; and although they are more educated than men (and the gap will grow, because women today constitute over 60% of all the students), their representation in the high academic ranks is still much lower than that of men. In summation, wherever they look, women encounter signals that society considers them inferior to men. These pervasive explicit and implicit signs of inferiority permeate women's consciousness and affect their perceptions, attitudes and behaviors.

The struggle is, therefore, far from over, and Israel still has a long way to go before gender equality in all life domains is attained. Israeli society needs to decide where it wants the struggle to lead: does it want equality in all life domains? Do all groups in Israeli society want to increase gender equality? How does Israeli society deal with gender differences: are the differences acknowledged and legitimized, or denied, forcing women to act like men if they want to succeed in the "men's world"? And what is the price of such equality?

In many Western societies, feminist ideologies contributed significantly to the changes in the status of women, but their impact was not uniform. The changes they brought vary from one society to another, according to the existing culture in each: from laws prohibiting gender discrimination to greater economic power for women; from changes in social norms that discourage sexual harassment to a growing acceptance of sexual preferences; and from a growing equality of parenting roles to increased visibility of women in the public sphere. In Israel, too, feminist ideologies are among the forces that enhance change, but their impact varies across social groups.

The main focus of this book is, therefore, the examination of the major forces creating and maintaining the barriers that hold women back, and the means with which some changes were attained. Assuming that equality in opportunities and rewards is a desired goal in Israel, as it is in many societies, the analysis of these factors may provide some insights and viewpoints on how to enhance social change for the betterment of society in general, and the status of women in particular.

The three parts of this book reflect the decision to analyze Israeli society, and some of the forces that made the shift from a traditional to a more modern society, in three time periods. The decision to delineate the first period—the traditional period—as lasting until the first formal feminist action groups appeared in the mid-1980s (Chapters Two and Three), the second period—the modern period—as being from the mid-1980s until 2000 (Chapters Five and Six), and the recent trends as being from 2001 onward (Chapter Seven), is a matter of convenience. It was made for practical reasons, showing how most of the processes seen today have their roots in earlier periods. Chapters Four and Five describe the factors that contributed to the shift from one period to the other.

The three parts also reflect the three major dimensions of social action defined by Anthony Giddens in his Structuration Theory (described in Chapter One; some of the more specific theories will be presented in relation to specific issues). Part I (Chapters One, Two and Three) focuses on the (unacknowledged) conditions that created women's inferiority in Israel. Chapter One presents the general theoretical framework. Chapter Two shows how demographic, economic, political, and social-cultural processes acted in tandem to maintain women's inferiority until the first organized feminist groups were established in the mid-1980s. Chapter Three deals with the major dimensions of women's inferiority (such as women's traits and identities, stereotypes, gender roles and division of labor, work segregation, and role conflict).

Part II (Chapters Four and Five) deals with the multi-tiered processes of change that correspond to Giddens' action, and explains how worldwide processes of change (like the spreading of democratic and/or liberal ideologies and the opening of diverse communication channels as described inChapter Four) affected processes of change in Israeli economy, demography, political ideology and society (as discussed in Chapter Five).

The last part of the book, Part III (Chapters Six and Seven) shows how the global and local processes were influenced by worldwide feminist ideas and affected Israeli women and how the feminist gender identity affected women's consciousness, the changes in women's assessment of their potential and their aspirations, their perceptions of and attitudes toward family and work roles, and their growing willingness to stand for what they believe they deserve (Chapter Six). The last section in this part of the book describes some of the future consequences of these changes and proposes several directions that such changes may evolve into (Chapter Seven), and raises numerous questions regarding the future changes in the situations affecting the lives of women and men, examining women's networks, the spreading of diverse feminist ideas to other groups of women, and the reactions of men to these changes.

Although the book focuses mainly on Israeli society, much of the analysis it presents is relevant to other societies in which modernity is not fully realized as well. Perhaps not all the forces that hinder the spreading of feminist ideas in Israel exist in some societies, but the impact of the factors that do appear across societies will operate in similar ways. Thus, for example, Islam is very different from Judaism (and there are many versions of Islam), but the obstructing potential of religion in Muslim countries will be similar to the hindering power of Orthodox Judaism described here.

The application of the theory to the Israeli society is described throughout the book. This is but a brief and simplified presentation of the theory which focuses on the elements most relevant to the analysis of Israeli women's impact on social changes in the last decades, and examines how societal processes limited women's ability to produce such changes. For a more elaborate understanding of the theory and its complexity, the reader may wish to turn to Giddens' many books.

Chapter 1

Structuration Theory and Gender Identity

The basic domain of study of the social sciences, according to the theory of structuration, is neither the experience of the individual actor, nor the existence of any form of social totality, but social practices ordered across space and time. Human social activities, like some self-reproducing items in nature, are recursive. That is to say, they are not brought into being by social actors but continually recreated by them via the very means whereby they express themselves as actors. In and through their activities agents reproduce the conditions that make these activities possible. (Giddens, 1984, p. 2).

1. The Structuration Process

According to Anthony Giddens, "Society only has form, and that form only has effects on people, in so far as structure is produced and reproduced in what people do" (Giddens and Pierson, 1998, p. 77). The Structuration Theory proposed by Giddens (1984) in The Constitution of Society[1] examines how the social context influences individuals, and how individuals attempt to change the social context. Giddens' Structuration Theory provides a balanced framework, attempting to deal with the influences of structure and agency equally, and attempts to reconcile the theoretical dichotomy of agency/structure (which relates to the micro/macro, subjective/objective dichotomies).[2] It focuses on the existence of the individual in a way that will match the concepts of social systems, their institutions, societies and cultures. Systems are "patterns of relations in groupings of all kinds, from small, intimate groups, to social networks, to large organizations" (ibid, p. 131). In this respect, systems are the patterns of conduct, the repeated forms of social action, or the "enduring cycles of reproduced relations" (ibid, p. 131).

Giddens defines structuration as "the structuring of social relations across time and space, in virtue of the duality of structure" (1984, p. 376). According to this view, agency and structure are not two separate concepts or constructs, but are two aspects or dimensions of social action. At the core of Giddens' Structuration Theory are three basic assumptions. First, social life is not the sum of all micro-level activity, and social activity cannot be completely explained from a macro perspective. Both levels must be examined simultaneously in order to understand structuration. Second, the repetition of the acts of individual agents reproduces the structure. Third, social structures are neither indisputable nor permanent (Gauntlett, 2002; Sewell, 1992).

The theory also posits that human agency and social structure are in a spiral relationship with each other: the repetition of actions of individual agents reproduces the structure, (but the resultant structure is not exactly the same as it was because the individual's acts have affected the structure). The structure thus reproduced then influences agents' actions. The balancing of agency and structure is referred to as the duality of structure (Giddens, 1979, 1981). The duality of structure includes on the one hand the situated actors who undertake social action and interaction, and on the other the rules, resources, and social relations that are produced and reproduced in social interaction (Cohen, 1987).

2. Structures and Agents

Giddens identifies three categories of structures in social systems: Signification, which produces meaning through the use of language; Legitimation, which produces a moral order by way of societal norms, values, and standards; and Domination, which produces (and makes use of) power through the control of resources. These analytical distinctions are interrelated and they both mobilize and reinforce each other. Thus, for example, the signification of the concept "gender role conflict" derives from—and contributes to—legitimation (which is reflected in the customary division of labor), and is based on forms of domination (e.g., patriarchy). One of the consequences of this interrelatedness which is relevant to the issues discussed in this book is that the concept "gender role conflict" is usually applied to women, not to men, as women are still expected to shoulder most of the domestic burden.

For Giddens, structures are resources, rules, traditions, institutions, moral codes, and established ways of doing things, which are organized as properties of the social system but also constitute its transformation criteria. Therefore, they may also be changed when people ignore them, replace them, or reproduce them differently.

The theory assumes that all actions of social agents are constrained by structures which are produced and reproduced by that action. Consequently, individuals (who are agents of the social system) do not create systems or cultures per se but "produce or transform them, remaking what is already made in the continuity of praxis" (Giddens, 1984, p. 71).

Agents are autonomous, knowledgeable, and skillful, although never fully in control of their actions. Agents' actions are always bound by historical-situational contexts, compounded by given power structures, which are not of the agents' choosing. However, agents are never fully culturally pre-programmed and have extended information about their social world. They are capable of offering "rational" explanations for the motives of their actions (Kimmerling and Moore, 1997; Thompson, 1989; Swingewood, 1991).

The social forces that limit agents' actions become apparent in those instances where agents attempt to disregard social rules. In those instances, people react strongly—even angrily—toward others who resist conventions or breach the accepted codes of "normal" behavior (even when the definition of "normal" is according to unwritten social rules: Garfinkel, 1984). In this respect, people's expectations define the rules for 'normality' of behaviors and are, therefore, part of what structures society (Gauntlett, 2002).

Every action involving agents combines three major dimensions that appear within circular loops: unacknowledged conditions of action, which are anchored in "sets of rules and resources"; the action itself—including verbal behavior—during which agents and their counterparts in social interaction monitor and rationalize their actions and motivations; and the unintended consequences of the action, which can or cannot reproduce or change the initial conditions on the micro or macro level (Giddens, 1976, 1979).

The continuous feedback generated by this circular movement creates the process of structuration. To the degree that these flows exhibit regular and uniform patterns, the praxis is reproduced. When the feedback shifts its course and creates new pathways, it shapes new practices. Changes in forms and patterns of social action are possible either when external conditions are modified or when a large group of people rejects the socially-accepted practices (or replaces them with practices that originate from different value systems in that society). Giddens gives no deterministic priority to any particular form of production of new practices or reproduction of old conducts; and correspondingly, no universalistic needs are implicitly or explicitly assumed, either for collectivities or for agents (Cohen, 1987).

Although the theory emphasizes the integration of agency and structure, the depiction of structuration processes describes the ways in which social systems are produced and reproduced in social interaction, but does not elaborate on the contributions of social agents and the constraints they impose on the process. Most of the discussion, therefore, relates to the mechanics of production and reproduction of cultures and collectivities on various systemic levels to which Giddens has made an enormous contribution (Giddens, 1979, 1981, 1984, 1990).

3. Structuration, Modernity and Identities

Giddens' Self-Identity

Until the 1990s, the theory provided but a partial and somewhat vague insight into the meaning of social agents, but the term "agent" remained practically devoid of significant social content (Kimmerling and Moore, 1997). For Giddens, "Actors are not inherently predisposed to sustained reasoning or existential reflection on the meaning of their conduct from moment to moment in everyday life" (1984, p. 134). It seems that a "discursive consciousness" emerges from critical circumstances. In these occurrences, "actors mobilize their efforts and focus their thoughts on responses to problems which will diminish their anxiety, and ultimately bring about social change" (1984, pp. 134-5). This emphasizes the subjective consciousness as a source of meaning and action, and the importance of praxis to the explaining of social action and interaction.

The process of structuration produces self-identities that are located on different levels of a given social order, from small groups to large national or even transnational bodies (Giddens, 1994). They also produce societal boundaries allowing individual members as well as groups, in communities, whether actual or desired, existing or imaginary, to make sense of the historical and situational context.

"What to do? How to act? Who to be? These are focal questions for everyone living in circumstances of late modernity—and ones which, on some level or another, all of us answer, either discursively or through day-to-day social behavior" (Giddens, 1991, p. 70). His handling of these questions, however, provides incomplete answers and only partially resolves the theoretical lacunae. Furthermore, his answers apply mostly to post-traditional (modern) society.

According to Giddens, self-identity becomes an inescapable issue in "societies where modernity is well developed" (Giddens, 1991, p. 73). In such societies all individuals will inevitably have to make significant decisions about who to be and how to act, and consequently about all spheres of their lives from relationships, beliefs and occupations to choice of clothes and lifestyles. In more traditional societies, the social orders are much less complex, change is slower, and structuration processes provide social agents with much greater stability and more clearly defined roles. Women, for example, have distinct though limited roles in traditional societies, but in modern societies they may choose from a more varied pool of options (though not all options are equally accessible).

In post-traditional societies, self-identity becomes a continuous reflexive endeavor. Social agents create, maintain, and revise a set of narratives that are based on their idiosyncratic understanding of their biographies. In this respect, self-identity is more than a set of traits or observable characteristics: it makes sense of a person's life, and his or her actions, and provides structure to his or her past experiences and creates continuity between these experiences and future expectations. Thus, the continuity of self-identity depends upon the effort to maintain a particular narrative, integrating events as they occur into the ongoing self-narrative.

Identity and Modernity

In order to understand Giddens' claim that self-identity can only be relevant in modern or post-traditional societies, we need to delve into his discussion on modernity, post-modernity and the post-traditional.

According to Giddens, no society existing today has reached the post-modern era. Some societies have fully advanced their modern cultures and that may seem equivalent to reaching a "postmodern" era, but these are merely the more advanced cases of modernity. He agrees that some societies have developed what other theorists have labeled "postmodern" characteristics – like skepticism towards meta-narratives, heightened superficiality, and consumerism—but claims that these characteristics are not so drastic as to define a new post-modern age, and no society has really gone beyond modernity yet (Giddens and Pierson, 1999).

He also claims that the significant distinction between cultures today is between traditional and modern (post-traditional) cultures. Traditional societies are those that prescribe social and cultural practices and define normative, sanctioned, and socially acceptable guidelines which social agents follow more or less closely. Thus, the free choice of social agents is limited by traditions and customs. As the traditional way connotes well-established modi operandi, it requires no reflexivity or individual choice.

In contrast, post-traditional (modern) societies are societies in which a larger repertoire of behavioral options is available to social agents and socially legitimated. Modernity implies changes not only in the structure, and its institutions and systems, but also in the related values, norms, attitudes, and actions. Members in such societies become more reflexive as they constantly make decisions and choices concerning all aspects of their behavior in a changing world. The same reflexive state can be found in macro-level systems (both national and global) as well.

Some of the societal systems are more resistant to change, and their power structures block trends that will decrease their advantage. As a result, attempts to enforce modernization (such as India's efforts to implement its democratic constitution on a highly traditional caste system) often fail, as they deal with but a segment of the system that needs to be changed, not with its practices, norms and values. When the fundamental institutions become modern, but traditions do not change, the attempt to modernize society is likely to fail (Giddens, 1998).

However, Giddens does not address the issue of differences within societies. In most societies, not all segments of society develop (or endorse) modern patterns at the same rate, and, therefore, within each society, some social categories may have developed (or endorsed) modernity more than other groups and categories, and diverse patterns will exist concurrently. In fact, the situation of diverse levels of modernity within a specific society may be the norm rather than the exception. The diverse patterns reflect the choices people make concerning the different identities they may choose, though the selection is not unlimited.

Even in the most "modern" states (for example, United States, England, Finland, Sweden, Norway and Denmark), some groups fight against modernity (such as groups of immigrants from third world countries who fight to maintain the way of life they brought from their countries of origin, especially in matters concerning family structure and gender roles).

4. Social Identities: Why They are Chosen and

How They are Structured

In contrast to most studies of social identities, which focus on defining the relationship between the individuals and society "from the bottom up" (i.e., from the "individual" to the "societal" level),[3] Giddens claims that although reflexivity is an ongoing individual (micro-level) endeavor, it cannot be viewed outside of contextual constraints and structuration (macro-level) processes.

According to Giddens (1991), any change in the individual level should take into account changes that occurred in other, macro-level systems. Giddens' approach suggest a more comprehensive view of identities than the uni-directional approaches present, but still leaves many important questions unanswered: how do agents choose who to be and how to act? What are their choices based upon? Can several identities exist at the same time? How does the socio-cultural context influence choices?

In order to answer these questions, the theoretical framework presented here suggests a Giddensian approach that combines the "from the top down" view (i.e., from the "societal" to the "individual" level) and the "from the bottom up" approach, and indicates how macro-level (societal) processes influence micro-level (individual) processes which then reshape existing macro-level processes or create new practices.

To attain that, and to provide a more comprehensible answer to Giddens' questions concerning how to act or who to be, the theoretical framework presented here elaborates on the Structuration Theory by adding components derived from Social Identity Theory (Tajfel and Turner, 1986).

This elaboration infuses a new meaning into the notion of "agent," to the different levels of the social order, and to the relationship between agents and social orders. Unlike Giddens, the approach suggested here refers to social identities rather than self-identities in order to emphasize the macro-level processes which are internalized and become an integral part of the (micro-level) individual.

Social Identity Theory

Social Identity Theory (SIT) focuses on the impact of group (or category) membership on people's perceptions and behaviors (Kalkhoff and Barnum, 2000). It analyzes social identification and group behavior that allows for the distinction between "us" and "them" or "ingroup" and "outgroup" (Tajfel and Turner, 1986; Turner, 1984). According to this theory, people tend to classify themselves and others into diverse social categories (such as those of religion and gender) using different bases of categorizations (Kalkhoff and Barnum, 2000). The different bases are defined by the specific socio-historical context of each society.

SIT posits that the self concept has two components: individual identity, which includes idiosyncratic characteristics of the individual (based on physical attributes, abilities, traits), and social identity, which includes the major group classifications in that society (Turner, 1984). The categories defined by the classification are dependent on the specific socio-cultural context, at a given time (Huddy, 2001), and may be considered among the unintended consequences of the structuration process. Some identity components are of a "more-or-less" structure (e.g., degree of religiosity) and others are bi-polar "either-or" choices (e.g., gender).

Social behaviors may be viewed as the result of interactions between two (or more) individuals, the result being influenced by both their individual characteristics and the social groups the interacting individuals identify with (Tajfel and Turner, 1986). In some social situations (e.g., when an intense conflict exists between two groups), interactions among members of those groups will be more strongly influenced by their group membership than in other situations, so that individual members of these groups will find it difficult to deal with each other as individuals (Bar-Tal, 2000; Hogg and Abrams, 1996; Moore, 1996, 2000b; Williams and Jesse, 2001).

Identification will develop when the person sees him- or herself as psychologically tied to the group, its successes and failures, its values and its norms. Many factors were cited as leading to group identification (Ashforth and Mael, 1989). The most relevant to our case: the distinctiveness of the group's values and practices in comparison with those of other groups, which provides individuals with a sense of unique identities (Oakes, 2002); the group's prestige, which may affect the individual's self-esteem (Chatman et al., 1986; Diehl, 1990); and the visibility of the outgroup, which strengthens the awareness of the ingroup (Levin and Sidanius, 1999).

We should remember, however, that a person belongs to several groups at the same time and may identify with more than one group. The question now arises: which identity will be more salient for individuals with conflicting identities?

Reflexive Interpretations of Social Identities

"...we come to know who and what we are through interaction with others. We become objects to ourselves by attaching to ourselves symbols that emerge from our interaction with others, symbols having meanings growing out of that interaction. As any other symbols, self-symbols have action implications: They tell us (as well as others) how we can be expected to behave in our ongoing activity... Persons acting in the context of organized behavior apply names to themselves... These reflexively applied positional designations, which become part of the 'self,' create in persons expectations with respect to their own behavior" (Stryker and Serpe, 1982, pp. 202-203).

This presentation of identities brings the notion of social identity closer to Giddens' self-identity. It assumes that in order to become meaningful, a person has to internalize the "positional designations" and thus turn the societal descriptions to self-definitions. These perceptions of identities are influenced by what the individual believes others think of him or her when they observe the individual perform in various roles (Desrochers, Andreassi, and Thompson, 2002).

Several researchers (e.g., Clark, Lipset and Rempel, 1993) emphasize that social identities are organized according to the issue the person deals with or according to the central debates in his/her society (Williams and Jesse, 2001). Thus, in societies in which national rights are a source of conflict, the structuration process tends to influence people to define themselves in regional or nationalistic terms, and in societies where religion is the major basis for social strife, the process will direct people to define themselves in terms of the religious component of their social identity (Abrams and Emler, 1992; Devine, 1992). In periods of intense gender equality debates, gender identities tend to become more prominent (see Chapter Four).

Hierarchies of Identities

Suggesting a hierarchical organization of identities, Stryker and Serpe (1994) provide a mechanism that emphasizes both the multiple parts and the singular whole that identities create. They posit that identity salience is the organizing mechanism underlying the hierarchical order (salience is defined as "a readiness to act out an identity as a consequence of the identity's properties as a cognitive structure or schema": Stryker and Serpe, 1994, p. 17). According to this approach, hierarchies may be composed of diverse identity components (some of which are more salient than others), depending on the groups and categories in a given society.

In Giddensian terms, because each social agent can create his or her own identity hierarchy by combining different identity components, several hier-archies can exist concurrently in any society, and each hierarchy reflects – and can reproduce—a different social order and its values. In this respect, identity hierarchies become codes for given social orders (Moore and Kimmerling, 1995; Weinfurt and Moghadam, 2001). In this respect, a given social order influences and reflects the values, norms, standards and practices that are al-ready embedded in the diverse identities which are included in the hierarchy. For example, when gender identity is included in individuals' identity hierar-chies together with a salient "conservative" identity, its meaning is different than when the gender identity is combined with a salient "liberal" identity. The different combinations entail diverse interpretations of "femininity" and "masculinity," and reward or punish diverse ways of performing gender roles. The values associated with the diverse combinations of identities are also dif-ferent: in the current example, when gender identity is related to liberal iden-tities and ideologies, the gender identity is that of egalitarian values; but when the same identity is related to conservative identities and ideologies, it con-notes the more traditional values of gender roles (Moore, 1998).

In societies where the definitions of political, ethnic, religious and class categories overlap, the related identities tend to overlap as well and become more salient than all other identities. Moreover, in such societies, the competing social orders and their related collective identities act as constraints on the choice of identities and decrease the agents' tendency to choose an alternative identity, which is not related to the societal divisions, as the most salient identity.

These alternative "free floating" identities often persevere in the system, and the option of adopting them does exist. Rare configurations do not constitute parts of the social order, but may be the nucleus for future orders and potential structuration processes. The choice of options (always culturally bound and context-related) is associated with an additional process that Giddens addresses—that of lifestyle.

Lifestyle

Traditional societies define specific social roles for all members of society, in all domains of social life. Moreover, in such societies, most aspects of behaviors and attitudes for each of these roles are predetermined, defined by traditions and social expectations that the individuals cannot influence. The more traditional the society, the more concretely it defines the roles of all individuals in all life domains. In some of these traditional societies, even the code of dress will be dictated to individuals, and they cannot "break away" from the socially defined normative dictates. The Jewish Ultra-Orthodox groups, for example, each have a specific code of dress (the types of hats they wear, the lengths of their coats, and the colors of their socks, for example) so that they are clearly "marked" and differentiated from other groups. Similar codes can be found for traditional Muslims, the Amish, and so forth. Disobedience is often severely punished.

The most basic roles delineated for individuals are related to gender and class. The main roles allocated to women in traditional societies are wife, mother, and homemaker; the roles allocated to men are mostly in the public sphere. Similarly, members of higher social classes are the potential leaders of their society and are trained for the role from early childhood. Thus, for example, in Saudi Arabia, women's roles are limited to the domestic sphere and women's work is discouraged, while in India the occupations open to women are limited by both their gender and their caste (other occupations will be deemed inappropriate). Failure to comply entails societal sanctions— often severe ones—against the "offending" individuals and/or their families.

In post-traditional societies, social roles are not prescribed. In fact, the more modern a society is, the more freedom its members have to choose the roles that fit them best, and interpret these roles according to their preferences (within limits). These preferences are influenced by the lifestyles the individuals choose. Choice of lifestyles is considered by Giddens not as a privilege, but as a necessity for all members of a society. In fact, "The more post-traditional the settings in which an individual moves, the more lifestyle concerns the very core of self-identity, its making and remaking" (Giddens, 1991, p. 81).

The options and possibilities open to members of different groups may vary, and some groups may have a wider range of options (depending on their membership in national, ethnic, class, or gender groups, for example). The choices they make are in all life domains—from selection of jobs and workplaces to political affiliation, from style of clothing to division of the domestic-work burden. Some lifestyle decisions are major, and affect diverse aspects of the individuals' life (such as the decision to join a career-like, time-demanding occupation or job), and others are more minor in nature, and affect specific domains (choice of type and location of vacation). All lifestyle choices reflect attitudes, values, and beliefs and are related to behaviors, and to societal reactions to the choosing (behaving) individual.

Choice of a particular lifestyle is in itself an acceptance of a template containing some pre-defined parameters, but for each choice there is a wide range of behavioral alternatives and specific options. Therefore, choices do not predict specific behaviors, and within every lifestyle, diverse narratives may be found, based on individual experiences.

The specific behavioral choices that individuals make in modern societies are limited by social definitions of right and wrong, appropriate and inappropriate behaviors, by how individuals perceive these societal decrees, and by the sense of relative freedom these individuals have. Each society defines a range of legitimate choices for its members concerning what to eat, what to wear, where to work, who to socialize with, and so forth. The perceptions of these decrees are influenced by the individuals' position in society (their standpoint) and the ideologies, beliefs, and attitudes that these positions engender, and by the sense of freedom to keep or discard the socially constructed normative definitions.

One of the major lifestyles relevant to the present analysis is related to the choices people make concerning gender. People can choose gender-typical lifestyles (according to the traditional division of labor between the sexes) or gender-atypical lifestyles. For example, a man may choose to stay at home and raise his children and take a part-time job that requires less commitment to work. Similarly, a woman may decide she prefers a fast-track career and decide not to have children or to postpone having them until her career is established. These choices will become part of the forces that define their chosen lifestyle.

However, such decisions are not made by a person alone. The deciding individual must take into consideration the desires and choices of his or her partner. A woman who prefers to invest most of her time in her job but wants children as well needs to find—with her partner—a solution to the question of who takes care of the children. The time-allocation decisions, and the solutions they entail are not, therefore, "ready-made templates for a narrative of self" but a family choice of lifestyle. These choices will be largely dependent, as Giddens claims, on the individuals' acceptance of tradition, and their sense of relative freedom, both of which will be reflected in their gender identity.

The next chapter deals with the forces that blocked feminist ideologies and identities in Israel until the mid-1980s, even though they were already spreading in modern societies, and thus prevented changes in women's status.

ENDNOTES

[1] Also in Giddens, A. (1979) Central problems in Social Theory: Action, Structure and Contradiction in Social Analysis. London: Macmillan.

[2] Others who tried less systematically to meet this challenge are Bourdieu (1977), Bhaskar (1979) and Collins (1981).

[3] See for example Howard (1994), Molm (1994), Whitmeyer (1994).

Chapter 2

Historical Perspective: The Conditions that Shaped Women's Inferiority

A review of women's rights in Israel shows that some egalitarian practices—like equal rights, social policies intended for women in the Israeli welfare state, and political representation—were granted early in the nation's formation, indicating, as Bryson (1996) claims, that women there enjoyed more equality than women in Western societies. However, despite the significant gains, the situation of Israeli women shows that male domination is more ingrained and widespread throughout society than is generally believed (Weiss and Yishai, 1980; Yuval-Davis, 1987), and a detailed examination of data relating to a variety of aspects of social life indicates that gender inequality is still prevalent in Israeli society (Ajzenstadt and Gal, 2001).

Equality between gender groups existed in Israel only in myth and ideology. The main examples of the mythical equality were the Zionist Socialist Movement and the kibbutz and its egalitarian ideology. The ideal according to which the Zionist settlements provided an opportunity to reassess women's traditional roles and expand their societal participation even before Israel became an independent state proved a myth by feminist researchers (Bernstein, 1983; Izraeli, 1981; Shilo, 1996). Similarly, women believed that the egalitarian kibbutz ideology would liberate them and put an end to the patriarchal social order (Agassi, 1989). However, a close scrutiny of kibbutz history reveals male-dominated institutions that involved subordination of women's positions (Reinhartz, 1984). Women could perform the social roles of men only on men's terms, and only if they acted like men, i.e., relinquishing all that is feminine (Bowes, 1978). Feminist ideas were perceived by some as of secondary importance to attaining equality, and by others as opposing—even conflicting with –the kibbutz values (Lieblich, 2002).[1]

The reality in Israel was and still is one of inequality and discrimination, when patriarchal Jewish law and practice, the military, employment and wage differentials, tax laws, public opinion, and political participation are examined (Bryson, 1996). Until the 1980s, most Israeli women lacked awareness of their inferior status and expressed contentment with the traditional role of wife and mother. A minority embraced feminism (Brandow, 1980). This lack of awareness may result from the perceived necessity to achieve national unity in response to existential threats and pressures of war (Bryson, 1996; Klein, 1997).

This chapter examines the main forces in the diverse spheres that interacted to limit –advertently or inadvertently—the process of change in the status of women. Israel was declared an independent state by the United Nations in 1947, but gained actual statehood only in 1948, after an existential war with all its neighbors—Egypt, Jordan, Syria, and Lebanon—and other Arab countries (Iraq, Yemen, and Saudi Arabia). Because Israel has a rather short history as an independent state, it is possible to examine how changes in diverse spheres—demographic, economic, political, social, religious, and military— contributed to changes in the status of women throughout the years. Changes in the various spheres are discussed and presented here as distinct categories but, of course, are all interrelated, and it is impossible to entirely separate the influence of one sphere from that of the others (see Figure 2.1).

Figure 2.1. The Spheres and forces that hinder changes in the status of women

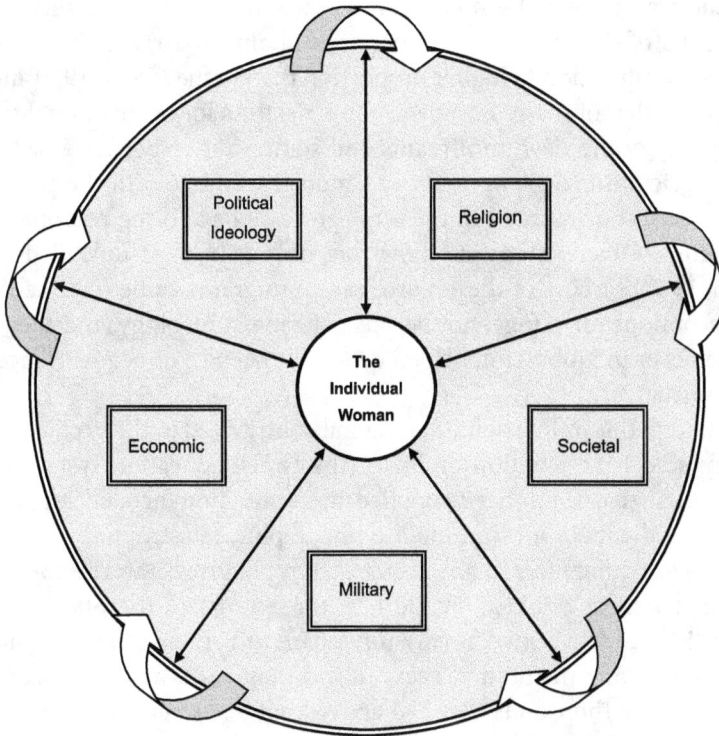

Demographic Factors

The demographic composition of Israel changed drastically after the war for independence in 1947: the Arab majority became a minority (close to a million Arabs either fled Israel or were deported from it; only about 150,000 remained) and the number of Jews increased constantly, mainly through immigration (Central Bureau of Statistics, 2010). Mass immigration started long before Israel became an independent state in 1948, and the Jewish population increased tenfold by the time of the Independence War: from about 60,000 in 1919 to 650,000 in 1947 (Central Bureau of Statistics, 1955). The major pre-independence waves of immigration came mainly (80%) from Zionist communities in the former USSR, ideologically-awakened Germany and anti-Semitic Poland (Central Bureau of Statistics, 1956).

The waves of immigration that arrived after the war included refugee Jews from every post-World War II European country. Many of the immigrants during that period were young (almost half were 15-29 years old), with at least some education. The level of formal education of the Jews in Israel at that time was among the highest in the world: over 90% of the men and almost 80% of the women were literate, and almost 10% of the men had a professional education (a higher proportion than in the U.S. in 1950 and more than double that of many European countries). As for occupational training, the majority of the new immigrants had some work experience or training: 15% in agriculture, 36% in crafts and industry, and 16% in the professions. Women were concentrated in the semi-professions and the personal-service occupations. Official statistics show that only 13% were unskilled workers (Sikron, 1957).[2] Many of these European immigrants came to Israel for lack of other options for refuge, not because of Zionist ideology, and they settled in the cities or in kibbutzim, helped by family, friends, or acquaintances from their homelands.

Although this inflow of human capital contributed to the expansion of the economy and Israel's nation-building (the Israeli education system by itself could not, at that time, have supplied the know-how needed for the task), all the ingredients of an imminent demographic catastrophe were in place, and immense difficulties in absorbing such rapid growth were expected. The population almost doubled in the first three years of the State's existence (1948-1951). Israel seemed totally unprepared to receive the huge numbers that were to come in the first years of independence, before it managed to fully absorb the thousands that had arrived but a few years earlier (see Table 2.1). Being in charge of the domestic sphere, women immigrants suffered more than the men from the day-to-day pressures that the mass immigration created throughout the country: they had to deal with the inadequacy of the infrastructure, which included limited food supplies (the State controlled the allotment of all food supplies via food-stamps), ill-suited housing (in tents or corrugated iron huts in the "Maabarot," the temporary townships), insufficient schools, lack of roads, and so forth.

TABLE 2.1. COMPOSITION OF THE JEWISH POPULATION BY COUNTRY OF BIRTH (1948, 1952)[a]

Country of Birth	Absolute Numbers		Percentages	
	1948	1952	1948	1952
TOTAL	716,678	1,450,217	100.0	100.0
Native-born[b]	253,414	393,873	35.4	27.2
Foreign-born	462,567	1,056,344	64.6	72.8
TOTAL FOREIGN-BORN	462,567	1,056,344	100.0	100.0
Asia	57,504	292,603	12.5	27.7
Africa	12,181	106,965	2.6	10.1
Europe/America	391,223	656,776	84.9	62.2

[a]   Adapted from C.B.S. 1956. Registration of Population. Special Publication Series, 53. Table XIV p.XXXI.
[b]   The proportion of those native-born is much greater among children (almost 90% of all the children under the age of four were born in Israel and 82% of those aged 5-14). Among adults the proportions are much lower—only about 8% of those over 30 years old were born in Israel.

Additional waves of immigration arrived in the 1950s, mainly from Islamic countries (primarily from North Africa and Middle Eastern countries , consisting of members of the group known as Mizrahi Jews). This changed both the ethnic composition of Jewish society and its culture, since many of these immigrants were religious. It also meant that the basically tradition-oriented late-comers from Asian and African countries were absorbed by mostly secular European Jews, many of who had come but a short time before them and were not fully integrated themselves.

The Mizrahi Jews began their exodus out of necessity more than as a result of ideological reasons, when it became clear that the new State of Israel was in conflict with the Arab world. The need to get as many people as possible out of these countries was urgent, and whole communities were uprooted and transferred to Israel (almost 90% of all the immigration from North Africa and 75% of all the immigration from Asia came within six years: Central Bureau of Statistics, 1956).

The massive Mizrahi immigration had different cultural and social characteristics, and it drastically changed the demographic composition of Israel. First, the newcomers from Islamic countries tended to have much larger families than did the veterans or European immigrants, so t the main breadwinner had more people to support (the average size of European families was 3.5; the average size of Mizrahi families was 5.0, and for those born in Israel, it was 4.1: Central Bureau of Statistics, 1957). Moreover, because in traditional Mizrahi culture women were not encouraged to work, they contributed very little to the economic support of their families.

Second, most of the Mizrahi immigrants had left their countries hastily, without selling their property or even taking all their possessions, thus arriving with few assets. Their predicament was further aggravated by their cultural distance and fewer associations with influential people in the European and native-born communities. Coming mostly from Arabic-speaking countries, and having little or no knowledge of Hebrew, made even language a barrier.

Furthermore, arriving from countries in which the level of technological development was far lower than that of Israel, these immigrants had, on the average, fewer human resources (such as education or professional training) than those who had emigrated from Europe, and many had no vocation in which they could find employment (Matras, 1965).

The issue of employment was aggravated by the fact that many of the Mizrahi immigrants who came in the 1950s were settled in small, remote development towns or in transition camps, where they became the majority of residents. Work there was more difficult to obtain and the immigrants who managed to find positions at allhad to settle for unskilled agricultural work or employment in labor-intensive, government-owned or -subsidized industries (such as textile and food production factories: Liron, 1973). Few women (fewer than 25%) found employment; those who did were employed as teachers, nurses and secretaries or as unskilled workers in personal services (like cleaning, caring for the sick or elderly, and so forth).

As a result, although many workers were needed in the newly established state, not all the immigrants were able to find jobs; most joined the ranks of the unskilled laborers (employed in manual relief work) or the unemployed (Eisenstadt and Lissak, 1984).

Between the mid-1960s and the mid-1970s, the immigration rate slowed as the potential reservoir of immigrants dwindled (the Jews who lived in the USSR were not considered potential immigrants at this time, because in 1967 the Soviet Union had cut all diplomatic ties with Israel. Shortly after the Six Day War, a massive propaganda campaign was launched in the Soviet Union denigrating Zionism and Israel. Relations between Israel and Russia were reestablished only in 1992, after the collapse of the Soviet Union). This had important implications for both the rate of economic growth and the production/consumption ratio. Fewer investments in housing were needed; fewer service workers were employed to help absorb the immigrants, etc. By the 1970s, the majority of the Jewish population in Israel was made up of immigrants from the Islamic countries or their descendants. However, the minority originally from Europe maintained positions of economic, social and cultural dominance.[3]

In the late 1970s, the former USSR changed its immigration policies and allowed Jews to emigrate. About a quarter of a million of them chose to do so, and more than 150,000 of them came to Israel. Many of these immigrants (65%) were highly educated and found work mostly in white-collar jobs and occupations (mainly doctors, dentists, engineers, teachers, and musicians: Ministry of Immigration Absorption, 1999). These immigrants were mostly absorbed in the occupations they held in the former USSR (unlike the later waves of immigrants, who had to find employment in alternative occupations, often suffering downward mobility). They were mostly secular and tended to be more egalitarian concerning the gendered division of labor than Israeli society was at the time (Sikron, 2004). The proportion of highly educated, independent women among them was high, and that influenced the labor market and the normative division of labor in Israeli society.

The Ideological-Political Context

A collectivistic socialist ideology, supported by the Labor Movement, ruled Israel from 1948 to 1977 and acted as a hegemonic and dominant ideology. An individualistic capitalistic approach, which advocated building the nation through private initiative and common (economic) interest groups existed, but was much weaker. This meant that in the first three decades of the State's existence, the Labor Party controlled national economic, political and administrative activities. In the first decade the emphasis was on absorption of immigrants and the creation of workplaces. Later, in the second half of the 1950s, the emphasis shifted to the expansion of economic development, diversification and the continuous increase in the standard of living. The distribution of Jews throughout the country was viewed as concurrent with economic progress.

Despite the centralization of economic power, and unlike other socialist countries, the State was not the single or even the major owner of the means of production or of industrial and financial enterprises (Eisenstadt, 1985). "Histadrut Haovdim," Israel's major labor union, acted both as a union and as an owner of many industries—a major employer. It thus created a huge, quasi-public sector.

This led to the development of a powerful public (and socialistic) economic sector parallel to a capitalistic one. The declared orientation of the Labor Government was toward a "mixed economy." This meant a policy of centralization of political and economic power combined with a strong awareness of the need to attract private investments through subsidization of private enterprises, privatization of governmental units, and so forth (Rosenfeld and Carmi, 1976). Labor-intensive industries received preferential treatment in an effort to create workplaces for the multitude of immigrants, and entrepreneurs who were willing to take risks and build their enterprises in remote, small development towns received extensive loans, tax exemptions, bonuses and the like. At the same time, state-owned economic enterprises were also initiated, specializing in creating infrastructure (housing and road construction, transportation and communication, electricity, water and sanitary services). The State thus became the direct or indirect employer of nearly one half of all paid labor (Central Bureau of Statistics, 1970).

The formative years were consequently marked by the rapid growth of public services and an extensive government administration. This was needed not only to replace the British Mandatory government and administration, but also to quickly supply the necessary health, welfare and education services for the huge influx of immigrants.

Moreover, ideological pluralism was depicted as a threat or a weakening force during that period. Ideological pluralism means that diverse—often competing—ideologies exist in a given society and are considered legitimate (much like the liberal and conservative ideologies in the United States). In contrast, when an ideological hegemony exists in a given society, the dominant ideology precludes the emergence of alternative views.

In ideologically pluralistic societies—especially in socially differentiated and conflict-ridden ones – diverse social groups tend to choose different ideologies in order to provide a sense of group identity, a motivating force for the conflict, and to justify their national ethnic, societal, economic, political or religious claims (Dickens, 1992).[4]

Israel, in those first 30 years, was construed as needing a unifying ideology to rally its people both in order to survive the hostility of its neighbors and to contend with mass immigration from post-war Europe and the Arab countries.

Moreover, by depicting Israel as a melting pot in which a new, distinctly Israeli identity is forged, the dominant ideology attempted to suppress almost all dimensions of ideological, social and cultural pluralism (only the distinction between religious and secular was granted legitimacy by the Zionist coalition formed after the first elections).[5]

The dominant ideology viewed the individual as a "bearer of collective ideals whose commitment to these ideals makes him or her subordinate to their imperative.... [T]his called on the individual to sacrifice private interests and to place him or herself at the disposal of a movement that purported

— 28 —

to serve collective goals and interests" (Horowitz and Lissak, 1978). It made similar demands from both men and women, and at the beginning women were supposed to be—at least ideally—men's equals. The hegemonic ideology also claimed to address the needs of all members of the collective, nullifying any attempt to form interest groups for the attainment of other goals (Hertzog, 1994; Kimmerling, 1989).[6] Lacking legitimacy to openly oppose the socialist hegemony, women, like other minority groups, attempted to advance women's issues through the hegemonic institutions. These attempts were mostly ineffective and had no significant influence on equality for women.

Any attempt to present an alternative ideology was considered counter-productive, and as encumbering the process of nation building and protec-tion. As a result, feminist ideologies have spread rather slowly.[7] Though femi-nist conceptions were apparent among some of the pre-state Zionist women, the small number of feminists and the lack of social and political support for gender issues rendered their attempts to gain equality ineffective (Bernstein, 1983).

The accelerated rate of development contributed to changes in the politi-cal power structure and social inequality. As public administration was applied to a growing number of spheres, access to administrative power turned into one of the major social benefits in Israeli society (Lissak, 1969). This access was not equally distributed among the different ethnic groups, and the newcomers from Islamic countries were deprived of an equitable share of benefits. However, as the immigrants who came to Israel after the 1950s had different ideological convictions, they, together with the dynamic economic development, instigated an ideological change that has continuously eroded the predominance of the veteran, mainly European, Labor-oriented administration.

In the late 1970s, Mizrahi Jews had undergone a political "awakening" process, and the majority of their voters turned to right-wing parties, away from the Socialist Labor Party, which had maintained its dominance until then. This switch is considered to be the result of their disillusionment with the existing socio-political system, in which they occupied inferior social, political and economic positions. The right-wing parties, with their pronounced liberal ideas and individualistic ideology, offered social change. Although this ideology endorsed the formal mobility ladders (e.g., education), it also provided legitimation for less formal ladders, such as entrepreneurship and the establishment of small businesses, and allowed for a higher status to be granted to the Mizrahi culture and value system. This combination of social recognition and greater legitimacy of alternative mobility ladders appealed to the Mizrahi Jews as a viable alternative to the Labor Party and its collectivistic approach, in whose institutions they had achieved so little. Furthermore, the political change reduced the power of the Labor Party apparatus, from whose positions of highest authority Mizrahi Jews were virtually excluded, and thus lessened the importance of personal connections within the existing administration. This created a paradox: the State administration continuously spread its control while its basic, grassroots support continuously diminished.

One of the unintended consequences of the hegemonic socialist ideology was the blurring of gender differences (as well as ethnic and cultural ones; see Smooha and Kraus, 1985), and the impeding of the formation of both significant gender group identity and feminist ideologies. Israeli socialism co-opted almost all other ideologies, parties and interest groups, and expected all members of society to contribute to the attainment of the collective goals as much as they could (Lotan, 1993). Women were expected to contribute to social propagation and regeneration of the Jewish people as much as to the work sphere. However, the reproductive role carries less power in society than the economic one, and women found themselves in an inferior social position despite egalitarian ideology (Izraeli, 1993).

Moreover, finding jobs for men was presented as a goal of paramount importance (especially for the many men who came from Asian and African countries and had more traditional—patriarchal—beliefs and ideologies). Encouraging women to work was seen as much less important (if not improper competition with men for limited resources) by the socialist government that ruled at that time (especially in the 1950s); collectivistic needs were viewed as preceding the need for equality for individuals (Rosenfeld and Carmi, 1976).

This led to the disillusionment of the Zionist women who found themselves placed in the very traditional role of homemaker. Furthermore, these women were unable to obtain massive social support for their desire for equality, even from other women. As a result, no group consciousness and hardly any group action developed. Attempts to redefine the major social goals or to fight for a better placement in the social hierarchy were weak and ineffective (Bernstein, 1983).

The right-wing capitalist coalition gained political dominance in Israel in 1977 by enlisting the support of the disenfranchised Asian-African ethnic groups (Peres and Yuchtman-Yaar, 1992; Roumani, 1988). The fact that women lacked both political and economic power seems to have made it easy for the new regime to ignore gender issues and postpone addressing the topic of women's rights, assigning precedence to social problems, such as ethnic equality, which those in power defined as more urgent.

Still, feminist interest and/or pressure groups became more active (e.g., The Women's Lobby, The Academic Women Association). This activity may be attributed in part to the unintended legitimation of ideological pluralism that the shift in government entailed (Klatch, 1990; Schlozman, 1990; Yishai,

1982). According to neo-Weberian analysis of capitalistic systems, each group attempts to guard its existing advantages while it encroaches upon the privileges of higher-placed groups (Calhoun, 1988). Thus, under the rule of the right-wing capitalist government (1977-1992), feminism attained a more significant foothold in Israel. Though right-wing ideology tends to be more conservative than left-wing socialism, its basic premises legitimize the existence of interest groups and competing ideologies (Dickens, 1992). Their influence increased slowly and its impact is discussed in later chapters.

Economic Processes

The basically underdeveloped, agricultural society that existed before Israel's independence had undergone a process of modernization and rapid development of its industry, followed by a tremendous growth of its service sector.

Economic growth had started in Israel even before it became an independent state, prompted by the waves of new immigrants arriving at its shores before and after World War II. Gaining momentum after the establishment of the State, the economic growth of Israel had undergone several stages that were in line with changing circumstances.

First, the tremendous inflow of both capital and human resources from abroad augmented the growth of the national economy. The very large number of immigrants led to a doubling of the population, and for more than ten years, the supply of labor was greater than the demand because the inflow of people exceeded the rate of economic development, even when that growth rate was rapid and extensive. This inflow brought about a two-fold effect: on the one hand, the demand for goods and services increased rapidly, making expansion of production necessary, while on the other, the supply of a much greater number of workers within the Israeli labor force enabled production of these goods and services. This allowed for large-scale projects such as construction of transportation and housing, establishment of commerce and banking systems, expanding health and education services, and so forth.

The rapid economic development from 1950 to 1955 increased the GNP per capita by 41%. The occupational structure also changed as immigration greatly expanded its variety, creating a swiftly growing class of hired professional employees on the one hand and a class of small-business owners on the other. The demand for highly skilled workers also increased constantly and was met mainly by the more highly educated European veterans and new immigrants, who were often employed in temporary jobs that did not require the use of all their skills. (The immigrants were willing to settle for any kind of employment when jobs were scarce, and many of them had to change occupations after coming to Israel [Halevi and Klinov-Malul, 1967].)[8]

This led to the creation of new pressure groups, changes in the power structure, and the adoption of a more materialistic and individualistic ideology (Ben David, 1963). As their numbers grew (reducing the relative weight of the agricultural and collectivistic enterprises), the Israeli social status system diversified and social and economic distances among occupational groups increased. Thus, as early as 1954, different occupational distributions are found for male and female new immigrants and old settlers (see Table 2.2).

Differences in occupational distribution are even more accentuated when one compares groups according to country of origin. Only 4% of Mizrahi Jews were in professional or managerial occupations, while the proportion was approximately 20% for European Jews. The highest relative concentrations of Jews of Asian and African origin were in agriculture and unskilled labor (22% of the total labor force [Central Bureau of Statistics, 1968].)

Moreover, because of their higher education and better connections, European immigrants were more able to progress from agriculture, transportation, industry and services to the more lucrative technical, professional and managerial occupations. The immediate result was the growth of income gaps and increased inequality between the highly educated workers and the unskilled ones, and between European and Mizrahi Jews. As they were divided by countries of origin as well as periods of arrival in Israel, the economic and occupational gaps coincided with the ethnic division of the Jewish population (Bernstein and Svirski, 1982). The frustration, perceived discrimination and feelings of deprivation grew and are still apparent today. They also led to the alienation between European and Mizrahi feminists (see Chapter Four).

The inflow of capital and material resources also had a significant influence on economic development. Between 1948 and the 1970s, Israel received over $10 billion in foreign aid from different states and international institutions (Zarhi, 1973). Imports of capital provided the means for large-scale economic investment and development activity, for example the creation of labor-intensive workplaces in remote areas of the country, which enabled dispersion of the population, and the devising of social services to ensure education, health and welfare for the entire population.

Nevertheless, the economy slumped in 1966-1967 (until the Six-Day War). The depression was caused mainly by the reduction of housing construction, which prompted a slowdown in industrial production. The rate of unemployment increased drastically (from 3.6% in 1965 to 7.4% in 1966 and 10.4% in 1967); the workers who suffered most from unemployment were Mizrahi Jews, and especially the women among them (Central Bureau of Statistics, 1968).

TABLE 2.2. EMPLOYMENT BY OCCUPATION AND GENDER, 1955-1986.[a]

Occupation and Sex	All Workers			Jewish Workers Only					
	1955	1958	1959	1960	1965	1970	1975	1980	1986
MEN									
Total (thousands)	443.0	492.9	510.8	521.9	576.1	598.3	645.9	695.4	716.8
Percent	100.0	100.0	100.0	100.0	100.0	100.0	100.0	100.0	100.0
Scientific and Academic	na	na	na	na	na	na	7.3	10.0	9.6
Professional/ Technical	6.9	7.7	8.0	8.4	10.0	12.3	8.4	11.5	11.7
Managers	3.0	} 14.8	} 13.4	} 13.8	} 16.2	} 17.1	5.0	7.4	9.3
Secretaries and Clerks	12.5						12.8	10.8	11.3
Sales workers	11.0	8.8	8.3	8.7	8.0	7.6	8.7	7.1	9.0
Agricultural workers	18.3	18.3	17.1	17.8	11.0	8.4	6.3	9.1	5.9
Industry workers	41.4	43.5	45.0	43.5	47.1	46.4	43.4	38.9	35.0
Service workers	6.9	6.9	8.2	7.8	7.7	8.2	8.2	5.1	8.2
WOMEN									
Total (thousands)	142.7	165.4	164.6	179.9	234.4	275.9	349.3	432.5	499.0
Percent	100.0	100.0	100.0	100.0	100.0	100.0	100.0	100.0	100.0
Scientific and Academic	na	na	na	na	na	na	7.3	8.3	8.9
Professional/ Technical	21.5	20.1	21.2	19.9	22.6	25.4	22.5	24.3	22.9
Managers	1.2	} 17.3	} 15.2	} 14.7	} 22.3	} 22.5	.7	.8	2.4
Secretaries and Clerks	15.2						29.7	31.0	30.4
Sales workers	12.4	9.2	10.5	10.3	8.5	7.9	7.0	6.6	6.5
Agricultural workers	13.4	14.8	12.4	14.9	9.0	6.2	3.3	2.6	1.7
Industry workers	14.6	13.9	14.8	14.0	15.5	15.9	10.7	8.7	8.0
Service workers	21.7	24.7	25.9	26.0	22.1	22.1	18.7	18.0	19.4

[a] Data for all workers (including non-Jews) are given when no other data are available.
Sources: Labor Force Survey, 1955. Central Bureau of Statistics, Jerusalem.
Labor Force Survey, 1962. Central Bureau of Statistics, Jerusalem.
Labor Force Survey, 1965. Central Bureau of Statistics, Jerusalem.
Labor Force Survey, 1970. Central Bureau of Statistics, Jerusalem.

After the Six-Day War in 1967, the economy recovered and growth resumed. Industrial production increased and provided workplaces for many of the unemployed, especially women and secondary breadwinners. This almost constant and continuous growth in national wealth and wages was accompanied by an unprecedented increase in the standard of living in Israel, but also by an increasingly unequal distribution of economic resources.

When the new waves of immigrants arrived from the former USSR in the 1970s, the Israeli economy gained additional momentum. Many of the newcomers were highly educated, work-motivated professionals, who joined the labor force and increased the need for housing, education and health care. Despite their contribution, the economy slumped in the early 1980s, the inflation rate attained horrendous levels (400% in 1984), and unemployment reached unprecedented highs.

These shifts and fluctuating trends further increased the inequality of income distribution in Israel. In the early 1950s Israel had a high degree of equality in its income distribution, as compared, for example, to the U.S. However, in the 1960s, inequality increased and has been growing ever since (Eisenstadt, 1985; Lissak, 1969).

These tremendous economic shifts—from agriculture and industry to services and the professions; from accelerated growth to "runaway" inflation; from creating relief work (such as road building and forestry) to an explosive growth of the service sector—either ignored women or marginalized them, and enhanced sex segregation.

The rapid growth of services and professional sectors, many of which were female-demanding and in the public sector (e.g. education, nursing and welfare), enabled many women to join the labor force. In fact, since 1955, the greatest (and most consistent) increase in the female labor force is in such sex-segregated occupations (Moore, 1992b). (This issue is elaborated upon in the following chapters.)

The Role of Religion

Religion is one of the major factors in shaping women's inferiority. Like most traditional religions, Orthodox Judaism hinders the spreading of feminist ideologies because of the codes of behavior it imposes and its conservative value orientations (Wuthrow and Lehrman, 1990).

Israel is one of the countries in which state and religion are not separated. However, in Israel, unlike most Western societies, Judaic principles are an integral aspect of the ideological justification for the existence of the state. Religion and nationality are equated, and "Jewish" refers to both a person's nationality and his or her religion. Religion is not by individual choice, and for all Israelis it is defined at birth, according to the mother's religion. No one remains undefined, whether he or she is practicing or not, whether Israeli-born or an immigrant. [9]

Because state and religion are not separated, and religion and nationality are intertwined, even laws like the Women's Equal Rights Law (1951), which aims to eradicate sexist stereotypes, failed to increase equality because it is insufficiently implemented (Lahav, 1977). The Israeli society is constantly torn between two clashing ideological value systems: the civic, universalistic-democratic and secular values on the one hand, and the nationalistic, particularistic and religious values on the other (Eisenstadt, 1985). Furthermore, two separate and completely independent judicial systems were created in Israel: the religious courts of law, which deal with family law only, and the secular, democratic system which handles the majority of legal cases.

The premises upon which the two judicial systems are based are inherently contradictory. According to the secular law all persons are equal; according to the religious law, inequality is a basic concept. The most frequently encountered inequality is the basic inferiority of women according to religious laws and in religious courts of law. For example, men divorce women, but not vice versa; a man can marry another woman if his wife refuses a divorce, but a woman cannot marry another man if her husband refuses to divorce her. A woman who has a sexual relationship with another man while still married may be divorced by her husband without her consent, without alimony or her share of the mutual property. She may even lose custody of her children. No such laws apply to men.

Until recently, through tacit agreement, religious law was always accorded supremacy, so that whenever a clash between secular and religious laws existed, religious law was upheld. This is in total contradiction with Israel's aspiration to secularism and universalism, according to which all are equal regardless of gender, race and religion, but social protest regarding the injustice has been negligible and ineffective so far.

One of the major individual-level reasons for the lack of support for attempts to separate state and religion is that more than a half of the Jewish population sees itself as "observing the major religious decrees," "tradition oriented," "religious" or "Orthodox," while the other half, the secular one, still sees religious tradition as an important part of its heritage and Israeli identity despite noncompliance with its decrees. Most of the Jewish population accepts, at least to some degree, the supremacy of religious institutions in molding the Jewish character of the Israeli state (Cohen, 1991; Kimmerling, 1985; Peres, 1992).

The prevalence of religiosity is problematic because the ancient codes of law (the Bible, Talmud and Halacha) upon which Orthodox Judaism is based define a distinct—and in democratic terms inferior—position for women within their families. Though often described as advantageous, the differentiation creates a hierarchy. Orthodox men and women have different obligations (Webber, 1983): Orthodox men are required to preserve and carry on the Jewish tradition through communal worship (there must be at least 10 men for that, and even a non-Jewish male is better than a Jewish woman), daily prayers, and religious study. Women are exempt from these religious duties because fulfilling them may interfere with their more important duties: taking care of their men, families and homes (the average number of children in Orthodox families is about six). Women come to pray in the synagogues, but they are segregated, sitting where the men cannot see them, and they are not allowed to raise their voices in song or prayer because their voices profane the house of worship (Kaufman, 1991). The religious duties of women are mostly performed at home, and are related to rules of modesty. (For example, a woman must go to the Mikve, the public bathhouse, where she must cleanse herself a week after the end of her menstrual cycle. During the two weeks from her period's beginning until she washes and purifies herself, she is considered unclean, and she is not allowed to touch her husband or be touched by him). When outside their homes, women must cover their bodies and hair. A woman dressed otherwise will be treated with contempt (El-Or, 1995; Hyman, 1979). Thus, Orthodoxy provides a well-defined, day-to-day, and season-to-season set of rules, regulating all aspects of women's behavior (Kaufman, 1994).

Moreover, unlike in the Diaspora, where Reform and Conservative Judaism are acceptable, Orthodox Judaism is the only legitimate and prevalent form of worship in Israel. As both Reform and Conservative Judaism are strongly influenced by liberal, humanitarian and feminist movements around them, they tend to be more tolerant and egalitarian (e.g., men and women pray together, women can be ordained and pray in public, and equal and integrated roles for both genders are emphasized).

The existence and power of religious institutions is another dimension through which religion hinders women's status. The Orthodox religious establishment and its all-male office-holders impede the spreading of liberal and feminist ideas by diverse means, but mainly by its hierarchical power structure, from which all women are excluded. Thus, women cannot set an example to others or act as role models, they are not allowed to address the congregation in any formal capacity related to religious services, and they cannot induce any adjustments that will contemporize religion and make it more egalitarian (Snyder, 1986; Woodruff, 1985).

Formal gender discrimination is legitimized and justified by Orthodox Judaism (as it is by the more conservative Catholic and Islamic denominations that steadfastly resist change) (Rhodes, 1983; Williams, 1987). Women still cannot become rabbis, although they can sometimes fill the roles of informal heads of congregations (Lehman, 1982). Thus, women do much of the informal work, but always in a gender-typical context (like visiting the sick, preparing food for the poor, and so forth), so that religious institutions reflect and reproduce the gender division of labor (McGuire, 1981). In contrast, in the United States, changes are occurring swiftly within Reform Judaism, with a growing degree of openness and willingness to reevaluate sexuality appearing (Nason-Clark, 1987; Snyder, 1986).

Another religion-related factor that hinders modernity and liberal ideologies in Israel is related to the existence of religious parties. Ever since the second elections (1951), there have been three to six religious political parties in the Israeli parliament (the "Knesset"). The political power of religious parties may be traced to the country's multi-party political structure. Ever since it became an independent state, Israel has had governments based on coalitions that included several political parties. As often happens, the only way to gain a majority (i.e., more than 60 representatives out of the 120) in the Israeli parliament is by assuring the cooperation of some strange bedfellows, and a religious party with two or three elected members may often demand—and receive—influence far beyond it elective power. Thus, religious parties were the cornerstones in many of those coalitions. The cooperation of these parties is granted to the party most willing to pass new religious laws and to enforce the existing ones more forcefully, which is possible because Israel has no constitution.

The influence of the religious parties and values has tremendously increased under Likud rule (since 1977). The right-wing coalition, headed by the Likud Party, had to deal with the profound political awakening of the Jews from Islamic countries, and the creation of the largest and most significant ethnic-religious political party in Israel.[10] As a result, the status quo has also shifted. Religious laws and decrees were more strictly implemented than in the past (for example: stricter control over abortions was implemented, disallowing abortions in any case except where an imminent hazard to the mother's health could be proven; and no advertisement posters depicting women were to be displayed in the streets of cities where Orthodox Jews live, even if they were not the majority in those cities [Lotan, 1993; Tal, 1987].)[11]

Once in the coalition, religious parties manipulate considerable sections of the domestic scene. This control is attained through their management of the budgets of ministries, and passing regulations which are in accord with their ideology or have high priority on their agendas (e.g., providing greater financial allocations to families with many children in order to encourage a greater birth rate. This provides greater funds for religious families, who are the majority of families with more children).

As their ideology tends to be particularistic (i.e., preferring to implement the Jewish religious traditions rather than egalitarian or democratic principles), they tend to use the funds they control to strengthen religious institutions and enforce traditional laws more forcefully. Thus, the democratic principle is twisted and subverted, and a minority of specific religious group determines the way of life in the country for other religious groups, for the secular, and for other religions.

In summation, the permeation of religious and traditional values and beliefs into everyday life hinders the spreading of modernistic, postmaterialistic ideas both at the structural-institutional level and at the individual one. At the structural level, religious parties fight to maintain the status quo or change it into greater Orthodoxy, which means greater conservatism; at the individual level, the wide support for traditionally Jewish values—even among the non-religious—limits the acceptance of postmaterialistic ideas.

As women are relegated to inferior positions according to Orthodox Jewish traditions, the political power of religious parties, and the wide support for a traditional (Jewish) way of life in Israel (even by the less observant), religiosity in Israel is one of the main forces that contributed to maintaining the traditional division of labor and the emphasis on the domestic, non-economic role of women in society. Because it is so well organized, it has been in effect a reactionary force ever since Israel became an independent state, and the sphere that has changed less than all the other spheres in the Israeli context.

The Inhibiting Force of the Israeli Army

The Israeli army was a national institution that recruited almost *all* men and women aged 18 for three years (for men) or two years (for women), and called many(mostly the men) back for reserve duty for as many as 60 days each year until they were 50 years old (married women are usually not called for reserve military service).[12] Several groups were, and still are, exempt from military service. The main exempted groups are Arabs, the handicapped, and the Ultra-Orthodox. Thus, service in the army is an almost universal experience of Israeli youth (Schilt, 1980). Moreover, Israel was the first state in which women were recruited to serve in the army through a national recruitment law. This was not only in times of national emergency or war, but was a permanent feature of army recruitment policy since the establishment of the state in 1948 (Yuval-Davis, 1981).[13] Hence, military service was required for full citizenship in Israel, and the conscription of women was thought to be a part of the egalitarian ethos of the new Jewish society, in which women contended that they "deserved" the "right to contribute" to the collective by becoming soldiers. Then, however, exemptions for any woman who declared that she was "religious" and for all married women and mothers were established, thereby re-gendering women's participation (Sasson-Levy and Amram-Katz, 2007).

The illusion of equality in the Israeli army derives from the pre-state period, and even then it was a myth. However, the sexual division of labor was less crystallized then because, first, there were no separate female units at that time, and, second, women were not restricted to the "rear" while most men were at the "front," because the war was not restricted to the "front" only. Once the differentiation was established, women's roles were clearly defined as "rear" only, and female soldierse were legally banned from actual war zones (Yuval-Davis, 1981).

The immense impact the army had on limiting the status of women and hindering their equality derives from its role as a masculine *total institution*.[14] It is considered a total institution because there are rigid barriers between the army and the outside world and because it controls the people who enter it by ruling all aspects of their lives: it determines what each new recruit is capable of doing, and uses this knowledge to allocate people to different jobs; it decides where a person will be stationed and for how long; it defines what a person will eat and when; where he or she will sleep and when, and so forth (Goffman, 1961). Although some ability to contend these decisions exists, most recruits serve their time when and where they are told (Schild, 1980).

The masculinity of any organization is determined by three factors: the proportion of men employed in it; the type of tasks required in the majority of its jobs; and the characteristics required to perform the work. The army is a masculine organization according to all three criteria. Men constitute most of its workers (though army authorities never release data regarding sizes of cohorts or their specific proportions); the tasks defined by its charter include high risk, high responsibility, protection of civilians, and field (combat) work. The characteristics necessary to perform most of the military tasks are also considered masculine (e.g., authority, use of physical force, taking initiative in stressful situations, and dominance).

As officially defined, the aim of the female soldiers' service in the Israeli army was to strengthenthe fighting force by fulfilling administrative, professional and auxiliary roles in order to release male soldiers for combat roles. The female soldiers also helped in the educational activity of the army, "in the areas of crystallizing the morale of the units and taking care of the soldiers of the units" (Office of the Prime Minister, 1977, p. 120).

All the women in the army belonged to the Women's Corps until the end of the 1980s, and had separate basic training and separate—sex-segregated – courses. However, most women soldiers worked under the authority of male commanders in the various corps. All *man*power decisions conscerning women were dealt with by the General Headquarters and the heads of various command units, who were all men. Senior female officers were given only consultant powers, and the head of the women's corps was one rank lower than other heads of command units (Yuval-Davis, 1997). As they were all in the Women's Corp, they could not ascend to the top military ranks.

Because of its practices and values, the Israeli army strengthened the existing gendered stereotypes and the gendered division of labor in several ways. First, because women are exempt from service more often than men, the message is that they are not as essential as men in the overall scheme of military roles (Klein, 2002). Second, because women serve less time than men, the army considered investment in them less productive. As a result, women were not sent to the lengthy courses that provide high ranks and technical/ instrumental knowledge as often as men (Yuval-Davis, 1985).

Moreover, female recruits served mostly in traditionally "female-typed jobs" (acting as secretaries, clerks, instructors or teachers) from which their advancement was limited (Chapkis and Wings, 1981; Megens and Wings, 1981; Yuval-Davis, 1981). Even within those female-typed jobs, the selection process included sexist criteria: women were placed in jobs not only according to skills and abilities, but also by their looks, so that the most beautiful amongst them were placed in the more prestigious jobs or at the best units (like the Air Force [Weiler, 1991].)

According to Weiler (1991), another women-depreciating dimension existed at the cultural level, because organizational messages were implicitly and explicitly sexist: examining texts of songs created by or for the military entertainment groups, he shows that some of the texts depict the naïve, pure, passive asexual woman-child, and others measure women by their beauty and present them as sex objects.

The immense impact of this institution as a hindering force for women's equality or their ability to rebel against the existing discriminatory practices is thus threefold. It supplies men with better qualifications then women, it blocks women's access to positions of authority and powerful social networks that enhance men's competitive ability once they leave the army, and it strengthens women's lower image of themselves (see also Marsden, 1986; Ojile, 1986).

The Impact of the Combined Influences on Women

These demographic changes had a tremendous effect on women. The Zionist, central-European women who came to Israel before its independence believed in their ability to be an integral part of the attempt to create a new society, one in which women shared the burdens and joys of being equal to men in all walks of life. They were soon disillusioned. Despite the myths, very few of them worked alongside their men. Most of them were placed in the very traditional role of "homemaker." Their very few and feeble attempts to change the situation were to no avail. The reversion to the traditional division of labor was enhanced by the interactive effects of changing ideology, social norms and needs.

During the first years of the State's existence, the need to supply wages and dignity to a large number of families that came from diverse cultural and social backgrounds led to differential policies towards the employment of men and women. Traditional norms according to which men are the breadwinners and women are the homemakers were dominant among men and women of both European and Asian-African origin, and were espoused by the ruling parties in Israel. Therefore, finding jobs for men was of paramount importance, while encouraging women to work was seen as of much lesser importance (if not downright improper competition with men for limited resources).

Most of the attempts to create work places were for men, not for women. The manufactured jobs—like road-building, foresting and construction – required little or no education, and minimal linguistic skills, but relied heavily on physical ability. No attempts were made to create jobs for Mizrahi women. Because it was understood that the division of labor in families from Islamic countries was traditional (i.e. men are the breadwinners and women are the home-makers), and the more traditional and religious immigration from Islamic countries looked upon women's work unfavorably as it implied that men were unable to properly support their families, reversing the roles meant the ruin of the family structure. If married women worked while their husbands did not, the men were considered incompetent. Moreover, in a market with limited demand for labor, working women were seen as depriving men of the opportunity to provide for their families and to gain self-esteem and social dignity.

The above led to a policy discouraging the entry of women into the labor market and, in fact, their proportion in the labor force decreased from about 32% in the 1940s to 25% in the 1950s, the first decade of Israel's independent existence (Bernstein, 1983). During that period women were able to find positions only when the supply of men was insufficient or when they had job qualifications which men did not have. As a result, women who joined the labor market found themselves mostly in lower-status, female-typed occupations (such as cleaning houses and doing other personal services) where they were not in direct competition with men. The limited job market in the 1950s led men into clerking, teaching and the like, and their proportion in these occupations was then much higher than it is now. The social standing of these occupations was higher at the time, and this provided men with greater incentive to join them (Ben David, 1963).

The attempt to find employment for new immigrant men served to reinforce traditional attitudes and reproduced the unequal division of labor in Israel, especially in Mizrahi families. European women were employed in greater proportion than Mizrahi women, but they, too, were limited to a small number of female-typed occupations. As these jobs require both education and knowledge of the Hebrew language, women of European origin were not replaced by the new male immigrants. However, many women who worked in agriculture or industry were gradually replaced by men. The justification the socialist regime provided for this trend was a need to supply at least one salary to each household.

The economic prosperity in the beginning of the 1960s brought about a growing need for workers, together with a normative change. Women were no longer seen only as a potential reservoir of workers but were encouraged to join the labor market for their own benefit as well as for national, economic reasons. The laws requiring equal pay for men and women which were passed at that time, making women's work more worthwhile, reflect this attitudinal change. (These laws' effectiveness will be examined in later chapters.) Women's proportion in the labor force has been increasing almost constantly (see Table 2.3). By the early 1980s, their proportion in the labor force rose to approximately 40% of all workers.

This shift is in accord with Rae Blumberg's (1979) claims that gender stratification and the position of women in society are the result of power differences which create an unequal distribution of privileges, and that the economic power of each gender is the main factor explaining their social status and life-options. In order to achieve economic power, labor is a mandatory, albeit insufficient, condition. Women were always a part of the production process, but their numbers in the labor force vary according to supply and demand for labor: when women's work was essential and could not be replaced or substituted by the work of other social groups, their participation increased. At such periods, they were able to turn their work into economic power. However, this was not translated into labor market equality.

When greater numbers of women entered the labor market in the 1960s, the occupational structure was already highly stratified, with the academic professions forming the top of the scale and the unskilled, blue-collar workers the bottom. Hence, while the expansion of the educational, welfare, and administrative systems created workplaces which enabled women to join the labor force, it also contributed to the strengthening of gender-typing of occupations in Israel (Bernstein, 1983). Women accounted for two-thirds of total labor market growth, but they found employment opportunities mostly in the rapidly growing public sector, in the services (mostly Mizrahi women), and the professions (mostly European women), creating "pink-collar" occupations as their numbers in certain occupations grew. The fact that women turned to these particular occupations or were accepted in them is hardly surprising. Considered an extension of the female family role, these occupations were seen as "natural" for women.

Even within these broadly defined occupational categories, most women are found in specifically female-typed occupations. When men work in these occupational categories, they join specifically male-typed occupations (for example, auditors, accountants and system analysts are mostly men, but they are in semi-professions which are predominantly female).

Table 2.3. Proportion of women in the LM 1955-2008

% Women	Men	Women	All Workers	Year
24.54	476.3	154.9	631.2	1955
25.69	546.7	189.1	735.8	1960
27.72	659.4	253.0	912.4	1965
28.59	692.6	277.3	969.9	1968
29.73	703.6	297.8	1,001.4	1970
31.93	765.1	359.0	1,124.1	1973
33.17	767.0	380.8	1,147.7	1975
34.98	816.0	439.0	1,254.8	1978
36.50	836.6	481.2	1,318.1	1980
37.92	896.4	547.7	1,444.1	1984
38.65	903.3	569.0	1,471.9	1986
39.58	938.6	614.7	1,553.0	1988
40.57	979.9	669.5	1,649.9	1990
41.80	1,080.9	776.6	1,857.8	1992
42.75	1,162.0	867.7	2,029.6	1994
43.54	1,217.7	939.2	2,156.9	1996
44.28	1,265.7	1,005.9	2,271.6	1998
45.65	1,323.4	1,111.6	2,435.0	2000
45.95	1,376.3	1,170.4	2,546.7	2002
46.35	1,436.8	1,241.7	2,678.5	2004
46.53	1,502.2	1,307.6	2,809.7	2006
46.55	1,546.7	1,347.1	2,893.8	2007
46.57	1,579.9	1,377.2	2,957.1	2008

Despite the increase in the proportion of working women, they were still a small minority in most of the more prestigious academic and administrative professions. Female-typed occupations were more attractive to women than male-typed occupations because they made concessions to women's needs, especially to those of mothers, allowing for shorter, more flexible working-hours and the availability of part-time jobs (England, 1982, 1988), which made it is easier for women to combine home- and work-life (Fuchs, 1989;

Polachek, 1991; Corcoran et al., 1985). Also, leaving and re-entering these occupations was easier because knowledge in them has fewer rapid changes and the required skills deteriorate at a slower pace (Blau and Ferber, 1986; Moore, 1987).

Another problem which faces workers (particularly women) in female-typed occupations is the loss of those occupations' originally high social status. Teachers, for example, were at first perceived as creators of ideas, cultural innovators, and representatives of the dominant ideology. When thousands of immigrant children joined the education system, many new teachers were needed. They were recruited from the highly educated, non-working reservoir of women, the main criteria for their employment being their willingness to work as teachers. However, the role of the teacher changed in time to that of a primarily technical role of transmission of information and development of specific skills. In addition, the rapid growth of the education system changed teachers' elitist status in yet another respect: because of its rapid expansion, the education system suffered financially and the professional activity of the teachers had to be curtailed. Salaries and benefits were lowered relative to other occupations, which led to the propagation of strikes and the tendency of men to leave the occupation and turn to more profitable employment, making way for women who were willing to work for lower salaries (Eisenstadt, 1967).

To summarize, women did not obtain men's cooperation in fighting for equality, and they could not accomplish it on their own. Whether because of the hardships of just trying to survive in the inhospitable land even without antagonizing their men, or because they found it more rewarding (or comfortable) to continue fulfilling their "traditional" roles, women did not fight for their equal rights and settled for the roles they were allotted, i.e. that of the supportive and loyal helpers to those who conquered the wastelands and built the State.

As a result, Israeli women faced all the problems that women in other achievement-oriented societies have to face, but their plight is more serious because of the complexity of Israel's immigrant and traditional society. The consequences for women, and how these processes maintained their inferiority, are dealt with in the next chapter.

ENDNOTES

1   The predicament of religious Zionist women was even more noticeable. Those among them who sought a part in the national endeavor, had to enter the public sphere which was—and still is—a male arena, and women found themselves at an inherently problematic juncture between tradition and change. Religious Zionism sought to preserve tradition, and grappled with the problem of giving women a part in the national enterprise while at the same time retaining their traditional function (Rosenberg-Friedman, 2006)

2   These data may be highly biased. Though education was indeed high among the newcomers, some of them called themselves "farmers," "technicians," etc. even if all they had ever done in that occupation was take a course and they had never worked in that occupation.

3   The disadvantages suffered by the "non-Western" immigrants in Israel are similar to those suffered by people of "non-Western" origin in other industrial countries which are dominated by Western culture.

4   These diverse ideologies can take the form of either competing or derivative ideologies. Competing ideologies promote alternative views of social order and social justice; derivative ideologies presuppose the existence of a dominant ideology and a distinct but contingent one (for example, radical feminism competes with other ideologies in most Western societies, while liberal feminism is related to—or derives from—general notions of freedom, equality and self-fulfillment [Andersen, 1993; Epstein, 1988; England, 1993; Renzetti and Curran, 1995].)

5   This means that although other ideologies and political parties (like the right-wing Herut) did exist in Israel at the time, they were marginalized and often de-legitimized by the ruling party and ideology.

6   The socialist government had pased several laws in order to reduce the growing gender gap (most of which were not initiated by women), but the changes that these laws have brought were minimal and superficial (Commission for the Advancement of Women's Status, 1995).

7   Therefore, feminism cannot be considered a derivative of this ideology. In this respect, Israel is different than other socialist countries, such as Scandinavia, in which Socialism does not act as a hegemonic ideology.

8   See also Central Bureau of Statistics. 1957. Labor Force Survey, 1954. Special Publications Series, 56. Jerusalem. Table 25 p.50-51.

9   The Law of Return recognizes the right of every Jew to immigrate to Israel, and prevents immigration from almost all non-Jews, even from Palestinian refugees who wish to return if they left Israel (or were deported from it). All immigrants are registered according to their religion upon arrival.

10   Previous ethnic-political parties (like the "Yemenites in Israel Association," "The Sepharadic and Mizrachi thnic groups," "Tammi") tried to gain power but had only one or two elected members.

11   Allocation of resources has also changed, with huge funds going to the educational, social and religious institutions supported by the "Sepharadi" religious party, thus strengthening their hold on the population even further..

12   This has changed in recent years; see Chapter Six.

13   These trends have changed gradually, as will be discussed in later chapters; nowadays more women declare themselves religious in order to evade military service, and the recruitment authorities make it is easier for women to do so. It is also easier for men to avoid military service and many more pretexts are accepted as legitimate causes for discharge or exemption.

14   "A total institution may be defined as a place of residence and work where a large number of like-situated individuals, cut off from the wider society for an appreciable period of time, together lead an enclosed, formally administered round of life" (Erving Goffman, 1961, Introduction to Asylums).

Chapter 3

Maintaining Women's Inferiority

The processes in the demographic, economic, political, religious and military spheres that were discussed in the previous chapter did not create women's inferiority, but contributed to maintaining this inferiority through their combined impact on the traditional Israeli society and its conservative culture. The inhibiting culture that was dominant in Israel until the mid-1980s (and in some segments of Israeli society still prevails) instilled in women low self-esteem and a belief that they were powerless outside their homes and, therefore, dependent on men.[1] The processes that led to women's dependence on men were supported by legislation, values and norms.

Legislation varies from one society to another, and became less discriminatory in most Western societies in the 1970s, as societies became more egalitarian. (For example, in many societies women were considered secondary breadwinners, and their taxes were calculated as supplementing their husbands' earnings. Therefore, they were not legally entitled to the benefits allocated to primary breadwinners. In Israel, this law was changed to include both spouses as equal only in 1998 [Income Tax command 64b]).

Values defined women's dependence on men as the right, the proper, even the desired state of affairs, and encouraged women to think of themselves as unfulfilled unless they were married and had children. In Israel, there were 2.14 million households in 2009; over 80% of them (1.72 million) were family households. 96% of these families were of formally married couples, and 75% of these had children. The other 4% were cohabiting couples, and only 26% of them had children (Central Bureau of Statistics, 2011).

The norms, which define how to implement the values, instilled in women the "right way" of attaining the goals that the values defined: be submissive, do not antagonize your man, do not be too demanding, nurture him, and so forth. These norms are still prevalent throughout Israeli society, mainly among its more traditional sections.

Several explanations for the almost universal existence of gendered socialization were suggested. Some theories assumed a sociobiological differentiation and diverse genetic development of men and women (Wilson, 1975). Other approaches supposed that social efficiency is responsible for the establishing of different characteristics in men and women: socialization is more efficient when the biological (sex) distinctions define the psycho-social (gender) categorizations, and males are socialized to become masculine while females are socialized to become feminine, regardless of their possible preferences (Zelditch, 1964a,b). Yet other theories claimed that the diverse socialization processes, which create different traits for men and women, are in accord with discriminatory and patriarchal practices, and are meant to maintain advantages for men (Millett, 1970).

Whichever theory one chooses to accept, they all lead to the same conclusion: the clear-cut distinction in characteristics and behaviors made both genders well suited to fulfill the roles they were socialized to fill— the expressive (nurturing), homemaking women and the instrumental, breadwinning men. This dichotomous division of labor was considered of utmost importance in societies that defined the traditional family as the focal point of all social life. The husband-and-wife families are still the dominant norm in most societies, though nowadays many diverse alternative patterns of families are tolerated (e.g., cohabiting, single mothers, gay and lesbian couples, and so forth: see Chapter Seven).

One of the main means with which a culture transmits its definitions of "correct" and "incorrect" behaviors is by stereotyping every trait, role, or activity as "masculine" or "feminine" (in other words, appropriate for men or appropriate for women). Sex-based stereotypes, like all stereotypes, result from the cognitive process of categorizing social groups. Due to the visibility and immediacy of sex as an attribute, sex stereotypes tend to be prominent elements in all contexts. "Crossing the lines" is discouraged and often leads to sanctions, and as a result individuals are brought up to expect specific behaviors from each gender group. We do not expect men in traditional societies to wash floors at home or do the laundry, and we do not expect women to work on a car's engine or lift heavy crates in a warehouse.

The stereotypes are often clear and obvious, but they may also be hidden or implied, and hard to pinpoint (as is the case with the "well meaning liberal male"[2]). Stereotypes derive from cultural values, attitudes and norms, and they also serve to strengthen the hold of these values, attitudes and norms on society. In Giddensian terminology, they reproduce culture in any given society and maintain the legitimation of existing cultural practices. The traditional cultures and stereotypes, which maintained women's inferiority and prevented (or slowed) social change, acted in three interrelated domains: the personal, the domestic, and the public. The interaction of processes in these domains rendered women unable to influence the system or initiate systemic changes.

The main assumption in this chapter is that the interaction of the three spheres both reflects and reproduces cultural definitions. Most important for this chapter's context is the combined impact of the personal, domestic, and public domains on how gender differences are presented, perceived and reproduced in traditional cultures and societies.

In the personal sphere—gender specific personality traits and abilities are attributed to men and women, and differences are assumed in their self-esteem, their trust in their ability to influence their life course, the social identities they choose to emphasize, and so forth (Stafford, 1984).

In the domestic sphere—traditional cultures consider the family to be one of the basic, almost sacred, social institutions. These cultures clearly define the division of responsibility and designate differentiated roles to each gender. Men and women complement each other, being two halves of the family whole: "mother"/"father," "wife"/"husband," "homemaker"/"breadwinner."

The public sphere encompasses all the domains outside the home, but mainly the work and political spheres. Traditional cultures not only define the "right" roles for men and women, they also "marginalize" women, relegating to women jobs and occupations that do not infringe on men's choices, and that men either reject or avoid (e.g., low paying jobs, personal services, working with small children, volunteer work).

This chapter deals, therefore, with cultural stereotypes and their impact on the personal, domestic and public spheres in Israel, changes that occurred in them, and the influence of these stereotypes on the lives of both gender groups. It examines issues such as how gender-specific traits led to different behaviors on the parts of men and women in the domestic and public spheres; which occupations were more "female-friendly"; what were the different strategies for combining work and family; how some people reduced role conflict; how stereotypes or social values influenced the behaviors of male and female workers; and which women reached higher positions, and how they did it. It also deals with the political/ideological activism women exhibited in the context of the prevalent ideologies of their time.

1. The Personal Domain

Gendered Traits

One of the major processes by which society instills its culture in its members is the socialization that begins in early childhood. In Israel until the mid-1980s, as in all traditional societies, the socialization processes were highly differentiated by gender, so that gender-typical personality traits were reinforced in boys and girls, defining different behaviors, attitudes and characteristics as legitimate and socially acceptable (e.g., physical ability and achievement motivation were more strongly emphasized for boys, while passivity, compliance and social skills were encouraged in girls [Auster, 1978; Canter, 1979; Maccoby and Jacklin, 1974]).

The prevalent socialization processes that existed at the time (and exist even today, in traditional segments of Israeli society) reflected the biases described by Broverman, Broverman, Clarkson, Rosenkrantz and Vogel (1970), according to which there is a double standard of mental health for males and females: "healthy" males have the socially desirable standards of health for all humans regardless of gender (rational, assertive, independent), and "healthy" women have the socially undesirable standards of health for all humans (emotional, hesitant, dependent). Marwit (1981) replicated their study, and found similar perceptions a decade later.

The pressure to develop only gender-typical traits was often taken to an extreme, and men were socialized to value characteristics such as competitiveness, ambition, and rationality to the exclusion of traits such as gentleness, nurturance, and being compassionate. This often created an imbalance, so that the adult male was frequently isolated from women, other men, and ultimately himself. In contrast, traits like self-sacrifice and putting others' needs before one's own were instilled in women, often coercing them into ignoring their own needs and desires (Walstedt, 1977).[3] The differences in traits led to differences in perceptions, attitudes, values and behaviors, conditioning men to succeed in all life domains, and women to succeed in the interpersonal sphere (Douvan, 1976; Molm, 1978).[4]

Moreover, in most Western societies until the 1970s, masculinity and femininity were considered the opposite ends of a single continuum of traits, preferences, interests, attitudes, and behaviors, which differentiated between men and women, and were practically synonymous with the biological categorizations "male" and "female" (Orlofsky and Stake, 1981; Pleck, 1977).

Stereotypes Concerning Gender Traits

Men in such traditional cultures were expected to be "masculine" (e.g., assertive, dominant, competitive) and women were expected to be "feminine" (e.g., gentle, affable, considerate), and, therefore, very different from each other. The presumed differences were attributed to all men and women, indiscriminatingly. Men and women who defied stereotypic expectations and exhibited traits that were considered atypical for their gender were labeled maladapted, strange, rebellious or queer, and were sanctioned according to the societal definition of their atypical behaviors. Thus, men who were considerate, soft-spoken, and/or uncompetitive were labeled "effeminate" and women who were assertive, dominant, and/or ambitious were considered "butch." The sanctions for noncompliance with the definition of gendered traits were many and diverse. Thus, for example, being considered unfeminine meant that a young woman was perceived as a less desirable mate and risked remaining "an old maid," a consequence few young women in traditional, family-oriented societies were willing to accept.

The gender-specific traits dictated gendered behaviors, and here, too, inappropriate behaviors were censured. Thus, for example, although no official policy ever barred Israeli girls, they were socially discouraged from taking courses like high-level mathematics, which were viewed as unnecessary for women, even "anti-feminine." Choosing such courses meant risking derogation, exclusion, even isolation. However, not taking such courses impeded women's ability to join the more prestigious faculties in the universities, as their attainments were considered insufficient and they were disqualified due to "objective reasons" (Hornig, 1984).

Similarly, those who aspired to atypical occupations risked the disapproval of their socialization agents (family, friends, teachers and co-workers) and the invoking of negative social sanctions. A man wishing to become a kindergarten teacher encountered the same ridicule as a woman who aspired to a career in nuclear physics. This was a heavy price to pay, and those who feared the consequences of such choices avoided contradicting social expectations. Moreover, as male-typed occupations were seen as requiring stereotypical "masculine" traits and female-typed occupations were seen as requiring "feminine" traits, young persons were led to aspire to gender-typical occupations, believing that they would be less successful in the atypical ones.

Consequently, most men and women acted in accord with what the socialization processes defined as the desired behaviors for their gender. Women were not expected to develop the skills most instrumental for competing in the public sphere (like the labor market or politics) and, in fact, were discouraged from doing so. They lacked the necessary competences to assert their abilities in all spheres except the domestic one. However, since the domestic sphere provides no tangible material resources, women were dependent on men for all their needs. Men, on the other hand, were brought up to become the providers for their families, and to consider themselves solely responsible for the family's material wellbeing. However, they were less adept in the ability to express emotions and were lacking in the skills necessary to deal with their own emotional needs or those of others.

This view of gender began to change when gender roles began to adjust and a growing number of women joined the labor force. New approaches (e.g. Bem, 1974) reached Israel in the 1980s, challenging the bipolar definition of masculinity-femininity and suggesting a dualistic view according to which, firstly, masculinity and femininity represent independent dimensions of personality traits, so that men and women can rate highly on both sets of traits. Such individuals were described as "androgynous" (Bem, 1981). Secondly, both masculinity and femininity are redefined as uni-dimensional, and, therefore, individuals who are masculine or feminine in one domain will be similarly masculine or feminine in all other domains (for example, individuals with salient feminine traits will also show a preference for feminine attitudes and behaviors). Thirdly, being androgynous is advantageous, because such individuals are psychologically healthier and socially more adaptable and effective (Spence and Helmreich, 1980).

Even according to this new approach, men were expected to be more masculine and women were expected to be more feminine, but personality traits were no longer considered the exclusive province of a specific sex group. "Rather, masculinity and femininity are seen as representing two sets of behavioral skills and interpersonal competencies which all individuals— regardless of gender—can use to interact with their environment" (Orlofsky and Stake, 1981, p. 219).

Such conceptions suggest that each set of traits represents—and leads to—a different type of coping behavior and, therefore, individuals who combine the two dimensions of traits have more varied and adaptable behavioral options. Bem (1974, 1981) has shown that men and women often attribute to themselves high levels of both masculinity and femininity, and that such individuals succeed in situations that call for assertive or independent behaviors as well as in situations that call for nurturance and sensitivity to others, whereas individuals who manifest only one set of sex-typed traits are effective only in situations involving these traits (see also Orlofsky and Windle, 1978).

This finding, according to which men and women are much more similar than had been traditionally believed, has significant implications for society. It indicates that the assumed psychological differences between the two gender groups are socially constructed, and that they were used to both explain and justify the differentiated gender roles, and to provide dissimilar rewards, privileges, advantages and spheres of responsibilities to men and women (Pleck, 1977).

In Israel, the only study reported in the literature concerning gender traits until the 1980s compared American and Israeli students in 1981 (Izraeli, 1983), and it showed that fewer Israeli males were classified androgynous than American males. No significant differences were found in the masculine or feminine categories, and Israeli and American females were very similar in terms of mean masculine and feminine BSRI (Bem's Sex Roles Inventory) scores. Israeli males had significantly lower BSRI masculine scores than American males.

Traits and Locus of Control

Intentionally or unintentionally, the socialization processes that created the gender differences also signaled to women that they are powerless in the societal sphere and should not expect to control their lives. They were expected to be dependent on men, and the dependence was translated into external locus of control and the lack of internal control for most women.

Rotter's (1966) definition of locus of control refers to the expectation that one's behavior is generally controlled by internal or external forces. According to this approach, individuals with internal locus of control believe that their behaviors and actions control their lives, whereas individuals with external control believe that arbitrary events over which they have no control (such as fate, luck, or society) rule their lives (Hong and Giannakopoulos, 1994). This approach, according to which a sense of control reflects personal mastery, is shared by many (e.g., Lefcourt, 1981, 1983; Prenda and Lachman, 2001), despite problems of definition and measurement (Antonucci, 2001; Skinner, 1996).

Women in traditional societies have fewer opportunities than men to develop internal control, and Israel until the mid-1980s was no exception (Long and Goldfarb, 2002; Mannheim and Seger, 1993). They were, however, often blamed for not assuming control over their lives, which required an ability they had no opportunity to develop. To attain some measure of control without seeming to act outside the gender schema, women in traditional societies occasionally resorted to "devious" means of attaining control, like becoming manipulative. They were then considered scheming, dishonest, underhanded, and so forth. Consequently, women often found themselves in a "no-win" situation wherein they were damned if they did (take control) and damned if they did not.

Stereotypic depictions of women at the time showed them using their weakness and powerlessness to control men and to attain their goals. Shows of emotions rather than exercises of rationality were considered "typically female manipulation," not the only means women had to achieve their objectives (Goh and Mealiea, 1984). Such perceptions were found especially among men who lacked personal control. These men also tended to oppose women working outside the home. Men with greater personal control, on the other hand, were more accepting of women in nontraditional roles than men with an external locus of control (Valentine, 1999).

Such perceptions led both men and women to devalue women's contributions in any public sphere activity. "Women are prejudiced against female professionals and, regardless of the actual accomplishments of these professionals, will firmly refuse to recognize them as the equals of their male colleagues," writes Goldberg (1968, p. 29). It is not only their intellectual ability that men and women undervalue; studies in that period claimed that a belief in male superiority and female inferiority was prevalent at the time, and that women and femininity were devalued by both men and women (Eichler, 1975); and that women in general were considered less intelligent that men (Crites and Fitzgerald, 1978). These attitudes have changed throughout the Western world, and even in the beginning of the 1980s, such findings were not replicated (e.g., Isaacs, 1981). In Israel of the early 1980s, such beliefs were rather prevalent (Izraeli, 1983) and may still be in effect today among some of the more traditional segments of society.

Gender Identity

Culture affects an additional aspect of the personal dimension—it leads to different meanings of gender identities. Gender identity connotes recognition of differences between the sexes as well as awareness that these differences are societally-directed, leading to differential treatment of men and women, creating diverse life-experiences, roles and statuses for members of the two gender groups (Gilligan, 1977, 1982; Ollenburger and Moore, 1992). Gender identity is considered one of the primary identities which are established early in life by the socialization process (like selfhood and human-ness). Primary identities are more robust and resilient to change in later life than other identities. Thus, although change and mutability are endemic in all social identities, they are less likely in these identities (Jenkins, 1996).

Unlike other social identities, gender identity may have two opposing meanings for both the subordinate (women) and dominant (men) groups. On the one hand, gender identity may reflect adherence to the traditional[5] division of labor according to which women's family role is their primary role, and men's breadwinner role is their primary role. This meaning of a salient gender identity indicates support of the existing patriarchal[6] social order. On the other hand, gender identity may reflect support of feminist and/or egalitarian ideas and rejection of existing social order and traditional gender roles (Hunt, 1980; Moore, 1998a,b; Wuthrow and Lehrman, 1990).

These two opposing meanings are linked to religiosity and what Giddens refers to as "the relative freedom" that individuals perceive (that is—how free to make specific choice the individual feels. For example, Orthodox Judaism and Islam define what women should wear. Women can choose which specific item of clothing to wear among the garments she owns, but she has no say concerning which styles of clothing or which colors are permissible—bright colors are frowned upon, pants are prohibited for Orthodox Jewish women, and exposing arms or legs is out of the question for Orthodox women of both religions).

These identities are also linked to the human images, and the distinction between central (or primary) and secondary human images (Scott, 1956). The primary human image, constructed by the dominant value system, cannot cover all social roles. Consequently, some of the vital roles require certain traits which contradict the primary image, and most societies develop secondary value systems. A secondary value system generates an additional human image which some of the social categories (usually weaker or inferior categories) are compelled to fulfill. Roles that are in accord with the traits of the central human image usually acquire higher status than those in accord with the secondary image (Scott, 1956).

In most societies the central human image is based upon achievement and universalism, which characterize labor markets, bureaucracies and science, and is associated with men and masculine traits. In contrast, the secondary value system is associated with ascription and particularism. It predominates in the family and the educational domain, and is considered women's main field of activity even in modern societies. Hence, women in modern societies have to contend with the demands of two contradictory value systems, while men cope with a single, uniform set of demands. Israel is no exception (Padan, 1968).

Like most conservative religious ideologies, Judaism is patriarchal, bestowing upon men higher status and privileges, and often legitimating the subordination of women. They have established different rituals and rules for men and women, and teach that men have the right to tell others (the women) how to be, what is right for them and what is wrong (Hunsberger, 1995).

Consequently, support of the traditional division of labor is more prevalent among religious men and women (especially those of the more orthodox denominations of Judaism, Islam and Christianity). As a result, Israeli researchers (El-Or, 1994) found that a salient gender identity among religious individuals indicates acceptance of the gendered division of labor, preservation of the social order, and resistance to change (Sered, 1997).

Thus, whether Jewish, Muslim or Christian, most Orthodox individuals with salient tradition-oriented gender identities do not support feminist, libertarian, or egalitarian ideologies as much as secular, nontraditional persons do.[7]

For secular, nontraditional persons, a salient gender identity seems to be based on egalitarian and/or feminist notions. According to egalitarian and some of the feminist ideologies, men and women are basically similar and, therefore, have a right to equal status, opportunities and rewards. Other feminist ideologies emphasize the uniqueness of each gender and the distinct perceptions, attitudes, and behaviors of men and women (Moore, 1998b).[8]

Like all identities, gender identity can only be chosen in post-traditional societies in which individuals need to make decisions concerning their lifestyles, and a feminist gender identity can only be prevalent in post-traditional societies in which ideological pluralism exists (ideological pluralism means that no ideological hegemony exists in that society and the emergence of alternative views is not blocked). In ideologically pluralistic societies, different ideologies are espoused by opposing sides, thus providing justification and rationalization for the identities. In this sense, ideology provides direction and motivating force for the identities. It seems logical to assume, therefore, that in countries where state and religion are not separated (as in Israel), this "tradition-oriented gender identity" may be more prevalent than in societies in which the separation formally exists (like the United States).

An additional constraint exists for feminist gender identities. Among women, if feminist awareness of a "common destiny" is reached at all, it is not in early childhood when the gender identity is acquired or imposed, but later in life when women experience what it means to bear the identity, and to be part of a differentially treated category whose social roles are often in conflict (Kaufman, 1991; Moore and Gobi, 1995). Some women do not reach this kind of awareness even when they face gender-related barriers, stereotypes and discrimination.

Hence, both ideological pluralism and awareness of discriminatory practices are necessary for women to develop a feminist gender identity (Moore, 1992), and only when these conditions exist will the awareness have the potential of being translated into organized social action (Izraeli, 1993; Moore, 1998b). It is no wonder, therefore, that the gender identity that developed in traditional Israel was related to the acceptance of socially defined differences between the sexes and the differential treatment of men and women.

Moore (1995a) assumed that collective social action to increase gender equality appears when defined gender identities are prevalent in a specific society, legitimized and directed by relevant - mostly feminist - ideologies, and showed that three factors hindered the crystallization of gender identities and the spreading of feminist ideologies in Israel: the lack of ideological pluralism, the prevalence of religious value systems, and the dominance of national and totalitarian masculine institutions. Ideological pluralism is essential for two reasons: to define the controversial ideological issues and to justify the social conflict that the rift creates. By definition, ideological pluralism implies that the opposing sides espouse diverse ideologies. The ideologies thus contribute to the definition of "us" and "them," and provide the framework for the social conflict that women's activism may create. Although the diversity can take the form of either competing or derivative ideologies, radical (i.e., competitive) feminist ideologies are, even today, less prevalent in Israel than liberal (i.e., derivative) feminist ideologies. This may have a significant impact on the gender identities of Israeli women, but these issues are beyond the scope of this paper.

Even when the socialist ideological hegemony was broken in Israel, the spreading of feminism was slow, as it had to overcome traditional and unequal value systems that both the Jewish religion and the Israeli total and masculine institutions (such as the army) sanctioned and reproduced.

Analysis of this specific political context shows that gender issues are often not related to other political issues and are not part of the political-ideological discourse. Defined by Israeli politicians—most of whom are men—the discourse focused on building a state, surviving wars, and encouraging economic growth; these issues were always presented as having higher priority than gender equality. Thus, feminist organizations and interest groups failed to elicit the support of other political parties and groups, and female agents' actions were bound and limited by a sociopolitical context which was not of their choosing.

2. The Domestic Sphere

Division of Labor and Gender Roles

> "The division and ascription of statuses with relation to sex seems to be basic in all social systems. All societies prescribe different attitudes and activities to men and women... There are very few societies in which very important activities have not been definitely assigned to men or women." (Ralph Linton, 1936, pp. 116-117.)

In traditional societies (and even in the less traditional ones), women learn at a very early age that their main social responsibility is to marry and raise a family, whereas men learn that they are supposed to be the major "breadwinners" for their families. This is presented to children of both sexes as the "rightful" division of labor. Women may work, and men are expected to "contribute" to domestic life, but as a secondary set of responsibilities, not the main one.

According to this cultural representation, family is the foundation of society. In Israel, the formal definition of a family (used by government organizations like welfare agencies or the Central Bureau of Statistics) is a group of 2 or more individuals who live together and are tied to each other as a couple or as parents. These include a couple, a couple with children or a single parent with children.[9] Until the 1980s, over 85% of the women in Israel were traditionally married.[10] Shainess (1980) even claims that in her early years as a psychotherapist, if a woman chose not to have children, she would have considered that woman's decision as "revealing some kind of neurotic difficulty in not wanting to fulfill their reproductive destiny" (p.377). This is most clearly shown in "The Good Wife's Guide" published in 1955:

The text, published on May 13, 1955, in Housekeeping Monthly, reads:

The good wife's guide
- Have dinner ready. Plan ahead, even the night before, to have a delicious meal ready, on time for his return. This is a way of letting him know that you have been thinking about him and are concerned about his needs. Most men are hungry when they come home and the prospect of a good meal (especially his favourite dish) is part of the warm welcome needed.
- Prepare yourself. Take 15 minutes to rest so you'll be refreshed when he arrives. Touch up your make-up, put a ribbon in your hair and be fresh-looking. He has just been with a lot of work-weary peopl (sic)
- Be a little gay and a little more interesting for him. His boring day may need a lift and one of your duties is to provide it.
- Clear away the clutter. Make one last trip through the main part of the house just before your husband arrives.
- Gather up schoolbooks, toys, paper etc and then run a dustcloth over the tables.
- Over the cooler months of the year you should prepare and light a fire for him to unwind by. Your husband will feel he has reached a haven of rest and order, and it will give you a lift too. After all, catering for his comfort will provide you with immense personal satisfaction.
- Prepare the children. Take a few minutes to wash the children's hands and faces (if they are small), comb their hair and, if necessary, change their clothes. They are little treasures and he would like to see them playing the part. Minimise all noise. At the time of his arrival, eliminate all noise of the washer, dryer or vacuum. Try to encourage the children to be quite.
- Be happy to see him.
- Greet him with a warm smile and show sincerity in your desire to please him.
- Listen to him. You may have a dozen important things to tell him, but the moment of his arrival is not the time. Let him talk first—remember,

his topics of conversation are more important than yours.

- Make the evening his. Never complain if he comes home late or goes out to dinner, or other places of entertainment without you. Instead, try to understand his world of strain and pressure and his very real need to be at home and relax.
- Your goal: Try to make sure your home is a place of peace, order and tranquility where your husband can renew himself in body and spirit.
- Don't greet him with complaints and problems.
- Don't complain if he's late home for dinner or even if he stays out all night. Count this as minor compared to what he might have gone through that day.
- Make him comfortable. Have him lean back in a comfortable chair or have him lie down in the bedroom. Have a cool or warm drink ready for him.
- Arrange his pillow and offer to take off his shoes. Speak in a low, soothing and pleasant voice.
- Don't ask him questions about his actions or question his judgment or integrity. Remember, he is the master of the house and as such will always exercise his will with fairness and truthfulness. You have no right to question him.
- A good wife always knows her place.

Today, about 75% of women up to the age of 60 are traditionally married. In addition, cohabiting couples were too few to count and the Israeli Bureau of Statistics had no category for them until the early 1990s.[11] The domestic role is portrayed as of paramount importance for both men and women, but for women, being "wife" and "mother" are the most valued functions, taking precedence over all others, especially over employment outside the homes (Izraeli, 1992a), despite the legitimacy of women's work (Brainerd, 2000; Dancer and Gilbert, 1993; Izraeli, 1991; Moore, 2000).

In Israel, such perceptions were augmented by essential needs: to counter the existential threat caused by unending wars, the scars of world-wide anti-Semitism, and the traumatic Holocaust. This dictated an emphasis on women's first and foremost obligation: propagation of the Jewish nation. Even today, after the number of births per woman has declined, Jewish women bear 2.9 children, twice the number found in Western Europe, for example.

As the data shows, almost all women in Israel until the mid-1980s got married, most of them before they were 40 years old. The proportion of women who chose to have children without a husband was negligible: in 1985, only 1.3% of all births were to never-married women. Even today, their numbers are rather small and only 3.3% of all births are to never-married women (these numbers include, of course, women who do have spouses but are not formally married).

The gendered division of labor placed a heavy burden on women since the industrial revolution, when a growing number of women began joining the workforce. Women became more valuable as workers, and at the same time, their domestic roles were reduced (e.g., education of children was transferred outside the home), made less significant (most products that were manufactured at home could be bought), and less satisfying. Economic necessity, egalitarian ideologies, and women's growing emphasis on what they wanted for themselves have all contributed to the growing participation of women in the labor market (Andersen, 1993; Fowlkes, 1987; Weitzman, 1984).

The problem then became one of juggling diverse roles: home roles (wife, mother, and homemaker) and work roles (including self-fulfillment). In traditional societies, in which the major part of the domestic responsibility is assigned to women, a heavy burden falls on women who work in addition to their household and family duties. Since raising children and taking care of them is predominantly women's responsibility (even in the more modernistic societies), their share of the domestic tasks is enormous.

Attempting to combine both home and work responsibilities created a situation in which women were placed in an impossible bind. They were expected to excel in all roles: be a devoted mother to well-adjusted children, be an attentive and indulging wife, run a well-organized household, and be a dedicated and efficient worker. Women were also expected to maintain a presentable personal appearance (Izraeli, 1983).

The tendency to accept the traditional division of labor is associated with Orthodox religious beliefs, which accord different roles to men and women. Orthodox women tend to support libertarian, egalitarian ideologies less than secular and nontraditional women (Greenstein, 1986; Kaufman, 1994; Moore, 2000).[12] In addition, acceptance of the traditional division of labor is associated with agreement with the stereotypes against working women and the devaluation of their work investments, especially against women who are mothers and wives (e.g., "Working women are worse mothers than nonworking women" [Antecol, 2001; Pelham, Hetts, and Stratton, 2001]).

Women who strongly support the traditional gendered division of labor tend to have heavier family responsibilities than women who do not support it (i.e., the former are more likely to get married and have more children than the latter; they also refrain from working when pregnant and/or when their children are young [Budig and England, 2001]).

Although the home-work dichotomy has somewhat weakened over the years as the number of working women grew, it was still highly significant until the mid-1980s (and in some segments of Israeli society it still is), and placed the burden for the domestic sphere almost entirely on women. Even NAAMAT, the largest women's labor union in Israel, reflected this traditional orientation in its mid-1980s advertising campaign, the slogan of which was, "Be a man! Give her a hand!" (i.e., don't share the burden equally; just help out from time to time).

3. The Public Sphere

Two domains are discussed in this sphere: women's socio-political activism and their participation in the labor market.

Women's Activism—With the Hegemony, Not Against It

Social activism is one component of the public spheres in which women historically had but a minor role, and their impact was almost nonexistent until the mid-1980s. Of course, Israel had a woman as Prime Minister (Golda Meir) long before other, more egalitarian societies, but that prime minister did nothing to advance women's issues. In fact, she was elected despite her gender, and may even be considered anti-feminist.

If social activism is represented by participating in political protests, less sociopolitical obedience, and attaining stronger social influence, then women were less active than men (Moore, 1998a). Moreover, most social actions taken by Israeli women until the late 1980s were either within male-dominated organizations (e.g., the existing political parties) or in women's organizations that supported the male-dominated institutions (like NAAMAT, the women's labor union, WIZO, the Zionist Women's Organization, and EMUNA, the religious women's organization).

Their actions in those years were directed mainly toward improving women's lives in the traditionally female domestic sphere but did not place these organizations in a position of competition with the state and its institutions. For example, these organizations focused their efforts on creating more—and better—subsidized day-care centers, which would enhance the ability of women to seek full-time employment.

Almost none of these actions were in conflict with the existing social order and its defined priorities. At best, when a possible conflict of interests seemed to develop (for example, when women's employment seemed to increase men's unemployment), women's attempts to improve their positions were portrayed as legitimately deriving from egalitarian ideas that were part of all the dominant ideologies.

This is hardly surprising. The willingness to participate in collective social action on gender issues to increase gender equality is related to salient gender identities and their prevalence in a given society. As we could see in the previous chapter, the more prevalent gender identity at the time was the traditional, non-feminist identity, and the necessary—mostly feminist—ideologies that were necessary to legitimize and direct feminist social action were nonexistent, or hardly existent.

The Labor Market

In contrast with the Western world of the 1950s, where most working women were young, unmarried and mostly immigrant, Israeli working women at that period were of varied ages, and mostly non-immigrant. The need for nation-building included women, though in Israel, too, women were allocated different types of jobs than men. Changes in the ages of working women soon appeared, in accord with other Western societies, and most married women with children left the labor market, so that they worked until it was time for them to fulfill their primary reproductive obligation. In the 1960s, when mothers of young children were returning to the labor market in the more advanced Western societies (Oppenheimer, 1970), Israeli women were leaving their jobs to raise their kids. It took Israeli women more than two decades to create the shift that enabled more women to return to work even when they were mothers of young children, and to recognize that children need not be a barrier (in this respect, they remain behind women in other modern societies).

The growing diversification of the Israeli labor market in the 1960s and 1970s, and the strengthening of the individualistic achievement orientation that accompanied the decline of the socialist collectivistic beliefs, exposed women to the limitations which this orientation imposes upon groups with weaker competitive abilities. It also reflected the conflict created by the primary and secondary human images, and the unequal reward allocation they generated. Moreover, it rekindled and intensified the conflict between the modern and the traditional value-systems which, under the collectivistic approach, had existed but had been somewhat less emphasized.[13]

In most societies, legitimization of unequal reward allocation and the different human images stem from the same normative basis. As men represent the traits attached to the primary image and as women are considered to be better suited to the secondary image, gender stratification evolves and corresponds with these images. Legitimization of men's advantages is maintained by presenting men as stronger, more intelligent, more energetic, and of higher moral standards, and therefore of being better able to hold positions that are more important to society.

As much as determining the criteria for reward allocation, societies also decide which rewards are most important. In most Western societies, money and material goods are the most valued rewards (Davis and Moore, 1945). The majority of societies in which individual achievement is the dominant value determine the hierarchy of positions according to the position's importance to society and its requirement of more extensive investment in human capital (i.e., education, on-the-job training and experience) and/or talent.

In the labor markets of most industrial societies, human capital factors which increase productivity are bases (or criteria) for the unequal allocation of opportunities and rewards. Changes in the amount of rewards over the years represent changes in the amount of human capital invested, so that more productive workers receive higher rewards in return for their work (Becker, 1964, 1971). According to both economic and sociological research, different social groups invest in acquiring human capital to different degrees so that their productivity tends to vary accordingly (Beck, Horan, and Tolbert, 1980; Bibb and Form, 1977).

Women, on the average, tend to invest in formal education more than men, and men invest more in specific on-the-job training and gaining experience, both of which are more highly valued and rewarded by the labor market. The different investments are not always because of women's choices: often, employers prefer to invest in training men, not women, believing that the returns on their investments will be higher, and will last for longer periods of time (Horan, 1978).

One of the "prices" women pay for their investments in higher education is their overcrowding in sex-segregated (female-typed) occupations, or in occupations regulated by credentials (mainly academic degrees [Oppenheimer, 1970; Wolf and Rosenfeld, 1978]).

Occupational Sex Segregation

Sex segregation leads to a substantially different occupational distribution of men and women, creating "female-typed" and "male-typed" occupations (Jacobs, 1989). Female-typed occupations (such as secretarial work, teaching and domestic work) are those in which women are the majority of all workers in the occupation (over 60%), and male-typed occupations (like piloting, managing businesses and construction work) are those in which men are the majority of all workers (i.e., women make up less than 40% of all people in the occupation). It indicates that there are different probabilities of members of both genders to take up particular occupations (Ruble, Cohen, and Ruble, 1984).

Out of the 100 occupational categories defined by the Israeli Bureau of Statistics,[14] 80% of working women are concentrated in only 12 specified occupational groups: academics in the humanities, teachers, social workers, nurses and paramedics, secretaries and clerks, switch-board operators, typists, domestic workers, hairdressers and beauticians, tour guides, dental assistants, and dressmakers. In contrast, men are dispersed over a much wider spectrum of occupations. Moreover, gender segregation is so acute that in the majority of male-typed occupations, the percentage of women is very low, and vice versa (Moore, 1992a).

But occupational sex segregation also means that there are different characteristics to occupations for men and women (Ruble, Cohen, and Ruble, 1984), despite the continuous growth of women's share in the labor markets of most Western countries (Oppenheimer, 1970).

Furthermore, the sex segregation prevalent in that period has not lessened despite the growing proportion of women who enter the labor market (Izraeli, 1979). Although many women joined non-traditional high-status occupations in the 1980s, many more entered either female-typed or mixed occupations which then became female-typed.[15] Moreover, in a study of Israeli society (1930—1971), Padan-Eisenstark (1973) found that concerning labor force equality, Israeli women were not better off than women of other industrialized countries, and they are predominantly in teaching, nursing, clerical, and sales occupations.

These female-typed jobs, which required a rather high level of education but a lower degree of commitment than male-typed occupations, offered fairly high status but low wages. These characteristics of women's work maintained the traditional division of labor with one major difference: additional responsibilities were added to women, without reducing their domestic roles. Thus, although the types of jobs open to women may have changed over the years until the 1980s, sex segregation did not diminish (see Table 2.2 and 3.1).

These occupations also provided fewer advancement opportunities and women who worked in them—that is, most women—remained in the status of secondary breadwinners, almost always contributing less to the family income than their husbands, never able to shake the secondary human image and to assume an equal-partner status according to the primary image (Borman and Guido, 1986; Kalachek and Pains, 1976).

Many explanations were offered for the continued existence of sex segregation. They may be classified according to the different analytical dimensions they represent: societal-structural, cultural-normative, and individual (Acker, 1990; Bradley, 1989; Cockburn, 1991; Scott, 1986). However, the explanatory power of these theories is still debated (Kessler and McRae, 1982; Ross, Mirowsky and Huber, 1983). Usually, feminist ideologies are not mentioned as a factor that may explain if and when women's participation in the labor market will lessen sex segregation.

TABLE 3.1. EMPLOYMENT BY OCCUPATION AND GENDER, 1990-2005[a]

Occupation and Sex	1990	1995	2000	2005
MEN				
Total (thousands)	746.3	931.9	991.8	1,052.8
Percent	100/0	100.0	100.0	100.0
Scientific & Academic	9.7	12.2	12.9	14.9
Professional/Technical	11.6	10.4	12.5	12.9
Managers	8.6	8.1	11.5	9.9
Secretaries & Clerks	10.5	9.0	8.7	8.7
Sales workers	10.3	15.0	15.4	17.7
Agricultural workers	4.9	3.4	2.7	2.4
Industry workers	35.5	34.4	29.1	25.9
Service workers	8.7	7.4	7.2	7.7
WOMEN				
Total (thousands)	565.5	783.4	927.4	1,003.2
Percent	100.0	100.0	100.0	100.0
Scientific & Academic	8.7	12.8	13.5	14.9
Professional/Technical	25.5	19.3	20.0	19.1
Managers	2.2	2.4	4.4	3.9
Secretaries & Clerks	29.0	29.0	28.8	27.7
Sales workers	7.0	20.9	22.0	23.5
Agricultural workers	1.3	0.7	0.4	0.4
Industry workers	7.2	6.2	4.2	3.9
Service workers	19.0	8.7	6.8	6.7

Source: Labor Force Survey, 2008. Central Bureau of Statistics, Jerusalem.

Some researchers relate changes in occupational sex segregation to shifts from the industrial to the post-industrial economic structure, linking levels of sex segregation to the size of the service sector and women's labor market participation (Charles, 1992; Jones and Rosenfeld, 1989). In post-industrial labor markets, service occupations have grown more rapidly than other occupations, together with increased societal bureaucratization, labor market rationalization, and meritocratic evaluation of workers (Tienda et al., 1987). A vast service sector would usually be female-demanding (Reskin and Roos, 1990); the reservoir of men is insufficient and women are encouraged to join these occupations when the demand for workers increases (Epstein, 1988; Novarra, 1980); women find service occupations compatible with their socialization (Marini and Brinton, 1984; Weitzman, 1984); or because the wages paid in these occupations are relatively low, and do not attract men (Blau, 1987; Bridges, 1982; Hearn, 1982; Madden, 1985).

But other research shows that a change in the proportion of women does not always lead to changes in sex segregation. For example, Semyonov and

Shenhav (1988) claim that when the service sector develops rapidly, and the proportion of women in the labor market increases, sex segregation will be stronger and fewer women will join managerial and professional occupations. In contrast, Pampel and Tanaka (1988) claim that when the proportion of women in the labor market increases, the sex segregation will decrease (see also Fuchs, 1989; Rytina and Bianchi, 1984). Nuss and Majka (1983) found that economic development and women's work are not related, and Charles (1992) claims that diverse structural and societal factors influence the relationships in varied directions, some of which strengthen sex segregation and others of which lessen it so that the end result is dependent on the specific combination of factors in each society. Beller (1984), Maret (1983) and Reskin (1988) claim that sex segregation exists in more detailed occupational categories (see also Kanter, 1982; McLaughlin, 1978).

In Israel, sex segregation hardly changed at all until the end of the 1980s. Women's proportion in the Israeli labor force increased steadily (from 25% in 1955 to 40% of all workers in 1989). However, Moore (1995b) shows that the changes in the overall sex segregation in that period were minor.

There are, of course, women who make it to the top echelons of male-typed occupations, such as science, business, academia, and politics, but they are but a few. Still, women's proportion in the academic, professional and technical occupations has increased significantly: from approximately 20% of all the working women in 1955 to about 32% in 1986. Particularly in the last two decades, women have become more inclined to enter male-typed occupations, increasing their numbers in occupations such as law, medicine and engineering, and altering the gender composition in those professions. (For example, 1600 new workers entered the medical profession between 1976-1980; half of them were women, thus reducing the percentage of men from 70% in 1976 to 65% in 1980). However, the differences in the occupational distribution of men and women are still greater than the differences between ethnic groups (Oriental and European Jews in Israel). In fact, forty to sixty percent (depending on method and/or year of measurement) of the women workers would have to change occupations in order to create an occupational distribution similar to that of men (Beller, 1984).

Like gender, occupational sex-segregation has a predominant effect on the formation of differential treatment and unequal opportunities in the labor market. Female-typed occupations are mostly service occupations in the "tertiary sector" (agriculture being the primary sector, and industry the secondary), which suffers from a low market-value. This means that even when their human capital investments are equal, workers in female-typed occupations have fewer opportunities and/or rewards in return for their work than workers in male-typed occupations.

The data for the Israeli labor market support the U.S. findings (Bielby, and Baron, 1984) according to which workers in female-typed occupations have, on average, more education than workers in male-typed occupations, but their accumulated experience (indicating the more specific job training) is much lower. This is mainly due to their younger age and earlier retirement, not to a greater propensity to leave the labor market or to stay out of it for extended periods of time.

It is interesting to find that workers in female-typed occupations have, on the average, lower status than workers in male-typed occupations (Blau and Ferber, 1986). These differences are even more salient when taking into consideration the hierarchies of specializations within occupations. As in educational attainment, here too women tend to be engaged in the less prestigious occupational specialties and the lower ranks in each of the professional hierarchies. In the universities of both the U.S. and Israel, for example, women occupy the ranks of lecturers and assistant professors in greater proportion than their share among full professors: 9% of the women vs. over 30% of the men (Bielby and Baron, 1984).

Occupational type differences were attributed to many causes. Like the gender differences, supply-side and demand-side factors interact to produce the inferiority of female-typed occupations. On the supply-side, women offer fewer resources: we have seen that women can expect shorter working lives; they join occupations from which they can exit to give birth to and raise their children; and in terms of general human capital, up-to-date knowledge in female-typed occupations is less important and deteriorates at a slower rate. Hence, re-integration is swift for those who choose to temporarily leave the labor market.

The lowering of their market value is also affected by the prevalence of female-typed occupations in peripheral (and public) sectors rather than core (and private) ones, in secondary labor markets rather than in primary markets, and in industries lacking market power more than in the "strong" industries. For example, teachers, nurses and social workers are employed mostly by the public sector, in its less influential segments, and workers in them usually cannot switch to alternative organizations (Bridges, 1980; Cohen and Pfeffer, 1984; Effroni, 1980).

Workers in male-typed occupations are more likely to be found in the private sector while workers in female-typed occupations are almost totally restricted to the public sector, which is almost the sole employer of those occupations (i.e., nurses, teachers, social workers and related occupations). Furthermore, almost all of the workers in female-typed occupations are employees (96%) whereas many workers in male-typed occupations are self-employed (only 74% are employees); and fewer among the workers in female-typed occupations are in positions of authority (26% vs. 48%, respectively).

In summation, gender biases and occupational sex-segregation interact to produce a very strong barrier for working women, whose options become limited not only in comparison to men in male-typed occupations but also in comparison to men who work in female-typed occupations: their accessibility to training and skill acquisition is limited, the quantity and quality of positions open to them is restricted, advancement systems do not treat them impartially, and less knowledge about opportunities within the system is available to them. Even trade union policy, according to which the most senior people in a position are entitled to more desired posts, acts against women. Considering their relatively lower seniority, especially within the blue-collar occupations, their advancement is curbed and they are the first to be declared redundant in accordance with the principle "last in—first out" (Deaux, 1984; Harlan and O'Farrel, 1982). The percentage of women in industry is on the decline since 1970, and we should expect that as long as economic growth does not create a manpower demand exceeding the supply of the male labor force, men will be preferred and segregation reinforced (Blau and Jusenius, 1976; Featherman and Hauser, 1976; Liss, 1975; Bartol, 1978).

In addition, "service" occupations, which are female-demanding, manifest the highest growth rate so that women are channeled to occupations already defined as female-typed, augmenting the disproportion in the occupational distribution (Ferris, 1971; Semyonov and Scott, 1983). Consequently, with a general increase in the number of workers, women's participation in the labor force will increase, but their relative status in the labor market will suffer due to growing segregation.

Inequality of opportunities exists at entry into the labor market as well as during the working life, so that female-typed occupations, and especially the women engaged in them, are discriminated against by market forces throughout their employment.[16] The sex-typing of occupations affects the structure of opportunities and rewards of men and women in the labor market and, as a result, influences worker attitudes and behavior both within and outside the context of work.

Although the inclusion of a work role to women's roles had a major impact on both the lives of individual women and the social structure, the attention of social scientists was significantly attracted to female labor force participation and its consequences only in the 1970s (in Israel, a decade later), especially when women began to indicate that combining the two worlds of family and work is not the idealized life style it was portrayed to be by some feminists. Studies focusing on role conflict first appeared in Western societies in the late 1970s (e.g., Catter, Scott and Matyna, 1977; Shainess, 1980).

4. The Clash of the Three Domains: Role Conflict and Labor Market Marginality

Role Conflict

Role conflict occurs whenever a person is required to perform diverse social roles that place excessive expectations on individuals and demand incompatible behaviors (Chassin, Zeiss, Cooper and Reaven, 1985). Home-work role conflict refers to the concurrent and incompatible time demands that people with both work and family obligations encounter (Cowan, 1983; Fuchs, 1989; Horowitz, 1982). The notion of family-work conflict is rooted in the broader theory of role-conflict, which is in turn associated with the problem of occupying a plurality of roles (Voidanoff, 1987). According to this theory, role conflict is inherent in the fact that any actor is the incumbent of a plurality of roles. Thus, being a woman entails being a daughter, wife, mother, teacher, volunteer and member of a religious community, and so on. In each of these roles, she interacts with others who compose a "role set" (Merton, 1957).

Role-conflict is created by contradictory expectations directed at the actor by others in diverse role sets, namely inter-role conflict. For example, a woman's boss demands that she should not be absent from work while her husband wants her to stay home when a child is sick. Here, two different role-sets are involved competing for a person's limited resources. Role conflict can also originate from discrepant or incompatible claims presented by people in the same role set, in other words, intra-role conflict; for example the role of a teacher who encounters incompatible demands from her supervisor, her students, and their parents.

The division of individual resources is accompanied and strengthened by work-related stereotypes and attitudes regarding working women and mothers, and it is related to gender ideology; that is, the perceptions and beliefs concerning the appropriate roles for women and men in family and society. Women who strongly support the traditional gendered division of labor tend to have greater family responsibilities than women who do not support the traditional gendered division of labor (i.e., the former are more likely to get married and will likely have more children than the latter; they also refrain from working when pregnant and/or when their children are young [Budig and England, 2001; Cappelli, Constantine and Chadwick,

2000]). Gender ideology is shaped by socialization processes and cultural expectations (Kirchmeyer, 1992).

In Israel, religiosity and acceptance of the stereotypical division of labor between men and women are usually related, so that religious individuals also adhere to the traditional gender ideology more strongly (Moore, 2000). Thus, to accord importance to her work as well as to her family, an Israeli woman needs to relinquish—at least partially—the traditional views.

The extensive research literature on the family-work interface, from different perspectives, reflects the salience of this issue in everyday life (Baltes and Heydens-Gahir, 2003). Work and family are the most important life domains of the adult person in modern society. Most of us participate in these "greedy" institutions, each demanding total commitment, for long periods in our lives. The separation of home and the workplace, the private and public spheres, the household and market, make family and work a classic case of potential inter- role conflict. However, "[b]y treating family and work as mutually constraining, these conceptualizations overlook how work and family are integrated in ways that contribute meaning to the everyday lives of individuals" (Bielby, 1992, p. 283).

The main classification of sources of role conflict distinguishes between two sets of factors. One—Insufficient Resources—is physical, pertaining primarily to time and place; the other—Incompatible Demands—is normative (attitudinal), related to values, ideologies, beliefs, and emotions (Katz and Kahn, 1966; Greenhaus and Parasuraman, 1999).

Insufficient Resources—Research was mainly concerned with time scarcity. This approach implicitly assumes that increasing time (and other resources, such as energy and commitment) in one role decreases the time that can be invested in other roles. In order to fulfill their various role obligations, working mothers need to allocate, manage or juggle the limited time at their disposal. Time pressures are frequently present also within a single role (intra-role), i.e., workers who feel that they cannot fulfill all their work requirements due to lack of time and energy, sometimes called work "overload."[17] Referring to the family-work interface, Hall argues: "...the conflicts between roles are often more a matter of role overload and competition for her time, a scarce resource, than an issue of intrinsic incompatibility." (Hall, 1977, p. 471).

Incompatible demands—The second source of role conflict stems from discrepant norms and values implicated in multiple role fulfillments. According to Thompson and Bunderson (2001), this issue is even more complex and confusing, referring to attribution of value and meaning rather than time scheduling. For example, in the context of work and family the competition is not only about the quantity of time that an individual devotes to home or job, but concerns the question of priority—which is of greater value and importance to him/her, to which is he/she more committed and loyal (hence the concept of "quality time")?

Despite the fact that home-work role conflict can befall both genders in all societies, it is usually applied to women, especially to women who are married and mothers of small children, rather than to men (Cooke and Rousseau, 1984; Crosby, 1987; Fox and Nickols, 1983; Gray, 1983).

The differential application of the term stems from the sex-typing of behaviors and characteristics and the socially constructed expectations regarding the two genders (Epstein, 1988), that were discussed earlier in this chapter. Sex typing of behaviors means that a majority of the people who behave in a certain way are of one gender, and there is a normative belief that this is "right" (Merton, 1957). Because in most societies family and domestic obligations are still considered primarily women's responsibilities, despite the legitimacy of women's work (Bernstein, 1983; Lehrer and Stokes, 1985; Marini and Brinton, 1984), choosing work over family is usually not a conceivable option for women (Izraeli, 1993).

In traditional societies, women used to quit the labor force once they married and had children. This is not the case in more modern societies, in which the proportion of women with small children who continue working outside the house has been growing continuously (Kessler-Harris, 1990), and many among them see their work as a career in which they invest much energy (Brinton, 1988; Novarra, 1980; Wiley, 1991). Still, because they are often expected to shoulder most of the domestic chores, the work roles are considered an additional burden to women's existing overload (Cowan, 1983; Polachek, 1985; Roos, 1985).

Because of the many demands on women's time, their labor market participation was greatly affected. First, only a few of them chose to add the work burden to their already heavy domestic responsibilities: until the mid-1980s, the proportion rose gradually in Israel, but remained lower than the proportion of women in other Western societies. Their proportion grew from 24.4% of all workers in 1955 to 40.6% of all workers in 1985.

Second, women in general, and mothers (or those who see themselves as potential mothers), in particular, tended to work intermittently, in part-time jobs or in less demanding occupations, or in employment where exits from and re-entries into the labor market are possible at minimum costs and loss of human capital.

The need to avoid a clash between their family- and work-roles limited women's occupational choices, and most of them turned to female-typed occupations in which flexible, part-time jobs are more acceptable and skills do not devalue as fast as in male-typed occupations (Aiba and Wharton, 2001; Hunt and Saul, 1975; Youssef and Hartly, 1979; see a more detailed analysis of sex segregation and sex-typing of occupations in the previous chapter). When they did turn to male-typed jobs, they entered the less demanding occupations within them in order to minimize home-work role conflict (Cappelli, Constantine, and Chadwick, 2000), and they sought advancement less than men in order to avoid increased responsibility and time-consuming obligations. Even women who expressed a high degree of motivation were disinclined to seek actual advancement.

While labor market entries and exits are easier from female-type occupations or from positions which demand less commitment and perseverance, women paid a heavy price for their choices: they accumulated fewer years of experience, their skills degenerated in the time they spent away from their work, and their knowledge became obsolete (Eriksen and Klein, 1981). The potential sporadic interruptions of women's work forced them to choose occupations in which the cost of interruptions is lower, usually those in which little on-the-job training is necessary, knowledge gets outdated more slowly, and the returns for experience are lower (Darley, 1976; Hoffman and Reed, 1981; Horner, 1972; Marini and Greenberger, 1978; but see Heath and Britten, 1984).

In addition, women who interrupted their work or quit their jobs for lengthy periods of time to care for children or other family members, as their major social role prescribes, expected employers to understand and accept their priorities. However, although this behavior was (and is) socially legitimated, even expected of women, such behavior was (and still is) detrimental to women's career development, as their productivity was considered lower than men's, and they were regarded as both less dependable and less deeply committed to their work (Gurin, 1981).

Despite part time jobs, joining female-typed occupations, choosing less commitment-demanding work, women often found themselves in role conflict, in which the demands of one role clashed with the demands of the other. The implicit assumption is that work obligations interfere with fulfilling the domestic roles of women, not vice versa. To minimize the interference and reduce role conflict, many working mothers curtail their work roles by turning to "Mommy tracks" (Bergman, 1992; Fowlkes, 1987; Weitzman, 1984).

"Mommy tracks" are career paths determined by work arrangements offering mothers certain benefits, such as flexible hours, but usually providing them with fewer opportunities for advancement (Gelbard, 2009). These tracks were often found to be traps for women who wanted to leave full time employment when they had small children but wanted to return to it once their children grew up. Joining such occupations is easy; leaving them is much more difficult (Noonan, Corcoran, and Courant, 2005).

Such tracks are more easily found in female-typed occupations (Charles, 1992; Moore, 1992), which tend to be more "female friendly" in terms of flexibility, less compulsory overtime, and adjusting working hours to women's needs than male-typed occupations, because of their reliance on women workers (Kaufman, 1992; Jacobs, 1989). They are also occupations in which finding a substitute for suddenly-unavailable (female) workers is easy (substitute teachers, pools of secretaries, interchangeable nurses, and so forth).

Male-typed occupations are not restricted by time-bound family obligations. In fact, their structure is based on the assumption that work roles are the workers' primary roles, and that their other (family) roles are less important. Therefore, in all societies, these occupations are constructed to accommodate the "breadwinner" or "careerist" roles rather than the "homemaker" role and demand less flexible, longer working hours and greater work commitment than female-typed occupations (Moore, 1992). Married women (and especially mothers) who select male-typed occupations are, therefore, more likely to be under pressing time obligations and role conflict than men or women who join female-typed occupations. Also, women's work in atypical occupations may be considered a deviation from the traditional expectations (Berger, Wagner, and Zelditch, 1985; Ridgeway, 1993),[18] which adds to the excessive expectations they encounter.

However, in Israel as elsewhere, because male-typed occupations pay higher wages than female-typed ones (Moore, 1990), women in these occupations are better able to pay for outside services such as child-care, cleaning, and cooking (Kulman, 1986; Thoits, 1987). Thus, women in male-typed occupations enhance their power position at home and induce greater sharing of home responsibility (Crosby, 1991).

Women's choices regarding work and family are not necessarily of an "either-or" type but rather of a "more-or-less" type. Their options are not limited to "family only" or "work only" and women may have different time allocation strategies. These choices represent a continuum, and without relinquishing either of the two roles, some women allocate more of their time to the domestic sphere and less to the work sphere while other women reverse the order of priorities (Anderson, 1993; Stacey, 1990).

Women's decisions regarding role priorities may be construed as different strategies for reducing role conflict: The "limited work role" strategy means reducing role conflict by limiting the time and burden at work, and the "limited family role" strategy means reducing role conflict by limiting the time and burden at home. The choice of strategy depends on women's preferences and needs, but also on the occupation-types, their time demands and rewards, and the occupational demands of their spouses. Male-typed occupations have less flexible working hours, and require women to spend more time at work and reduce the time they allot to family work. In female-typed occupations, where working hours are more flexible, women may choose to spend less time at work and more time on family roles.[19]

Moore and Gobi (1995) show that controlling for marital status and number of children in Israel, women who worked in male-typed occupations did not report stronger role conflict than women in female-typed occupations. They perceived the domestic roles as less central, spent less time on their family obligations and more time at work, and experienced domestic work as less burdensome than women in female-typed occupations did.

The "limited family role" strategy does not mean that women in the male-typed occupations undervalue their family roles. These roles were found to be as important to women in male-typed occupations as they are to women in female-typed occupations. However, unlike women in female-typed occupations, women in male-typed occupations perceive their work roles to be as important as their family roles. Because of that, and because these occupations demand greater investments of time and commitment, they work longer hours and are more likely to have additional tasks than women in female-typed occupations. They spend less time on family obligations and their balance of time allocation is different from women in female-typed occupations. Also, women in male-typed occupations earn higher wages than women in female-typed occupations and can purchase more domestic services. In that, they seem to choose a strategy that is similar to men's. The "limited family role" strategy seems to be more effective in reducing role conflict than the "limited work role" strategy.

The "limited work role" strategy accords highest priority to family and domestic roles. This strategy is possible for persons employed in part-time work or in time-flexible jobs. Because they work shorter hours and for lower wages, workers in such occupations need—and can afford—less help with domestic obligations. They spend more time on family and domestic obligations than women in male-typed occupations, and they also feel more burdened by these responsibilities.

Deconstructing the dissimilarity between those who espouse each of the two strategies, Moore and Gobi (1995) show that the differences are due to distinct basic dispositions and attitudes exhibited by women who turn to male-typed occupations and those who turn to female-typed ones in Israel: the former were more egalitarian than the latter. However, occupations also shape the behaviors of those who enter them. In this sense, occupations impose the strategy, and women are not entirely free to choose a strategy. They may be "forced" into certain occupations in which they can implement the strategy that fits their needs and the constraints of their lives.

Moore and Gobi (1995) concluded that the different strategies are due to a combination of the two influences so that workers with a certain disposition turn to occupations in which a specific strategy is required while workers with different dispositions turn to occupations in which a different strategy is more prevalent. (The question of which of the two elements precedes the other remains open.)

It may also be that work in male-typed occupations is adjusted to the traditional division of labor that attributes greater importance to men's work roles than to their family roles and, therefore, all workers in them are forced to follow the "limited family role" strategy. [20] In contrast, female-typed occupations have no inherent or predetermined strategy and therefore workers in them can prefer to emphasize either the family sphere or the work domain. In either case, women cannot be treated as a homogeneous group, for whom a single and specific strategy is applicable.

In summation, it seems that heavier load in one sphere leads to stronger role conflict only if the load at the other sphere is not reduced. Thus, heavier family load leads to stronger role conflict if the workload is not reduced; similarly, a heavier workload leads to stronger role conflict if the domestic load is not reduced. The decision to allocate more time to one role than to the other may be construed as dependent on preferences, needs, culture, or socialization. It may also depend on the occupation types and their time demands: in male-typed occupations, where working hours are less flexible, workers tend to spend more time at work and reduce the time they allot to family; in female-typed occupations, where working hours are more flexible, workers may choose to spend less time at work and more time on family roles.[21] Though women usually spend more time on domestic obligations than men, time allocation decisions apply to both genders.

Consequently, women who turn to male-typed occupations tend to be less home-oriented and attribute less importance to their traditional feminine roles (i.e., parent, spouse and homemaker) than to their work roles (i.e., breadwinner and careerist) as a strategy to reduce role conflict.

Labor Market Marginality

As there were few women in such jobs until the mid-1980s, the number of potential female role models was negligible and, in addition, women had to deal with diverse factors that exacerbated their plight. Two of them are discussed here: the problematic nature of their "token" status, and the difficulty in finding mentors and female role models.

Tokenism and the Queen Bee Syndrome

The tokenism approach (Kanter, 1977a,b) explains some aspects of the working lives of the few women who joined male-typed occupations, especially in the early years (the 1960s and 1970s in the U.S., the 1980s in Israel). According to this approach, the proportion of each gender in a specific occupation or organization is one of the main factors affecting the work behaviors of individuals. Kanter (1977a) found that when women were a small minority in a group (15% or less), their gender made them highly visible, separated from male co-workers, and unable to assimilate in the majority group. As a result, women in male-typed occupations were compelled to conform to the dominant male culture, which they were powerless to influence or modify to their needs. Any deviation caused immediate, often harsh, sanctions (in the form of ridicule, isolation, loss of status, and so forth).

This led most "token" women to follow the norms and standards that emphasized individualism, attainment, self-efficacy and effort. Alternative ways of attaining the same goals were not considered as legitimate. Any attempt to "change the rules" and act in a more feminine way (e.g., share power and responsibility with team members or show emotions), was considered an indication that they were incapable of doing the job. To minimizing the salience of their gender and avoid sanctions, women tended to lower their visibility by dressing conservatively, in cloths that mimicked men's garb, strictly following the rules, and trying hard not to be different. Therefore, "tokenism" constrained the female minority's interactions with their male colleagues and limited their choice of behaviors.

According to Laws (1975), tokenism can be found in every situation in which a dominant group comes under pressure to share its privileges, power and resources with a group which has previously been denied them, and it represents one of the means by which the dominant group enables some potential mobility for the weaker group while nonetheless limiting it.

It should be added that token status is not attached to all who are minorities within a larger group. When men join female-typed occupations, for example, their visibility is an advantage, not a detriment (Floge and Merrill, 1986; Izraeli, 1983). They are given more opportunities for advancement, are more highly respected than women, etc. Kanter's (1977) theory should, therefore, be amended: heightened visibility, contrast between majority and minority groups, and the inability to assimilate are drawbacks only when the primary (external) status of the minority group is lower than the status of the majority. The same preconditions are neutral factors or even an advantage when the primary status of the minority group is higher than that of the majority.

Being a "master status," gender dominates relationships even before professional skills can be assessed, and it reduced expectations for members of the "inferior" group. The sex structure of occupations strengthens these processes even further by relating the occupational role to the sex role, defining what is "suitable" for each sex group (Epstein, 1971; Holahan, 1979; Keller, 1984).

Moreover, being a "token" led the women involved to believe in their superiority over other women, and to avoid encouraging or supporting other women interested in breaking through the boundaries of the system. Hence, the socialization process these women went through deterred the development of class awareness among women[22] and turned many of them into "queen bees." It is interesting to note that there are no studies of tokenism in Israel, although the phenomenon exists, perhaps because of the small size of the Israeli female labor market.

The **Queen Bee Syndrome** refers to the phenomenon according to which successful women in male-typed occupations or organizations are likely to be critical of other women and to endorse negative gender stereotypes more than their male colleagues. To succeed, these women had to prove that they were not like other women, that they did not fit the gender stereotypes, and that therefore they deserved to be treated differently: to get promotions, positions of power, and more responsibility. The very strategies that women employ to counter the negative impact of gender in their work settings in order to achieve career success are likely to cause them to discriminate against other women (Heilman, 1995), and the phenomenon has been found in different settings, and different societies.

For example, Ellemers, van den Heuvel, de Gilder, Maass and Bonvini (2002) analyzed women in academic settings and argued that while male and female PhD students showed equal work commitment and work satisfaction, senior *female* researchers showed a consistent bias against the female students. No such negative stereotypes were found among senior *male* researchers. Ellemers at al. (2004) attributed this bias to the female researchers' struggles to show that they differ from "regular" women, and thus merit their senior positions.

Another example is Rediger's (1979) examination of ordained female clergy, and his analysis of the resentment among the new members of their cadre who could not find jobs easily and were looking for someone to blame. While some of them were angry with denominational executives who refused to fight for their placement, others were disillusioned by people who were unwilling to accept women as ministers. Some, according to Rediger (1979), put the blame on "queen bees" who achieved their own ambitions and then held other women back.

Furthermore, women who attained high managerial levels in male-typed work settings tended to oppose organizational changes more than other women, because they wished to maintain the organizational culture in which they managed to succeed (Gibson and Cordova, 1999). They were also more likely to oppose the women's movement than other women or men (Staines, Tavris, and Jayaratne, 1974). However, when the proportion of working women increased, more among them joined male-typed jobs and organizations, and greater numbers of them attained positions of authority, the "queen bee" experience that led to greater sexism among women than among men diminished. In Israel in the mid-1980s, though, it was probably still very much in existence, as there were but a few women in such positions of power and authority.

The Difficulty in Finding Female Mentors and Role Models

Generally, mentors are supposed to be wise and trusted guides and advisors, open-minded and nonjudgmental, consistent and supportive. Protégés are the people who receive career support, protection, and advocacy. Mentoring has generally been perceived as a positive relationship that enhances the lives of protégés, mentors, and organizations (Kram, 1985). Having a mentor has been linked to career advancement (Scandura, 1998; Whitely, Dougherty and Dreher, 1991, 1992), higher pay and greater career satisfaction (Burke, 1984). For mentors, the relationship is an opportunity to make productive use of knowledge and expertise in middle age and to learn in new ways (Burke and McKeen, 1996).

Mentoring relationships may be critical to the advancement of women in organizations, especially when they join managerial roles in which the competitive pressures are more emphasized than in other jobs (Morrison and White, 1987).

Research on mentor relationships increased about two decades ago (Fagenson, 1989; Noe, 1988; Ragins, 1999), and continues to be reported (Johnson and Huwe, 2003; Waters, 2004). This is not surprising, given the fact that empirical research shows significant gender differences in availability of mentors and benefits from mentoring (Kram, 1985a,b; Thomas and Alderfer, 1989).

Gender issues have become increasingly important as the instrumental role of mentoring in career development has been recognized. Mentors have been identified as an important factor in the career success of men, but may be even more critical to the career success of women (Morrison and White, 1987; Ragins, 1999). At this time, because of organizational demographics, most mentors are men.

Ragins and Cotton (1991, 1999) found that women reported more perceived barriers to gaining a mentor than did men. Cross-gender mentoring may raise additional issues that are absent in the typical male-male relationship (Clawson and Kram, 1984). Noe (1988) has identified six potential barriers to the establishment of cross-gender relationships. Clawson and Kram (1984) discuss the developmental dilemma existing in cross-gender relationships in which the pair must manage closeness/distance in the internal relationship as well as perceptions of the relationship by outsiders. In addition, there have been suggestions that the costs and benefits associated with being a mentor may differ for women and men (Kram, 1985b), although some studies (Ragins and Cotton, 1993) did not find this to be the case.

Women may bring unique competencies and needs to the mentor-protégé relationship (McKeen and Burke, 1989). Fitt and Newton (1981) observed that female protégés needed more encouragement and had to be sold more actively at higher levels than did males. Burke (1984) studied male and female protégés and found that females reported receiving more psychosocial functions from mentors than did males. Reich (1985) supported these findings when he reported that the affective, emotional aspects of the relationship were more vital for female protégés than for male protégés, and that women were more likely than men to stress caring, nurturing, and teaching when describing the mentorship. Relationships involving a female protégé were also more likely to develop into a close friendship than were those involving only men. Kram (1985a) found that female protégés were more likely to experience greater social distance, discomfort, and over-protectiveness from male mentors than male protégés. Furthermore, women considered the mentor's role in providing feedback about strengths and weaknesses to be more important than did men (Kram, 1985b).

Noe (1988), in a study of successful assigned mentoring relationships, found that mentors matched with opposite-sex protégés reported that these protégés used the mentorship more effectively than did protégés with same-sex mentors. He hypothesized that protégés in opposite sex mentoring relationships worked harder to make the relationship successful because of the possible difficulties of cross-gender relationships at work. He also found that mentors believed that women more effectively utilized the mentorship than did men. Women may be more strongly motivated than men to use mentors because of their knowledge of the importance of such relationships to their careers. Noe (1988) collected his data in an educational setting. Women in this setting were engaged in occupations that were congruent with occupational role stereotypes. Men in upper-level administrative positions may not have been inhibited in dealing with female protégés, and female protégés may have been supported to develop mentorships to advance their careers in this particular environment. The study had several objectives, including comparing the experiences of women who had female and male mentors and examining the influence of cross-sex mentoring relationships. The research focused on the experiences of female protégés, since cross-sex mentoring has not been sufficiently studied (Ragins and McFarlin, 1989).

However, there are gender differences in perceived barriers to obtaining mentors. First, women may be reluctant to initiate a relationship with a man for fear that the mentor or others in the organization will misconstrue such an approach as a sexual advance (Bowen, 1985; Fitt and Newton, 1981). Men may perceive mentoring women as complicated and may select men over women as protégés to avoid destructive gossip and innuendos (e.g., Clawson and Kram, 1984; Fitt and Newton, 1981). A second reason for expecting gender differences is that traditional gender role expectations encourage men to take an aggressive role and women a passive role in initiating relationships (Maccoby and Jacklin, 1974), which makes it difficult for women to initiate cross-gender relationships (e.g., Bushardt and Allen, 1988; Hill, Bahniuk, and Dobos, 1989). Women may fear that assertive attempts to initiate relationships will threaten potential mentors, and may therefore wait for the potential mentors to initiate the relationships. Finally, women have fewer formal and informal opportunities than men for developing mentoring relationships. Women lack access to many of the informal settings potential male mentors frequent, such as men's clubs and sports activities (Hunt and Michael, 1983; Zey, 1984). Also, since women tend to occupy low-level positions (Blau and Ferber, 1987), they may be less likely than men to get involved with projects that lead to mentoring relationships.

Though no studies of these issues were performed in Israel, it seems logical to assume that the same processes and constraints on finding mentors limited women in Israel in the same manner as elsewhere.

Conclusions

In summation, the different socialization processes and diverse prospects curbed women's actual aspirations and expectations, limiting their choice of careers in Israel as in other Western societies. This caused their crowding into a relatively limited number of occupations that accepted such work-behaviors (e.g., working part time, in female-typed occupations, with low commitment) that allow the family to remain womens' first priority. As a result, an excess of women workers was created in these occupations, reducing both their professional status and their salaries (Bergman, 1974, 1986). The process also affected employers' expectations: because women were seen as less stable workers and less committed to the labor market, and because on-the-job training requires a large investment, the employers made the "rational" calculation of expenditure and preferred engaging men for positions requiring extensive training and practice (Amsden, 1979).

These processes strengthened the stereotypes against women, and they became more entrenched. Stereotypes are based on "a grain of truth" that turns them to actuarial biases (Blau, 1977). In order to exist, prejudice requires some reality-based data according to which statistical generalizations can be made. Once formed, these stereotypes tend to remain rigid even when faced by contradictory information, and to become a stereotypical reaction to ambiguous or uncertain situations (Kiesler, 1975). Moreover, women who worked part-time, or in female typed occupations, or showed low commitment because they had family responsibilities, were taken as "proof" that the stereotype is true for all women, not as demonstrating the compromise that women had to make in order to combine family and work. Women's labor market behavior was interpreted as indicating that "this is what women want," or "this is all women are good for," or "women shouldn't try to combine family and work once they have children."

In addition, the political sphere contributed to strengthening the stereotypes and the social expectations: no public funds were allocated to the construction of day care centers for young children and no social legitimation for such institutions was created; expenses for care-givers, private day care centers, or other solutions that women tried to use when they had young children were not recognized as tax-deductible, often making women's work not worth the effort. Women's dependence on men was high, and their contribution to family income low. As domestic work and raising children lack monetary value, they were considered to have low-status.

ENDNOTES

[1] Since feminism was not established in Israel until the early 1980s, and feminist research was practically nonexistent at the time, most of the definitions are based on research in more advanced societies.

[2] The well-meaning liberal male (WMLM) is a man who expresses liberal ideas but behaves inconsistently with his professed beliefs (Gackenbach and Auerbach, 1975).

3   Women who did not accept the "altruistic other orientation" were more likely to be self-supporting in their middle years and attain more academic degrees than those who did.

4   Douvan (1975), for example showed that the psychology of women (i.e., their self-perception and traits) did not correspond to the demands of the academic world, and that men tended to enter college with a more highly developed sense of assertiveness and autonomy than women, who emphasized empathy and investment in fantasy.

5   The term "traditional" is used in its literal sense (according to Webster's Thesaurus) to denote generally accepted, customary, habitual, widespread, sanctioned, prescribed, doctrinal, and well established cultural norms.

6   Following Eisenstein (1983), Kourany, Sterba and Tong (1992) and Andersen (1993), I define patriarchy as a hierarchical system of social relations among men and women that creates and maintains the domination of women.

7   Some religious denominations are more liberal and more egalitarian than Orthodox denominations. In Israel, however, these denominations are not common (they constitute less than 5% of all Israelis) and only Orthodox Judaism is *formally* recognized in Israel. The more egalitarian denominations are strongly influenced by liberal, humanitarian and feminist movements around them. Among Muslims, the trend seems to be reversed so that *all* religious Muslims are devout, but the Fundamentalists see themselves as more devout than others (Haddad, 1985). Thus, all Muslims are bound by a powerful cultural and religious ideology linking family honor ("ird") to female virtue, entrusting men with safeguarding family honor through control over female members (Mernissi, 1987; Moghadam, 1992). Certain newer Muslim movements like Hamas and Hizbollah enforce a more literal interpretation of Islam that complicates gender relations and promotes a more traditional division of labor.

8   In order to avoid a lengthy discussion of differences that is not entirely relevant in this context, the concept "feminism" is used for a variety of political perspectives. A more elaborate discussion can be found in Chapter Four.

9   Same sex couples are not included because they are too few to count in Israel.

10   Traditional marriages in Israel are performed only by Orthodox rabbis. No other types of marriage are recognized by Israeli law. Among the Palestinian citizens of Israel, the marriage rate is even higher, whether they are Muslim or Christian, and is 95% and 93%, respectively.

11   Today, only 2.9% of Israeli couples are cohabiting and not married by the Orthodox establishment. Almost all of them are Jewish couples. In comparison, 7.4% of couples in the US are cohabiting, 10% of couples in England, and 23% in Sweden.

[12]   In contrast, some Christian denominations as well as Reform and Conservative Judaism are more liberal, and more egalitarian. The more egalitarian denominations are strongly influenced by liberal, humanitarian and feminist movements around them. However, such denominations are not common in Israel and only Orthodox Judaism is currently formally recognized, so that only Orthodox rabbis can determine who is Jewish, perform marriage ceremonies, etc.

[13]   The lesser emphasis may be due to the more urgent nation-building problems that Israeli society faced in the first years, when collectivistic ideals were stronger. If so, the intensity of the conflict should not be attributed to the ideology, and the observed concurrence is not a causal relationship.

[14]   Over 400 occupations (3-digit classification) have been defined by the Central Bureau of Statistics, but the proportion of men and women in each occupation is published only for about 100 occupations in the 2-digit classification.

[15]   The data are for 1984 because it is closest to the year when the sample's data were collected·

[16]   However, not all inequalities mean discrimination. Part of the apparent inequality is the result of differences in the personal characteristics of the two genders employed in the various types of occupations. Discrimination refers, therefore, to the presence of inequality which results from stereotypes and prejudices.

[17]   Men, too, report experiencing role conflict (see, for example, Moore, 1995). However, the prevalence and intensity of that conflict among them tends to be lower than for women. Moreover, like Crompton and Harris (1998) and others, our study focuses only on women.

[18]   The logic may also be reversed: i.e., women who are less traditional in the sense that they perceive their work as very important are those who join male-typed occupations.

[19]   The choice between the two strategies may have been made *before* the person chose a specific occupation and therefore may have affected the occupational choice. It could have also been made *after* joining the labor market and therefore influenced by the occupation.

[20.]   In fact, Harlan and Jansen (1987) show that women working in traditionally female-dominated occupations showed more psychological and physical distress than those working in male-dominated, or neither-sex-dominated, occupational categories.

[21]   The choice between the two strategies may have been made *before* the person chose a specific occupation and therefore may have affected the occupational choice. It could have also been made *after* joining the labor market and therefore influenced by the occupation.

22. Another group of researchers in the above subject has concentrated on breaking down the boundaries of sex segregation in specific occupational categories (i.e., medicine, engineering, sciences, law, physics and management). These researchers analyze the conditions and limitations and the causes of women's acceptance into a specific male-type occupation, but it is impossible, on the grounds of these specific occupational characteristics, to draw general conclusions concerning women's integration in male-typed occupations. (See, for example, Exum, Menges, Watkins and Berglund, 1984.)

Chapter 4

Feminism Changes the World

Feminism, which is a world view that originally developed from general liberal ideologies, emphasizes advancing women's status in all domains of society that influence the relationships between men and women: the political, economic, social, and cultural spheres. It now includes diverse theories, beliefs, ideologies and movements that focus on different aspects of status, and varied routes to attain the goal of improving women's circumstances.

When did feminism begin in Western societies? When the ideology was defined? When organized groups took feminist action? When a significant proportion of women in a specific society defined themselves as feminists? We may argue about definitions and dates, but we cannot argue with its achievements if we consider social equality a worthy goal. Its impact is not uniform across societies, and the changes it has brought varies from one society to another, according to the existing culture in each society: from laws prohibiting gender discrimination to greater economic power for women; from changes in social norms in order to prevent sexual harassment to a growing acceptance of sexual preferences; and from a growing sharing of parenting roles to increased visibility of women in the public sphere.

The struggle for equality is far from over, and society still has a long way to go before women's contributions are recognized and valued in all life domains. Or before we even decide where the struggle is leading us. Or where we want the struggle to lead: do we want equality? Do we want it in all life domains? Do all groups in our society want to increase gender equality? Do we want to acknowledge existing differences in how their achievements are attained, or to emphasize differences in what they want to obtain? Or do we require women to act like men if they want to succeed in what used to be a men's world? And what is the cost for such equality?

These questions are but a few of the basic dilemmas that led to different answers provided by diverse feminist ideologies and movements (e.g., Liberal, Marxist, Radical, and Postmodern). What is considered "right" by some ideologies may seem "wrong" to others, and feminists today are far from agreeing on which goals to pursue and what the best way is of attaining them. Moreover, each ideology and set of goals is interpreted differently in each society in which feminist ideas are spreading, to suit the needs of the existing culture (Chafetz, 1988, 1990).

Opposing gender discrimination is common to most feminist ideologies, as is the fight against the patriarchal world-view that sees men in the center and as superior to women, or which produced Aristotle's words, "it may be said that a woman is an inferior thing and a slave beneath consideration" (Okin, 1979, p. 89). Still, there are significant differences among them. Some ideologies focus on equality, others on empowerment, and yet others on offering an alternative view of reality to the hegemonic (male) view. Many extensive studies of the development of diverse feminist ideologies and their impact on society exist today (e.g., Anderson, 2000; Botting and Carey, 2004; Burke, 1986; Caine, 1997; Daley and Nolan, 1994; Fuller, 1941; Habermas, 1999; James, 1990; Keohane and Gelpi, 1982; Mellor, 2002; Stanton, Anthony and Gage, 1889; Taylor, 2004; Thompson, 1983; Windle, 2000).

This chapter focuses on how the different feminist ideologies affected Israeli society in general and the psychology of women in particular. It deals with the impact of feminism more than with the assumptions of any specific feminist approach. Moreover, the chapter is based on several suppositions: that increasing gender equality is a desirable goal for both individuals and society; that gender equality does not imply "sameness," so that men and women may have different ways of doing things, but the differences may lead to similar results (for example, men and women may have different management styles, but equal economic results); and that to increase gender equality, some major social changes need to be made, and those who benefit from the existing unequal situations are bound to resist such changes.

This analysis examines the social and psychological impact of feminist ideas in three periods: (1) the hegemonic socialist era of nation-building in which feminism had only a minor influence on the psychology of women and on social processes (until the late 1970s); (2) the liberal opening to "imported" Western ideas like capitalism and individualism, a period in which feminist psychology contributed to changes in the gender schema, and the gendering of traits, roles and stereotypes (the 1980s until the mid-1990s); and (3) the multiculturalism and globalization period, with its local nuances, in which feminist psychology influenced the perception of the female body, leading to a significant change away from the presentation of menstruation as "unclean" and the hiding of the pregnant body, and more recently open and natural breastfeeding in public places (since the mid-1990s).

These periods roughly correspond to the feminist waves that emerged in Europe and the US, but each wave commenced in Israel a few years after it impacted Western societies. The beginning and end of each period cannot be unequivocally defined, as they are part of the on-going structuration process; they are presented separately because the spreading of feminist ideas in them was hindered by different forces, and their accumulated social and psychological consequences tended to influence different domains.

The chapter then turns to the examination of the impact of feminism on gender identities and gendered activism. Feminists in Israel attempt to influence the relationships between men and women and advance women's status in the political, economic, social, cultural, and psychological spheres. The struggle for equality is far from over, and as do many societies, Israeli society often fails to recognize and value women's contributions in diverse life domains. Moreover, feminism in Israel developed slower than it did in most advanced Western societies. Though strongly influenced by global changes, it had to work around specific psychological and cultural limiting forces, mainly the myth of equality that was prevalent in the pre-state ("Yeshuv") and the highly traditional and patriarchal views of the religious establishment.

1. The Three Waves of Feminism

The First Wave

The first wave began in the eighteenth century as part of the spreading of liberal ideas proclaiming emancipation, freedom and equal rights for all. One of the clearest feminist voices at the time, Mary Wollstonecraft, demanded protection of women's rights in 1792 (*Botting*, 2006; Wollstonecraft, 1995). Another voice is the combined work of Elizabeth Cady Stanton and Susan B. Anthony, who fought for women's right to vote (Stanton, Anthony and Gage, 1889). The wave ended around World War I, when severe economic depression forced women to relinquish their dreams of equality.

The spreading of liberal ideas that emphasized personal freedom and equal rights in the early twentieth century was noticeable among women as well as among non-white men, the two groups that did not benefit from such ideas in the past. It may be said, therefore, that liberalism and egalitarianism competed with traditional patriarchal and racial values and ideologies for dominance. Many of the liberals supported values like freedom and equality because they saw them as just and fair; others supported these values because they saw them as instrumental to the attainment of other values like solidarity, improving the status of disadvantaged social categories, increasing the ability of all individuals to control their lives and so forth (Chafetz and Dworkin, 1986).

The main premise of Liberal Feminism is that it sees all humans as rational beings, with a right to self-actualization. Its supporters saw the emancipation of women as crucial to creating a liberal and advanced society, and fought for legislating equal rights for women, especially the rights to protection and independence. On the basis of their emphasis on universalistic principles that unify all individuals, they accentuate the similarity between men and women, and the need to integrate women in the public sphere (Thompson, 1983).

The main objective of this ideology was to fight the existing division of labor according to which men are actively seeking personal fulfillment and success, mainly through work, and women are passively dependent on men and interested in a stable family life (Friedan, 1963). Instead, the ideology suggested that women should become as active and achievement-oriented as men. It claimed that this would benefit not only women, but also society in general, as it would increase the reservoir of human potential in each society. Seeing women as well as men as rational beings meant believing that women are capable of sensible, realistic and coherent choices and decisions, and should be, therefore, making their own choices in both the public sphere (work and voting) and the private domain (family [Marso, 2003]).

During World War II, when men were away from their jobs, women took their places in offices, production lines, and agricultural work. Their accomplishments indicated that they are fully capable of participating in the world of work, and able to take care of themselves and society. However, when the war ended and men came back home, women had to vacate their jobs and return to their traditional family roles. The taste of freedom remained, and though feminism was set back and its gains slowed down, women's dreams of equality and freedom, like those of African Americans, fueled social change (Fisher, 1999). The main achievement of the first wave was attaining women's voting rights.

In recent decades, new liberal feminist trends became apparent, legitimating gender differences in how to attain goals and recognizing typical gendered behaviors which derive from these basic differences (Thompson, 1983). For example, female managers are considered more egalitarian than men and more people-oriented than the task-oriented male managers. The emphasis, therefore, became that of equal worth, according to which a job can be carried out in different ways, but performed just as well by men and women (Shainess, 1980).

The First Wave's Impact in Israel:

The Hegemonic Socialist Era (Until the Late 1970s)

Israeli feminism developed slowly. It had to work its way around the myth of equality[1] that was prevalent in pre-State Israel (the "Yeshuv") as well as the highly traditional and patriarchal views of the religious establishment (see Chapter Two). The myth prevented discussions of women's human rights for many years (Fogiel-Bijaoui, 1992; Izraeli, 1981).

The first wave became visible even before Israel became an independent state. At first, feminist ideas grew within prevalent ideologies in the pre-state: mainly Zionism and Marxism, which emphasized equality of social classes (Bowes, 1978). Although these ideologies did not see the status of women as a separate issue from the status of all other social categories, they were aware of the need to create gender equality and took for granted the notion that attaining equality for all social classes will bring equality to women too (Bernstein, 1983).

The first wave emphasized voting rights and the right of representation for women. The third Zionist congress (1899, Basel, Switzerland) recognized women's right to vote and recommended letting women elect representatives to Zionist organizations (like the "Histadrut"). This decision was not implemented in Israel for 20 years because of opposition from religious and Ultra-Orthodox representatives. Only when women organized and took militant action (e.g., strikes, protests, marches, disruption of political meetings) did they manage to attain their voting rights (Elboim Dror, 1994; Safran, 2006).

Several women's organizations have operated in Israel (than Palestine, or Eretz Israel) since the early nineteenth century. They were all based on liberal feminist ideologies which did not conflict with any of the major premises of the then-hegemonic Zionist ideology, and only acted to improve the lives of women in ways that were sanctioned by the male-dominated establishment. Among them: the "Female Workers' Movement" ("Tnuat Hapoalot"), which was created before World War I to improve the working conditions of female workers, mainly in agriculture; Hadassah Zionist Organization, which was created in the US in 1912, and in Israel in 1913, as an organization for strengthening Jewish ideals and institutions in Israel; WIZO (Women's International Zionist Organization) which started in Britain and opened its first branch in Israel in 1920, and focused on the welfare of women and children in Israel, especially creating and operating day-care centers, improving living conditions, and providing professional and agricultural education for girls; and NAAMAT, which was formed in 1921 on the basis of the "Female Workers'

Movement," as part of Israel's largest labor union ("Histadrut"), and reflected its main ideological premises (see Chapter Three). In 1926, Golda Meir, later Israel's prime minister, became chair of the organization (Bernstein, 1992).

These organizations relied on volunteers and focused on educating new immigrants, securing the rights of female workers, and providing day-care centers to enable women to work and become financially independent (Shilo, 1996). As Chapter Three indicates, their activities in those years were in tandem with the state and its institutions, not in competition or dispute with the patriarchal order they maintained (Brandow, 1980).

The only women's rights organizations that fought against the social order at the time were the "Hebrew Women's Union for Equal Rights" and the "Histadrut of Hebrew Women." The first, formed in 1919, included urban, secular, educated Western women, and worked to provide voting and election rights for women. When that was attained, they shifted their focus to the establishment of legal aid bureaus. The second, founded in 1920, was composed mainly of immigrant women from the US and focused on women's health issues (e.g., abortions and post-natal issues [Herzog, 1992; Izraeli, 1992]).

The power of women's organizations was low-key but stable since voting rights were obtained, and for many years the voices of women were practically silenced. Feminist action declined drastically when equal rights were attained (at least in declarations) when the State of Israel came into being (1948), a little after it ended in other Western societies. Then, pressures that threatened the very existence of the new state (wars, creating economic infrastructure, absorbing huge waves of immigrants, and so forth) forced feminist issues out of the sociopolitical discourse. The aforementioned women's organizations continued to operate the institutions they created, and provide the services for women and children, but they were not feminist in ideology. Even the few women in academic institutions were silent. In the late 1970s less than 8% of all associate professors and less than 5% of full professors were women. Feminism was rejected by male professors in all academic institutions; none of the academic publications accepted feminist manuscripts, and no feminist progress can be seen in that period. Very little documentation of these practices exist, for obvious reasons (see Moore and Toren, 1998, for further discussion).

Between the First and Second Waves

The period between the two waves (1940s and 1950s in the US, 1950s to 1970s in Israel) was one of two contradictory forces. On the one hand, post-World War II societies needed to recuperate from traumatic events and start rebuilding. Survival, economic rehabilitation and returning to "normal" life were of paramount importance. Liberal ideas like equality and social justice were accorded far less importance. The emphasis on materialistic values also brought back the traditional division of labor that had faded during the war when women had to work to earn a living and to replace men in factories and agriculture (Gornick and Moran, 1971). The need to employ women while men were at war now became a need to send women back home to make room for men, and to increase childbirth to replace the portion of the population that was lost. The "happy housewife myth" reached its peak in the 1950s in the US (Friedan, 1963). It was apparent in Israel as well (Brandow, 1980), where it was strengthened by traditional and religious values; "career women" were frowned upon.

On the other hand, French feminism became noticeably activist, and enjoyed a significant following in France and elsewhere. Works such as Simone de Beauvoir's "The Second Sex" (1973), in which she claims that women were always defined as the "other" sex, a deviation from the "normal" male (first published in 1949), led to major changes in the understanding of women. Translations of such works into diverse languages had a significant impact on many societies (Butler, 1986).

Although, at the time, the return to the traditional division of labor was a stronger trend then liberalism and feminism, and had a more significant impact on women in particular and society in general, in a historical overview, the feminist ideas that kept the ideological spark going proved to be stronger and longer lasting, and served as the basis for the second wave.

The Second Wave

Liberal ideals began spreading in the US in the early 1960s, and revolutionized society. Among them: equal rights movements, the American Civil Liberties Union (ACLU), and the Blacks' Movement, which all fought for equal individual rights; the students' revolution; and the sexual revolution that followed the approval of the birth control pill by the FDA (1961).

The atmosphere of transformation created optimal conditions for the reawakening of feminist ideals and movements, but it also changed the thinking of women about themselves, their goals, and the ways to attain these goals. Many feminist organizations were formed during this period, and among the first of them is the National Organization of Women (NOW), formed in 1963 by Betty Friedan and her colleagues. The liberal ideology of the organization emphasized similarities between the two gender categories, and fought to change the system that creates inequality between them (Chafetz, 1990; Cook, 1994).

The center of their fight was redressing inequality at home and in the workplace. The sociopolitical actions of the organization focused on equal rights legislation, and their major accomplishments were the Presidential Commission on the Status of Women (1963), which led to the Equal Pay Act, paid maternity leave and affordable child-care; Affirmative Action (1967); and abortion rights (1968 [Friedman, Tzukerman, Wienberg, and Todd, 1992]).

The changes in women's perceptions and actions were noticeable, as Shainess (1980) wrote in her conclusions: "The sense of a woman's obligation in marriage to 'please' the husband, is lessening. The sense of priority of children, and devotion to them, seems dulled. The desire to have children is weaker. The need for personal accomplishment seems greater. The choice of career over relationship with a man is growing in frequency. Intense affectional ties to husband and children are diminishing. First the extended family, and now the nuclear family, is fragmenting. Women are becoming more group-oriented through work in the corporate structure" (Shainess, 1980, p. 384).

Alternative Second-Wave Feminist Views

However, the social transformations gave rise to more extremist feminist schools of thought as well, and women who disagreed with and criticized liberal ideologies or were impatient with their slow, accumulative and deliberate achievements formed the radical feminist ideology and its organizations (like the Women's Liberation Movement [Echols, 2002]).

The ideology advocated a revolution in social relations that would lead to non-hierarchical and leaderless structures, and focused on women's lives and experiences as constructing a counter-culture in which women could become conscious of the meaning of their womanhood. The shared experiences and understanding led to the formation of a "Sisterhood" from which all men were excluded (Eisenstein, 1983).

Claiming that because all social institutions were created by men and for men they are unavoidably biased against women, radical feminists concluded that no amount of change would enable women to express their unique feminine essence. No matter how hard they tried, women would never be able to change the aggressive, male-dominated hierarchies to suit their needs, and therefore they saw joining these organizations as accepting patriarchy. Instead, they advocated creating alternative organizations in which feminine values and preferences (like cooperation, equality, support and empowerment) would flourish: organizations meant only for women, which would operate by a different set of rules (Whittier, 1995).

Another type of alternative feminist ideology that became noticeable at the time (and later affected Israeli society) is Marxist feminism. Marxist feminism follows Friedrich Engels' reasoning, according to which the family represents the wellbeing of one side (men) as attained through the oppression of the other side (women [Engels, 1884, translated 1972]). Women's dependence on men began when private property was established, when men's interests defined monogamy as indispensible for women to ensure that the property they owned would be transferred within the family, i.e., only to their rightful heirs (Berkeley, 1999; Okin, 1979).

The ideology claims that women are exploited both at home and at work, that freedom and equality will be attained through social revolution, which will abolish private property, and through women's work in the public sphere, which will enable them to achieve economic independence (Ramazangalu, 1989). Thus, they will not need to be dependent on men. According to this approach, housework should be considered a type of production which has financial value, like any other work. Therefore, "Wages for Housework," which would provide women with economic independence and status, should be demanded, and so break the gender hierarchy which places men at an advantage over women. The problem with this argument is that this would bind women to their homes and the housework instead of enabling them to break the bonds. Critics of Marxist feminism claim that it ignores gender differences and emphasizes only the domains common to both genders.

The main gains of second-wave feminist activists include attaining fundamental rights in both the work and family spheres, the creation of domestic shelters for abused women and children, access to contraception and other reproductive services, the legalization of abortion, the creation and enforcement of sexual harassment policies for women in the workplace, child care services, equal educational funding for young women, and women's studies programs. Information about these achievements spread throughout the world and influenced the awareness and consciousness of women in diverse societies. The empowerment of American women ignited the hopes of women even in very different cultures (Taylor, 2004; Whittier, 1995). Israel is among them.

The Impact of the Second Wave on Israeli Society: The Liberal Opening to "Imported" Western Ideas (1980s—mid-1990s)

The second wave reached Israel in the early 1980s. The non-conflictual courses of action changed in the late 1980s both at the individual and the collective levels. At the individual level, several highly publicized sexual harassment and gender discrimination cases were brought to the legal system

(Barak-Erez, 2007). For example, Naomi Nevo's fight for an equal-to-men's retirement age (i.e., 65 years instead of 60) was won (Supreme Court Ruling 104/87, given October 22, 1990), and set a precedent according to which women are given a choice regarding retirement age (Kamir, 2002).

No longer bound by the hegemonic socialist ideology, feminist activism increased around the mid-1980s. The lack of widespread feminist ideologies that could define the gender boundaries and rationalize the conflict was balanced by an increase in feminist activity in the Knesset, the establishment of women's studies programs in the universities, and the spreading knowledge about success of programs such as Affirmative Action throughout Israel (Herzog, 1999).

At the same time, the psychology of women changed and women began to legitimize gender differences and women's "different voice" (Gilligan, 1982). For example, the traits that women attributed to themselves became more varied. The legitimacy of feminine traits such as empathy, warmth and caring increased, while greater acceptance of masculine traits like assertiveness, determination, self-confidence, and competitiveness in their gender schema can be seen (Moore, 1991, Moore and Gobi, 1995). Their behaviors changed accordingly. These changes contributed to changes in gender roles and the gendered division of labor, and had a significant liberating influence on their values and attitudes, increasing their willingness to participate in social action (Moore, 1995a,b, 1996b). Thus, the changes in the psychology of women simultaneously reinforced feminist activism and were strengthened by it.

Women's demands for equality became clearer and more determined, accompanied by collective social action that reached wider audiences. The non-aggressive women's organizations embraced more radical feminist ideologies and became more uncompromising in their attitudes toward the dominant institutions: NAAMAT's department of legal aid for women attained greater publicity, and increased its involvement with fighting against masculine establishments; several shelters for battered wives (and their children) were formed by women's organizations; elected women members of the Israeli parliament (the Knesset) became more involved with legislation to ensure equal opportunities for women, regardless of party membership;[2] and the women's lobby gained more power and status and supported parliament members who were willing to be involved in women's rights activism (Herzog, 1994). They emphasized the differences between the perceptions and needs of men and women, suggesting alternative interpretations of womanhood (Safran, 2006).

These organizations operated mostly in the big cities, but their ideas affected peripheral areas as well. The ideologies of most of these groups tended to be radical, and many among them considered themselves left-wing (e.g.,

'Isha LeIsha in Haifa, Bat Shalom in Jerusalem [Dahan-Kalev, 1997; Rozin, 2005]). The organizations were voluntary, non-parliamentary associations. They preserved their freedom from the institutionalized male-dominated sociopolitical system that maintained the disadvantages of women (Fogiel-Bijaoui, 1992). The most prominent among these associations is the Women's Lobby, which was formed in 1984. Being mostly grassroots organizations, they spread feminist ideas to almost all national, ethnic, economic, religious and education groups and categories (Shadmi, 2005, 2007).

The main thrust of all their actions was to raise public awareness of women's status and rights, create laws to ensure equality, deal with family issues (domestic violence, legalized abortions, divorce, shelters for battered women and so forth), help pass laws in the Knesser that would protect women's rights, and define politically correct language that would enable egalitarian ideas to spread. This was attained by linking diverse activist groups, collecting data, and sharing knowledge, thus revealing the ways—both sexist and "benevolent"—by which oppression and marginalization was carried out in the everyday lives of women (Herzog, 1999).

One of the main activities that the liberal women's organizations undertook in the early 1990s was legislation. The major thrust was to increase women's representation in politics (both national and local) and power positions in the economy. They achieved rulings of the Supreme Court for women's representation in government offices, local authorities, in the higher ranks of the military, and in directorates of government-owned companies and corporations (Izraeli 2003; Kamir, 2002). Their pressure on the government, together with international developments (like the UN's ratification of the treaty concerning abolishing all types of gender discrimination) led to the creation of the Committee for Women's Status in the Prime Minister's Office (1992), which enhanced the efforts to increase gender equality.

A further step was the formation of the Committee for the Examination of Women's Inclusion in Government Service (1993—1996), which led to the creation of diverse national institutions in charge of advancing the status of women (for example, the Inclusion and Advancement of Women Unit at the Public Service Commissionership [1995] and the Authority for the Advancement of Women's Status at the Prime Minister's office [1998]. These institutions often acted together to increase equality: e.g., increasing pay for women in the public sector, lengthening maternity leave, promoting women to high management, and so forth [Herzog, 1999; Himen-Reish, 2008; Svirsky, 2004]).

The Third Wave

Since the early 1990s, the rate of psychological, social, cultural and ideological changes in Israel has increased significantly, and the diffusion of ideas occurs more rapidly than in the past. The critique of previous feminist notions and the desire to address issues, like sexual harassment and violence against women, that were insufficiently dealt with by earlier feminist movements has led to the creation of new feminist trends (Rosen, 2000). Most of these trends have challenged the binary definitions of femininity and masculinity, which often assume a universal female identity based on the experiences of upper middle class white heterosexual women, ignoring the different experiences of members of other races, classes, or sexual preferences (Code, 2000; Hoff Sommers, 1995).

Supporters of third wave feminism are mainly "Women of Color," a broad category that includes all non-white women, for whom race is an added source of oppression. Often, poverty is added as a third source of deprivation. For women who are both non-white and poor, the interaction of the three factors leads to consequences which are harsher than each of the separate factors (Harris and Ordona, 1990; Walker, 1990).

Emphasizing the ambiguity of gender boundaries, third-wave theory is essentially postmodernist, but it also incorporates ideas derived from diverse sources such as critical theory, post-colonial theory, transnationalism, queer theory, transgender politics, women-of-color consciousness, ecofeminism, libertarian feminism, and new feminist theory (Henry, 2003; Heywood and Drake, 1997).

Third-wave feminism introduced the idea that feminism can change with every generation and individual, and emphasized the need to enable all women to define feminism for themselves, based on their life experiences and according to their own perspectives (Baumgardner and Richards, 2000, 2005). This idea derives mainly from post-modernistic notions, according to which: there is no absolute, objective truth, and each person sees the world from his or her specific point of view; meaning is produced by political processes that are controlled by those who have power in a society; there is no constant identity but a wide array of shifting identity components that gain salience and meanings at different times (Cashmore, 1996; Gillis, Gillian and Munford, 2007).

Because there is no feminine psychology or identity, and there is no meaning to the feminine collective experience, the whole rhetoric of earlier feminism is rejected (Code, 2000; Jones, 1994). The deconstruction of what being a woman means, and the negation of all categorizations, made "truth" relative, dependent on the culture from which it arose (Ludlow, 2008;

Kinser, 2004). According to extreme interpretations, this makes all conflict redundant, but most post-modernist feminist claim that struggles for equality are legitimate if they are undertaken for a specific group (i.e., not a general struggle for equal rights, but a fight for the rights of a specific group to whom the rights are denied [Faloudi, 1993; Rosen, 2000]).

These notions fragmented the collective action of earlier feminism. Instead, a profusion of small, uncoordinated, unrelated grassroots organizations appeared, each dealing with a specific issue (e.g., Code Pink, an anti-war group against the Iraq War, Vox: Voices for Planned Parenthood, a program designed to educate and mobilize students and youth in support of reproductive healt, the Feminist Majority Leadership Alliance, a network of feminist organizations operating in US college campuses to inform young feminists about abortion access, women's rights, affirmative action, and lesbian and gay rights, and to protect these rights from threats by right-wing extremists at the grassroots, national, and global levels [Jones, 1994; Rosenberg and Garofalo, 1998; Schilt, 2003]).

The Impact of the Third Wave on Israeli Society: Multiculturalism, Globalization and their Local Nuances (Since the Mid-1990s)

The third-wave appeared in Israel around the mid-1990s. One of the main activities that women's organizations undertook in the 1990s focused on legislation. The major thrust was to increase women's representation in politics (both national and local) and in positions of power in the economy. They achieved rulings of the Supreme Court for women's representation in government offices, local authorities, in the higher ranks of the military, and in directorates of government-owned companies and corporations (Izraeli 1992, 2003; Kamir, 2002). Their pressure on the government, together with international developments (like the UN's ratification of the treaty concerning abolishing all types of gender discrimination) led to the creation of the Committee for Women's Status in the Prime Minister's office (1992), which enhanced the efforts to increase gender equality.

A further step was the formation of the Committee for the Examination of Women's Inclusion in Government Service (1993-1996), which led to the creation of diverse national institutions in charge of advancing the status of women.[3] These institutions often acted together to increase equality, in areas like increased pay for women in the public sector, lengthening maternity leave, promoting women to upper management, and so forth (Herzog, 1999; Himen-Reish, 2008; Svirsky, 2004).

The unity of feminist groups has been declining since the mid-1990s, with the appearance of specific women's groups, including groups for Mizrahi, religious, Palestinian and lesbian women, which demanded recognition for their uniqueness[4] and needs (Luzzato and Gvion, 2007; Dahan-Kalev, 2001; Safran, 2005; Shalom, 2005). Their lack of equal representation in the larger organizations, and their rejection of what they declared the "oppression by the dominant categories of women" (mainly Western heterosexual Jewish women), fragmented and diversified Israeli feminism. This, however, weakened the power of feminism in Israel (Lind and Farmelo, 1996).

Third-wave feminism found tentative support especially among feminists in academia and among women of Eastern origin. It has not yet attained a strong foothold in grassroots organizations in broader Israeli society, but it is expressed as a negation of liberal feminism, which is the mainstream in Israel. Although the new approach to feminism is taught in academic institutions in Israel, the programs have not grown significantly in the number of either faculty or students. Feminist research is growing in most of these institutions (e.g., Benjamin and Barash, 2004; Dahan-Kalev, 2006; Gal Ezer, 2006; Kampf, 1996; Sasson-Levy and Rapoport, 2002), but it still has minor influence on the curricula of other social science departments.

Supporters of the new feminist trends in Israel attempt to change the liberal discourse to create a multicultural one that will accord equal status to women of diverse ethnic backgrounds. According to this approach, liberal feminism made no attempt to account for the differential treatment of women based on ethnicity or socioeconomic status. For instance, these feminists believe that women from Asian and African origins ("Mizrahi") had distinct characteristics and life experiences which are similar to those of Women of color in the USA (in Israel, Women of color do not include Arab women or new immigrant women from either Ethiopia or the former USSR [Benjamin and Barash, 2004]).[5]

Mizrahi women claim that traditional theories fail to explain their plight adequately. Although they are not a homogeneous group, the cultural differences among the diverse Asian and African cultures (e.g., from Morocco, Egypt, Libya, Iraq, Yemen, and Syria) are minor in comparison with the considerable differences Mizrahi women perceive themselves to have from from Western women (the veteran Ashkenazi women and immigrants from Central Europe or the US). Despite their cultural differences, Mizrahi women share a sufficiently similar predicament that they identify with one another and communicate and act collectively on the basis of solidarity to better their socio-economic positions and achieve greater equity. Their similar experiences of economic deprivation, political marginalization, and social exclusion minimize the differences among them. In respect to common history, they even see themselves as closer to Mizrahi men than to non-Mizrahi women (Dahan-Kalev, 2006). Viki Shiran, one of the Mizrahi leaders, claimed that Ashkenazi women act as oppressors toward Mizrahi men and women, behaving as part of the hegemonic and advantaged group (Shiran, 2002). According to Dahan-Kalev (2002), Western women exclude Mizrahi women, turning a blind eye whenever Mizrahi women are deprived of their rights by the system.

Marxist feminism and intersectionality provided the basis for the claims that third-wave Mizrahi women made concerning the interaction between ethnicity and class. Mizrahi women encounter a double disadvantage: first, they are disadvantaged as women (vis-à-vis men); second, they are disadvantaged because of their ethnic origin (vis-à-vis Western women). Intersectionality claims that in each society, diverse categories of discrimination interact on multiple levels, leading to complex patterns of social inequality, so that in each society, a different hierarchy of oppression and inequality exists (Collins, 2000, Ritzer, 2007). The interaction often leads to a more-than-double price to pay, so that the limitations on these women's life opportunities are greater than the limitations on either women or Mizrahi men. Some claim that there is a third dimension of oppression—that of poverty—that contributes to these women's social inferiority. The significant correlation between ethnicity and economic status indicates that Westerners tend to be better off than the Mizrahi. One of the consequences of the double (or triple) disadvantage is that it leads to different life experiences of Mizrahi women, which precludes their sharing in the general (Western) feminist narrative (Dahan-Kalev, 1996; Herzog, 1999).

Since the 90s, several activist feminist organizations have been created in Israel. One of their main organizations, "AHOTI" ("my sister"), created in 1991 by Mizrahi feminists, is a movement which acts to strengthen solidarity among women of low socioeconomic status to advance economic, social, and cultural justice. The movement operates a meeting place in Tel Aviv and organizes cultural events in which Mizrahi women present their thoughts, beliefs, and creations. Members of the movement were the first to point out that Mizrahi women in academia, who come from less privileged backgrounds than Western women, have to take on heavier workloads or even search for additional jobs outside the university (like teaching in colleges) to earn enough to support their families. They cannot, therefore, advance as quickly as men or even as other women (Dahan-Kalev, 1997).

Other feminist groups, movements, centers, and forums include Palestinian, religious, and lesbian organizations.[6] The fragmentation of women's identification enables women from diverse backgrounds to find a group or organization to belong to, but it also prevents a unification to enhance general causes that are common to all women.

Unlike the first wave, who fought for and gained the right to vote for women, and the second wave's struggle for equal opportunity in the work sphere and an end to sex discrimination, third-wave feminism has diverse causes that most women cannot join or support because they are excluded by the group members for not being part of the specific group fighting for that cause.

The lack of a cohesive goal that typifies third-wave feminism also opens the possibility of attaining many, diverse and simultaneous goals, not a single, major goal. Each group of women fights for an issue which is highly relevant to the specific group. For example, lesbian feminist organizations were instrumental in the changing of the law which now permits each partner in a lesbian couple to adopt the children of the other (Yaros-Hakak Verdict against the Legal Advisor to the Government 10280/01, obtained in 2005, after 9 years of litigation [Goldstein and Spielman, 2005]).

As third-wave feminism began before the second wave ended, the former is often seen as an extension of the latter (Rowe-Finkbeiner, 2004). Baumgardner and Richards (2004) claim that the difference between the second and third waves is a cultural one, so that only young feminists, who grew up with the achievements of feminism, and for whom feminism is a part of culture, are truly third-wave. Unlike their mothers, who had to fight to separate feminist issues from other pressing social issues, young women in the third millennium grew up in a society that recognizes—and in most cases legitimizes—feminist social action, and are more inclined to take the legitimacy of feminism for granted (Friedman, Tzukerman, Wienberg, and Todd, 1992; Ichilov, 1994).

This distinction often leads to generational tension between older and younger (third-wave) feminists. The older (second-wave) generations of feminists, with their clear definitions of feminism and its goals, and their sense of unity of purpose, are often intolerant of the less militant younger generation, who often choose to solve problems in a "no-fight" way. For example, women today often relinquish their high status jobs and choose to become "stay-at-home moms" or even to embrace the ideology and practices of the "Continuum Concept," according to which human babies require constant physical contact with the mother to achieve optimal physical, mental and emotional development.[7] This solves the home-work conflict (Liedloff, 1977; Shtarkshall, 1987), but it is considered by other feminists as self-defeating, a return to the traditional division of labor, or even a reversion to economic dependence on their spouses (Henry, 2004).

Although they do not openly criticize third-wave young mothers for choosing this option, or for intensive motherhood, older feminists frown upon these choices because they see them as going back to the conventional economic dependence of women on their partners, and the reaffirming of the traditional division of labor. Moreover, if the main achievement of second-wave feminism was securing equal opportunities for men and women in the labor market, they have yet to achieve equality in responsibility in the domestic sphere. Adopting the "Continuum Concept" prevents such equality, as men cannot contribute much to the family if they are the sole (or main) breadwinners and must work for many hours. This dilemma is addressed more fully in later chapters.

2. Feminism and Gender Identities

One of the undeniable influences of feminism is the impact it had on the social identities of women. Social-psychological identity develops when the person sees him- or herself as psychologically tied to the group, its successes and failures, its values and its norms (see Chapters One and Three). Questions of individuals' identity in modern society are, according to Giddens (1991), both a consequence and a cause of changes at the societal level, and, therefore, the micro–individual and the macro–societal levels cannot be dealt with separately. Examination of changes in the individual level should take into account changes that occurred in other, macro-level, systems. It is, therefore, necessary to examine how the institutional changes discussed in the previous chapter, and the spreading of feminist ideas, influenced the structuration of gender identities, and how gender identities contributed to the macro-level changes.

As seen in Chapter Three, gender identity was considered a salient identity amongst a fifth of Jews in the 1980s, but the identity could be interpreted as reflecting either adherence to the traditional division of labor and support of the existing patriarchal social order or support for feminist and/or egalitarian ideas and rejection of the existing social order (Moore, 1996a,b; Moore and Gai, 2006). Hence, if only about 20% reported a salient gender identity, and some of them supported the traditional division of labor, feminist ideologies were not prevalent in Israel.

A more recent (2007) examination of gender identity shows that in a representative sample of 800 Jewish Israelis, 48% of the women (and 39% of the men) defined themselves as feminist when asked directly, "Do you consider yourself a feminist? (1=yes; 2=no.)" (See Table 4.1) This constitutes a major change, which indicates that feminism has spread to a grassroots level, and is no longer the ideology of a few highly educated women.

Table 4.1. Percent of men and women who agreed or disagreed with the statement

		Gender		Kendall's tau-b
		Men (%)	Women (%)	
In general, do you consider yourself a feminist?	No	60.8	52.4	2.036*
	Yes	39.2	47.6	
Are there equal opportunities for men and women	No	61.1	69.4	2.036*
	Yes	38.9	30.6	
Should there be equal opportunity for men and women?	No	10.6	5.4	-2.611**
	Yes	89.4	94.6	
In most jobs, can men and women succeed equally?	No	28.3	17.0	-3.744**
	Yes	71.7	83.0	
Should men and women who work in the same type of jobs get the same salaries?	No	5.9	2.6	-2.228*
	Yes	94.1	97.4	
In your opinion, will men and women perform the same work in different manners?	No	27.2	18.8	-2.726**
	Yes	72.8	81.3	
In your opinion, is it a problem that men and women perform the same work in different manners?	No	84.2	77.7	2.305*
	Yes	15.8	22.3	

* p≤ .05

** p≤ .01

When specific questions concerning gender equality were asked, support for egalitarian ideas was even more significant: 95% of the women and 89% of the men agreed that "there should be equal opportunities for men and women," and even higher proportions (97% of the women and 94% of the men) believed that "equal salaries should be paid to men and women who perform the same types of jobs." Many (83% and 72% respectively) believe that "men and women perform the same work in different manners," and most of those (81% and 73%, respectively) believe that this is not a problem.

These findings reflect a significant change already seen in other societies that may indicate that women are no longer satisfied with their allotted roles and their place in the social order (e.g., Crosby, 1991; Crosby and Jaskar, 1993; Rothbard, 2001). A more interesting finding is that Israeli men tend to support them.

Moore (2004) claims that in a tradition-oriented society like Israel (with 57% of the Jews defining themselves as "observant," "religious," or "Ultra-Orthodox"), the espousal of feminist gender identities is a two-stage process: women first have to move away from (or relinquish) traditional gender identities before they can develop a liberal and egalitarian gender identity. Relinquishing an identity is more difficult than is automatic identification with a membership group, and this may account for the resistance many women feel against feminist ideas. According to the present analysis, secular Jewish women (with salient gender identities) seem to have entered the second stage, whereas religious Jewish women (with weak gender identities) seem to have entered the first stage.

This interpretation can also explain the finding that religious women with weak gender identities and secular Jewish women with salient gender identities participate in social protest more, and are less socially obedient. According to the study's second hypothesis, women with salient gender identities have a greater propensity toward social activism, indicating a declining support for the existing social order. According to the suggested interpretation, this hypothesis should be revised to indicate that nontraditional, egalitarian gender identities have a greater propensity toward social activism.

The salience of gender identities among secular Jewish women and the rejection of a salient gender identity among religious women, together with their greater willingness to participate in social action, may also indicate that these women have become more aware of the gender differentiation that exists in Israel and the inequalities it creates. Thus, the placement of gender identities within the hierarchy of identities may lead to conflict with their collectivistic identities and thus curb their adherence to collectivistic values and ideologies. Moore and Kimmerling (1995) have already shown that collectivism has weakened in Israeli society in favor of individualistic and instrumental ideologies similar to the American syllogism, which states that individuals are personally responsible for social and economic advancement and individuals' place in the distribution of rewards is dependent on skills, effort, and attitudes (Mirowsky, Ross, and van Willigen, 1996).

If traditional gender identities are weakening among religious women and feminist gender identities are strengthening among secular women, the inequality-inducing sociocultural value orientations may also be weakening in Israeli society (see Inglehart, 1990; Inglehart and Abramson, 1994, for support of this interpretation). For the time being, cooperation between secular and religious women seems unattainable due to both geographical accessibility and political orientation.

As often happens in conflict situations, the two sides become more aware of the divisive issues, ignoring the non-conflictual issues and similarities between themselves. Studies such as this can (and perhaps should) be applied to the understanding of ongoing societal processes, such as the struggle for social equality, by highlighting the issues on which religious and secular women agree and making them widely known. This knowledge of mutual interests and shared values is a precondition—and the basis—for mutual understanding and women's joint ventures. NAAMAT, WIZO and the Women's Lobby are some of the organizations in which religious and secular women work together, regardless of religiosity and political agenda, but the representation of Ultra-Orthodox and religious settler women is much lower than that of secular ones.

These conclusions may apply to many societies. In democratic and heterogeneous societies, many women aspire to the full realization of pluralistic values. This entails coexistence based on equality among the different groups in each society, which, in turn, should lead to equal influence in matters of state and society. However, in many of these societies, women are more aware of their differences than of consensual issues, and they often fail to unite to achieve common goals. Black, white, Asian, and Latina women in the United States, for example, have created many fragmented and racially segregated organizations, even though many of their goals are similar. As a result, each organization fights alone. United, they might be able to achieve much more for women. A study focusing on gender identities may show which of the women in these groups and organizations share a common ground and what their areas of agreement are.

How are these relationships affected by women's gender identities? Does a salient gender identity lead to greater participation in social action? And, if so, does a salient gender identity have different meanings for women who are at the polar ends of the political spectrum? Is religiosity one of the forces shaping the interplay between gender identity and the willingness to participate in social action?

Moore (2000) examined the meaning of gender identity for religious and secular women in Israeli society and the relationship between gender identity and the willingness to participate in social action. The study analyzed the existence of salient gender identities in relation to other identities, that when adopted by diverse agents from the larger repertoire determine large parts of the competing sociopolitical orders as carried, produced and reproduced by these agents. It also examined the socio-political correlates of salient gender identities, and analyzed the demographic characteristics of these women.

The findings indicate that gender identities of secular and religious Jewish women may reflect diverse social orders. The analyses seem to support the assumption that social identity has a broader meaning than is usually given to it in sociological theory, which almost always disconnects identities from their role in the formation of social order and social change. Locating the identities within the context of the construction of social orders, the analyses suggest that the hierarchy of identities and the sociopolitical attitudes of religious women indicate a consensual acceptance of the social order more than the hierarchy of identities and the attitudes of secular ones.

The analyses also show that women do not form a single well-defined group. The demographic "profiles" of the two groups differ as much as their attitudinal ones: more among the religious women than among secular women are of lower-income families, married and with large families. Many among them also have less formal education, and fewer among them work. Thus, there are many differences between religious and secular women, but it is hard to imagine that any these could make cooperation difficult if it was to be based on shared goals.

The willingness of these women to participate in collective social action on gender issues to increase gender equality seems to be related to salient gender identities and their prevalence in a given society, legitimized and directed by relevant, mostly feminist, ideologies. Thus, the dissatisfaction with social systems directs the structuration processes away from reproducing the existing sociocultural systems and toward social change. Religious women are less active in this sphere, though they are politically active (especially against the peace process). Social activism (represented by participating in political protests, and demonstrating less sociopolitical obedience) is strongest among secular women with salient gender identities and weaker among religious women with weak gender identities.

The number of "women only" organizations is increasing, claims Himen-Reish (2008), and she offers several reasons why women operate within such organizations: women have a different way of doing things; women are not fully integrated, so they need to create a space of their own; and women address issues that men are not interested in, and in order to advance these issues they need to organize as women. She categorizes these organizations into groups according to their sphere of action (i.e., the main issues the organization deals with: social service, equality, national security, or welfare); content (i.e., the main spheres in which they act: political issues, gender, or welfare issues); form of activity (i.e., whether the activity is organized or not); scope (i.e., whether the organization is local, national or international); participants (the socioeconomic status of most of the participants); and feminist expression (i.e., the main domain of feminism, distinguishing between organizations that focus on feminist content, feminist ways of action, or issues of motherhood that are unique to women only [see Table 4.2]).

Another dimension that should, perhaps, be added is that of time: some organizations tend to be "durable" and survive social, economic, and political changes, while others tend to be short-lived, "fluctuating," or are disbanded once their goal is attained. Organizations involved in social issues tend to be long-lasting, as they never run out of issues to deal with; other organizations seem to be fluctuating according to events that are external to the organizations (e.g., when significant political events occur, or seem likely to occur, political movements and organizations may become more noticeable; when economic crises threaten, the welfare organizations may become more visible). Yet others (like Vicki Knafo's fight for social welfare for single mothers in 2003, which led to a grassroots movement of single mothers) disband after either attaining their goal or failing to do so (Gal-Ezer, 2006). To understand women's social action we need to examine the context of the political environment as well.

Table 4.2. Types of Feminist Organizations in Israel*

Sphere of Action	Organization	Content	Form of Activity	Participants	Scope	Feminist Expression
Service	NAAMAT	Women's issues	Organized	Middle class	National	Content
	Emuna				National	
	WIZO				International	
Equality	Women's Lobby	Women's issues	Organized	Middle class	National	
	Feminist Movement		Unorganized		National	
National Security	Women in Black	Political	Unorganized	Middle class	International	Ways of Action
	Women in Green				Local	
	Women of Rehelim				Local	
	Four Mothers				National	
Welfare	Single mothers	Personal welfare	Unorganized	Low class	National	Motherhood
	Mothers of Shderot	Local welfare			Local	

* Translated from Heiman-Reish (2008).

3. Gender Identity and Social Action in Israel:

Redefining the Social Order?

Political Environment and Women's Activism

Israeli women engage today in social actions to increase social equality and are more willing to fight the social system and its institutions. Thus, the dissatisfaction with social systems directs the structuration processes away from reproducing the existing socio-cultural systems and toward social change (Kampf, 1996).

However, the process is not linear. In some periods the activism of women's groups increases and in other periods it declines, in accordance with broader political processes. For example, between 1992-1996, when the left-wing coalition pushed the peace process forward (i.e., the signing of the peace treaty with Jordan, the Oslo agreements in which Israel and the Palestinians negotiated a Palestinian independent state, and the peace talks between Israel and Syria), Israelis felt more nationally secure and therefore able to address other issues such as social justice and gender equality. The discourse shifted to include human rights and equality for the Palestinian citizens of Israel as well (Sasson-Levy and Rapaport, 2002).

The shift of power in the 1996 elections (and again in 2009) to a right-wing coalition put a stop to the peace process. Violence escalated and the threat of imminent war was reintroduced, lessening Israelis' interest in equal rights and feminist issues (Herzog, 1999). Still, the number of Israeli women in the Knesset in 2009 rose to an unprecedented number (21 out of 120 members), among them women known for their feminist ideology (like Shelly Yehimovich, Yuli Tamir, and Hanin Zoabi).

Moreover, the 1996 coalition, in which about 50% of the members were tradition-oriented, religious, or Ultra-Orthodox, wanted to set back these egalitarian trends. Representatives of some of the Ultra-Orthodox parties in the coalition declared that they would attempt to restore the status quo to its pre-1992 level, eradicating women's gains by legislative actions to change some of the supreme court's rulings in favor of women (and against the rabbinical courts of law) and to curtail the power of the supreme court so that no new rulings of this sort would be possible (Herzog, 1999). The 2009 coalition attempts to do the same, as evidenced by the dispute over who will head the Ministry of Justice and who will have the strongest influence to counter the "liberal" Supreme Court.

The current shift in power also indicates that materialistic values like physical and economic security (Inglehart, 1990) are still highly salient in Israeli society. As analysis shows, feminism is unable to flourish in an otherwise materialistic and traditional society in which national security, economic growth, and conservative values are perceived by most social agents to be of highest importance (Moore, 2007, 2008).

As ideological pluralism exists in Israel today, and the army has begun to include women in hitherto exclusively male jobs (like piloting fighter aircraft) and advance women to the highest ranks, the major hindrance for feminist ideas is the hold of religion. It seems that the intense nationalism depicted by religious Jews in the past decade has increased the distance between secular and religious Jews, forcing a reevaluation of the relationships between them. It remains to be seen how they will use their increased power in the coming years.

Israeli women seem to have learned that they need not accept their inferior social position as an immutable fact, and that free-thinking, nontraditional, liberal women can induce changes in social processes and reproduce social structures in which their abilities and contributions are more highly valued. No longer complacent (Moore, 1998, 2011), women are less hesitant to demand acknowledgment of their abilities and exercise their right to choose their life options, their work involvement, their parenting style, and so forth. The gender identities which developed gradually but are widespread at the beginning of this, the third millennium of the common era, may also indicate that achievements which women fought hard to gain are now being taken for granted by young women who were born into a more egalitarian world.

Two Examples: Left- and Right-Wing Activism

To show how women operate in "feminine" ways, this chapter presents two unorganized, political, activist groups that deal with national security issues and are made up mostly of middle class women (see Himen-Reish [2008] categorization). The mass media shows Israeli women participating in the Arab-Israeli conflict, on both the left and right, in many stereotypical and non-stereotypical ways (Lemish and Barzel, 2000; Schachter, 2005). Left-wingers (the "peaceniks") fight to end the occupations and for a two-state (Israel and Palestine) solution; right-wingers (mainly the "settlers") support continuing the occupation of the territories Israel conquered in 1967.

The "Women in Black" movement was started in 1988, in response to the first Palestinian Intifada (uprising), by Israeli women who opposed the occupation and decided to act for peace, justice and nonviolence. Most of them were secular, liberal, "modern" women, depicted by the media as mostly left-wing (though some consider themselves part of the center [Helman and Rapaport, 1997]). Their form of protest was new and unique: once a week, at the same hour, and in the same location (a major traffic intersection) they dressed in black and raised signs upon which the slogan "End the Occupation" was printed (Shadmi, 2000). The media coverage created interest and women throughout Israel joined the protest, chose additional locations and elaborated on the message (Berkowitz, 2003). The continued activity, week after week, throughout the country, has become a constant public reminder of the unresolved conflict (Baum, 2006; Gaynor, 2006).

Later, the movement became international and women throughout the world joined it to speak out against violence and injustice in their own society. In Italy, Women in Black protests a range of issues, from the Israeli occupation to the violence of organized crime. In Germany, Women in Blacks protest neo-Nazism, racism against guest workers, and nuclear arms. In India, Women in Black holds vigils that call for an end to the ill treatment of women by religious fundamentalists. And during the war in the Balkans, members of Women in

Black in Belgrade set a profound example of interethnic cooperation that was an inspiration to their countrywomen and men (Berkowitz, 2003; Kaufman, 2008; Meyer, 2004; Svirsky, 2004).

Though they were independent chapters at first, internet connections and electronic mailing lists brought women from different nationalities together to support the fight against the occupation:

> "The movement of Women in Black has empowered women and men in many countries to mobilize for peace. It is an international movement, so that the voice of conscience in one region now echoes and reverberates throughout the world. And it provides a worldwide support system for victims of oppression, exposing their injustice to the light of day and the pressure of world opinion. The movement of Women in Black assumes many forms in many countries, but one thing is common to all: an uncompromising commitment to justice and a world free of violence." (*http://coalitionofwomen.org/*).

The right-wing activist group of Jewish female settlers, "Women in Green," began in 1993, in response to (or as a force against) "Women in Black," and was headed by Nadia Matar and Ruth Matar. Its members, who define themselves as "pioneers" in the occupied land of the West Bank, participate in recapturing the land that God promised the Israelis, and fight to continue the occupation.

"Women in Green" began with mostly older women, but soon changed its name to include "Women for Israel's Tomorrow," and became a more inclusive movement. It now includes grandmothers, mothers, wives and daughters, housewives and working women, and most of them appear[8] to be Orthodox.

The movement organizes demonstrations and mobilizes women to join male settlers when they take action against Palestinians in the West Bank. Most of their actions were channeled toward fighting the decision to dissociate Israel from the Gaza Strip and protesting against the Oslo Agreements and the attempts to create a Palestinian State:

> "In addition to weekly street theater and public demonstrations, we write weekly articles, commission posters, advertise in newspapers, and lecture to groups in order to educate the electorate on the consequences of certain government policies, such as abandoning the Golan Heights for an illusory promise of peace.... We insist that Israel remain a Jewish state. We are actively and intimately connected with the fight to preserve a united Jerusalem. We support and encourage the brave Jewish community in the ancient city of Hebron, and sponsor annual Hanukkah and Purim parties with gifts and professional entertainment for the isolated Jewish children in that community." (*http://www. womeningreen.org/*).

Though it is not associated with a specific political party, the movement is defined as right wing and religious, and associated with the messianic extremist settlers willing to be arrested in their violent confrontations with the army.

Little is known about "Women in Green," and there is little academic research on their actions (El-Or, 1993, is one of the few). Although they claim to have thousands of supporters (men and women, young and old, religious and secular), the activists in demonstrations are mainly youths, infused with righteous religious zeal. There is no ideological platform other than the Bible and their deep belief that the land of Israel was promised to the people of Israel. Their actions were directed against the soldiers and the state when the "dissociation" (Hitnatkut) took place in 2005, and against Palestinians in the West Bank since then.

Summation, Implications and Conclusions

The examination of these issues is important for several reasons. First, some studies indicate that salient gender identities can indicate a weakening of collective identities (like civic or national identities) and a dispute over the existing social order. Other studies I carried out (Moore, 1998a,b, 2011), indicated that salient gender identities may also be associated with a very different trend in that they strengthen collective (patriarchal) ideologies. However, these diverse relationships may be a by-product of another factor – religiosity. Second, feminist ideologies have only begun to spread more swiftly to the grassroots levels in Israel in the past decade, and their impact on the nationalist discourse has not been extensively assessed in Israel. Third, although this chapter focuses on Israeli society, its conclusions may be relevant for diverse societies in which gender identity, religion and nationalism interact, and thus enhance understanding of the correlates of salient gender identities in other societies, particularly in the Middle East.

The development of civil society throughout the world and the spread of feminism served to promote women's activism. Consequently, the number of women's organizations and movements is growing in many societies, including Israel (Gabriel, 1992; Meyer, 2004). The unique characteristics of these organizations is that they contribute to the interests of women, that they contend with and often provide different solutions than mainstream organizations, but that they may also act to remove women from the main spheres of influence, leaving them male-dominated.

The social, political and ideological changes discussed in this chapter significantly influenced the psychology of women in Israel. From fighting for voting rights in the new State, the feminist struggle shifted and, in the

80s, focused on striving to attain equal rights in employment, political representation and economic attainment. In the 90s, it shifted again to a more individual type of feminism, with an emphasis on multicultural aspects. This trend has weakened the mobilization of women to attain general goals, as previous generations of feminists attempted to do, but has strengthened the ties among women who see themselves as part of smaller, more homogeneous groups, attempting to attain their individual and group goals.

Less bound by a rigid, clear-cut, male-delineated definition of "femininity" and "womanhood," secular women today are more free to define these terms for themselves. The religious value system still treats women as inferior beings, but their hold on some aspects of Israeli secular lives has decreased. As there are diverse types of feminism, there are diverse types of being feminine or being a woman, and all are socially legitimate (at least in some sections of society). Consequently, women can choose which traits to develop, their values and norms, their sexual preferences, lifestyles, beliefs and attitudes concerning the relationships between men and women, and the behaviors that accompany these choices. The multitude of types seems to defy categorization, so that each woman can be a "type" and choose her "womanhood style." This is apparent especially among women who are secular, highly educated and young.

The new patterns of being are spreading already: more women choose to befriend other women, and women-only support groups focusing on different topics proliferate (e.g., "La Leche" groups around breastfeeding, "Continuum Concept" groups around constant contact with babies, home schooling support groups for women who wish to remain at home with their children, etc.). Though these patterns may be considered "self-defeating" as far as the fight for equality is concerned, they seem to indicate that women are now finding new ways of shaping their lives, patterns more suited to women and formed by women, not by men. Most of these patterns emphasize quality of life rather than level of income, work careers, and other extrinsic signs of status. A growing number of women are choosing to stay at home when they have children, but in contrast with tradition-oriented women, they are empowered, highly aware of their rights, and have the ideology to support them (Gillis, Howie and Munford, 2007).

It may also be said that the changes in the psychology of women are influencing men as well. More men are choosing to work fewer hours than before (Stearns, 2003). The trend began with divorced fathers who wished to share custody of their children and so left work earlier to be with them, homosexual men who chose to raise children, and metrosexual men who were more attuned to their feelings. However, the trend appears to be spreading to other young men, especially those of means, who do not wish to invest in time-consuming, enslaving careers (Gauntlett, 2002; Moore 2010). Hence, it seems that societal changes influenced the psychology of women while simultaneously being influenced by these changes in women. These issues are elaborated upon in Chapter 7.

ENDNOTES

[1] The Zionist socialist movement and the Kibbutz (with its egalitarian ideology) asserted that they could create social equality (Bowes, 1978). Women believed that the egalitarian kibbutz ideology would liberate them and put an end to the patriarchal social order (Fogiel-Bijaoui, 1992). However, feminist researchers (e.g., Bernstein 1983; Izraeli, 1981; Shilo, 1996) have shown that the ideals of the Zionist settlements failed to create gender equality or to change the psychology of women and the traditional perception of roles in the kibbutz in pre-State Israel (Bernstein 1983; Izraeli, 1981; Shilo, 1996). A close scrutiny of kibbutz history reveals male-dominated institutions that involved subordination of women's positions (Moore, 1998b). Feminist ideas were perceived by some as of secondary importance to attaining equality, and by others as opposing—even in conflict with—the Zionist Kibbutz values. For example, fighting for gender equality was seen as hindering the goal of assimilating thousands of new immigrants. Finding jobs for new immigrants so that every family would have at least one breadwinner was presented as highly important. As most of the immigrants arrived from highly traditional societies (e.g., Libya, Morocco, and Yemen), finding jobs for men was seen as far more important than finding positions for women. Women who insisted on working were depicted in the media as anti-social, egotistic, or blind to the welfare of the collective, unless they worked in jobs that required knowledge that the immigrants did not have (like fluency in Hebrew [Izraeli, 1981]). Moreover, for many years, the equality principle was taken to mean that women should work like men, even in physically demanding manual jobs. Any request to adjust quotas to women's different physical abilities met with derogation. On the other hand, men left all "feminine" jobs (e.g., kitchen duties, taking care of children) to women. The ideal of equality was a fiction, but a fiction that took years to expose (Bernstein 1983, 1992).

[2] Laws that increase equality and improve women's work conditions were passed even before the 1980s (like the cancellation of the law according to which women needed official permission to work at night). These were often initiated by men, not by women. Some of these laws may have hindered women's work opportunities more than they enhanced them (like the law according to which a mother of small children is required to work seven hours per day instead of eight hours for full pay).

[3] For example, the Inclusion and Advancement of Women Unit at the Public Service Commissionership (1995) and the Authority for the Advancement of Women's Status at the Prime Minister's office (1998).

4   The organizations include the Feminist Lesbian Community (KLF, formed in 1987); the Palestinian Feminist organization (El Phanar, formed in 1991); and the Mizrahi Feminist Movement (AHOTI, formed in 1996).

5   This may be due to decades of oppression of Mizrahi Jews by the hegemonic Ashkenazi Jews (those primarily from Eastern Europe), and the need to unite as a homogeneous group in terms of history, experiences, and perceptions (Dahan-Kalev, 2006). It may also be due to the fact that a trickle of immigrants from Ethiopia began reaching Israel in the 80s, broken, traumatized survivors of a long trek through Sudan. At the beginning of the 90s, their numbers increased, but by then the Mizrahi women had already defined their goals. The poor, less educated, underprivileged, and submissive Ethiopian women were not considered an asset, and attempts to include them were not undertaken. As for women from the former USSR, they were considered part of the Ashkenazi group and were, therefore, shunned. Palestinian women, like all Palestinian citizens of Israel, were never part of the Jewish collective, and the Mizrahis (who share greater cultural similarity with them than other Jewish groups do) tend to maintain greater distances from them to emphasize the differences between the two groups (Horowitz and Lissak, 1989).

6   Among them: Kayan (an organization of feminist Palestinian citizens of Israel), Asawat (Israeli Palestinian Lesbian Women), Isha LeIsha (The Haifa Feminist Center), Bat Kol (Religious Lesbian Organization), Bat Shalom (Women's Network for Peace Advancement); Help Center for Sexual Assault Victims (a volunteer organization hot line), Itach (female lawyers organization for social justice for women), KLF (Feminist Lesbian Community), and Kolech (Religious Women's Forum).

7   The source of the concept is Liedloff's observations of the Yequana tribe in Venezuela, which she then adapted to Western parenting. The concept includes breastfeeding whenever the baby signals, and for as long as the child wants to suckle, carrying the infant close to the mother's body, co-sleeping (i.e. the baby sleeps with the parents) and so forth. This concept is considered highly feminist by some, as it allows women to fully accomplish their gender role.

8   Many of the more religious individuals tend to choose clothing that signifies their exact religious affiliations (headdress for both women and men, length of women's skirts, color of socks, type and color of coats worn by men, and so forth). Though some of these 'signals' are not known to the secular population, they serve to create a sense of identity. Thus, for example, the headdresses that married women wear (wigs, hats, or scarves tied in specific ways) signify not only their religiosity but also their more specific religious affiliation within Orthodoxy.

Chapter 5

Changes in Israeli Society since the 1980s

The spreading of feminist ideologies, together with globalization processes, and the intense modernization throughout the Western world reached Israel in the last twenty years, and their impact—combined with changes that are specific to Israel (e.g., intense privatization)—became increasingly more noticeable. This chapter focuses on the many and diverse macro-level changes that occurred in Israeli society from the mid-1980s until the beginning of the third millennium, leading to considerable changes in the status of women. In fact, changes can be seen in all the spheres analyzed in Chapter Two.

1. Demographic Changes

Life Expectancy

The life expectancy[1] of women has grown significantly. In the early 1970s, life expectancy was 73.8 years for women and 70.6 for men. In 2001, women's life expectancy has reached 82 years and men's 80 years. Men's life expectancy is ranked eighth of 192 countries graded by the World Health Organization (WHO, 2003), a decline from fourth rank in 1999. Women's life expectancy was ranked 20th of the 192 countries, in comparison with 24th place in 1999. Thus, although women's health is improving vis-à-vis the health of women in other countries, the health of Israeli men is still graded higher than that of Israeli women's. Women's relatively low life expectancy is attributed to a high rate of death from cancer and other illnesses, and the heightened stress and pressure which is due to lack of power and status that may reduce pressure (for example, men have military as well as civilian sources of power, while women only have civilian sources [Women's Lobby, 2004]).

Still, as data gathered by the Israeli Bureau of Statistics (2005) shows, retirement homes have a predominant majority of women, many more women remain single when their spouses pass away (while single elderly men tend to remarry), and women prepare themselves better than in the past for a situation in which they have to live alone (e.g., more among them have pension funds, make arrangements to move to protected housing and so forth).

Immigration and its Impact

In 2002, 6.5 million people lived in Israel, among them 75.6% Jews, 20% Arabs and 4.4% "others."[2] The composition of Jewish Israeli society has changed in this period mainly because of mass immigration from the former Soviet Union (about one million Jews arrived between the end of the 1980s and 2000), and Jews of Western origin became the majority (about 52%) of the entire Jewish population. Beginning in the 1980s, under Mikhail Gorbachev's rule, the emigration rules that forced citizens desiring to leave the former USSR to relinquish all rights to their property were changed, and people were no longer required to give up their Russian citizenship upon emigration. The trickle of "Russian" immigrants to Israel in the 1980s became a torrent in the early 1990s.

In contrast with previous waves of immigration to Israel, the motives for the immigration of the "Russian" Jews were economic rather than ideological (many of them tried to emigrate to the US rather than to Israel: 200,000 Jews from the Soviet Union immigrated to the USA until American policy changed in the 1980s and the gates were closed). Unlike the "Russian" immigrants of the 1970s, these new-comers were not Zionists, and had not prepared themselves culturally to assimilate in Israel. Most of them did not learn Hebrew before migrating to Israel, and many knew very little about Israeli society, its culture or its religion. Most of the "Russian" immigrants are secular (only 11% are religious), and the proportion of those among them who married non-Jews (before coming to Israel) far exceeds that of previous immigration waves.

Because of its composition, this wave of immigration has had a significant impact on Israeli society. First, most of the immigrants (88%) came from European areas of the former Soviet Union (such as Russia, Ukraine, and the Baltic states; the other 12% came from the Islamic republics like Kazakhstan, Uzbekistan, and Georgia [Ben Rafael, Olshtein, and Geijst, 1998]), thus changing the ethnic composition of Israeli society, in which Jews from Asian and African countries had been the majority (53% of all the Jews in Israel at the end of the 1980s were from Muslim countries [Central Bureau of Statistics, 1992]).[3]

Moreover, although the immense wave of immigrants was directed mostly to temporary mobile homes ("caravans") that were built for them in peripheral cities, their human capital and their willingness to work hard enabled many of the immigrants of European origin to move to one of the big cities within a few years. In many cases, the immigrants created "Russian enclaves" in which Russian is spoken as much as (or more than) Hebrew, supermarkets sell Russian products, and shops carry signs in both languages. This separatist process has slowed their integration. The many newspapers in Russian, libraries for Russian books, and the creation of two "Russian" political parties (one headed by Nathan Sharansky, the other by Avigdor Lieberman) have further slowed the process and strengthened the new immigrants' perception of cultural superiority.

This trend was further enhanced by the high human capital of these immigrants (67% of them had more than 13 years of formal education, and 97% were in professional occupations in the Soviet Union, according to Ben Rafael, Olshtein, and Geijst [1998]). A high proportion of them joined the labor force, and they were integrated in most economic sectors, significantly improving the human capital in Israel. Many entered high-tech workplaces or joined start-ups that were aided by government funding in order to supply new arrivals with jobs. As many of the "Russian" doctors and engineers could not find suitable jobs in the already-saturated Israeli labor market, they settled for employment as technicians, high school teachers and so forth, forcing the veterans (many of them Asian-African Jews) out. This trend created a conflict with the upwardly-mobile Jews from Asian and African origin, some of whom were pushed away from the better-paying professional and technical occupations or pushed out entirely, into unemployment. Moreover, studies show that while the wages of highly educated newcomers (with 16+ years of education) tended to be about 40% that of veteran Israelis, six years after arrival their average wages tend to be similar to those of veterans. (Among the young adults [ages 22-40], there is even a 6% advantage for the immigrant group.)

Other demographic changes in Israeli society may be seen, some of which are related to the characteristics of new immigrant women. More women than men (53% vs. 47%, respectively) arrived with the waves of migration in the 1980s and 1990s; many of them arrived as single parents. Most of these women worked in the Soviet Union, and a high proportion of them sought work in Israel too. Being highly motivated—and often the sole supporters of their families—these women were willing to work in whatever jobs were available, if they could not find jobs in their former occupations: engineers became industry workers, nurses became beauticians, and teachers became domestic workers. Many were willing to take on more than one job in order to enable their children to enroll in the best schools and to provide them with the suitable conditions for succeeding in their studies (and, indeed, the children of these new immigrants are over-represented in all academic institutions).

These trends increased the need for changes in the educational system, and contributed to both changes in the curricula and the decision to prolong hours at school, which allowed working mothers longer hours of work.

Being mostly secular and egalitarian concerning the gendered division of labor, these immigrants contributed to the attitudinal shift in Israeli society:

they enhanced pluralistic tendencies and openness toward different life styles, family structures, and cultures. The "melting pot" ideology was abandoned, and the idea of an all-fitting "ideal type Israeli" was deserted.

2. Changes in the Ideological-Political Context

Israel had a European (at first socialist, later democratic) orientation from its beginning. Since the 1980, most of the political alliances and economic associations of Israel have been with Europe and North America, and Israelis look to the West for cultural trends, identification, and criteria with which to evaluate their lives. According to Samocha (2005), most Israelis prefer to be aligned with the Western block rather than with the Arab/Muslim block in political, economic and cultural matters, and this preference has grown significantly since the mid-1980s: improved mass communications, the decline of the Socialist ideology, and increased individualism have contributed to the acceleration of "Westernization" of Israel. The ideological shift from collectivistic socialism to individualistic capitalism is an important contribution to these trends.

After Menachem Begin and the Likud Party broke the hegemony of the Labor party and its Socialist ideology in the 1977 elections, the Likud was in power and won most elections until Ariel Sharon created the centrist party ("Kadima") and became Prime Minister in 2001. In addition, ideological and cultural pluralism became more noticeable in Israel. New governing structures were created, like "unity (Ahdut) government" in which the two main parties – the right-wing Likud and the left-wing Labor—formed a coalition in 1981. The two political leaders took turns as Prime Ministers in order to provide stability.

This has brought about a paradigmatic shift, and a "center" was created between the Left and Right ideologies. Parties like "Shinui" were formed in the 1970s, but became significant only in the 1990s ("Shinui" gained two seats of the 120 in the 1981 Knesset, six seats in 1992, and fifteen in 2003, turning into the third largest of the thirteen parties in the Knesset). The liberal-capitalist ideology they presented focused on the interests of the secular, well-educated, middle class, and emphasized economic rather than the national security issues that both Likud and Labor emphasize. In this respect, "Shinui" is the complete opposite of the religious parties, which also emphasize the economic aspects, but focus on welfare policies and the interests of Orthodox families, many of whom are poor and lower class, demanding that child-support pensions with greater funds be allocated to families with a large number of children.

"Kadima," Ariel Sharon's party, was created in 2005 as another "center" party and replaced "Shinui" in the political arena ("Shinui" collapsed in 2006, and did not have a single representative in the elections that year). The desire for a more balanced approach turned "Kadima" into the largest party and, therefore, Sharon was chosen as Prime Minister and the head of the coalition.

The paradigmatic shift also allowed ethnic parties to flourish (among them parties of "Russian" new-immigrants, Arabs, and separate religious parties for Jews from Islamic countries and Jews of Western origin). These parties reflected sectarian interests more than either left- or right-wing attitudes. (For example, the "Russian" party, "Israel Ba'aliya," headed by Nathan Sharansky, represented right-wing political and economic attitudes, but left-wing positions regarding welfare and social policy.) The only social category that has never succeeded in forming a political party is women.

The paradigmatic change reflects the shift found in advanced industrial societies, in which social and political attitudes have changed so that the relative salience of postmaterialistic values and ideologies has increased (Flanagan, 1987; Inglehart, 1985, 1987).

Materialist-Postmaterialist, Old-New Politics in Israel

Materialist-postmaterialist values were first examined in Israel by Gottlieb and Yuchtman-Yaar (1985). Taking into account social class, their analysis shows that applying Inglehart's (1977) measures, 71% of the lower class, 68% of the middle class and 43% of the higher-class respondents espoused materialistic values. But in contrast to Inglehart's predictions, when asked about their opinions on related social and economic issues, materialists and postmaterialists were indistinguishable (e.g., those who were found to be postmaterialists at the individual level tended to support materialistic goals at the national level as much as those who were found to be materialists at the individual level). In fact, they claim that postmaterialists were those who believed more strongly in the importance of economic growth and in workers' productivity as the basis for reward allocation. In general, Gottlieb and Yuchtman-Yaar (1985) found less distinction between materialists and postmaterialists than did Inglehart. Their explanation of these findings: Inglehart's research was conducted in rich countries, where there are weak relationships between the economic success of the nation and the individual, while in Israel, with its much weaker economy in the 1980s (rapid inflation, slow economic growth, growing unemployment), there was a much stronger relationship between the nation's and the individual's economic well being.

The lack of differentiation may also be due to timing: Gottlieb and Yuchtman-Yaar (1985) may have attempted to discern Israeli postmaterialism too early. The values and issues most relevant to postmaterialism (e.g., civil rights, preserving the environment, individual freedom) may not have been widespread or crystallized at the time of the research (1982). Wider support for this orientation can be seen since the late 1980s, when the ideology shifted its focus to the more pressing issue of attaining peace, which caused more people to support this ideology (Peres, 1992).

In addition, the Left-Right distinction, which both Inglehart and Flanagan consider an important generalized orientation for politics in advanced industrial societies, may have a different meaning for Israelis. As Arian and Shamir (1983) point out, the Left-Right continuum in Israel has become a "super-issue" or "critical referent" (Kerlinger, 1967, 1984) which connotes the mapping of diverse issues like voting behavior and political ideology and the more specific behaviors that political parties elicit by using the Left-Right labels as cues (see also van Deth and Guertz, 1989; but Robinson and Fleishman, 1984). However, there seems to be a clear distinction between political and economic orientations (Left-Right on the one hand, and Socialist-Capitalist on the other) in the Israeli context (Peres and Yuchtman-Yaar, 1992), and both are critical to the understanding of materialism and postmaterialism (Inglehart, 1977, 1985; Flanagan, 1979, 1982b).

Throughout the years since 1948, when Israel gained its independence, the rift between Left and Right focused on three major issues: foreign policy/national security, the economic system, and the state-religion relations (Cohen, 1985, 1991; Gottlieb and Yuchtman-Yaar, 1985). In the 1990s, foreign policy and national security became the focus of Left-Right schism. The Left advocates making peace with Palestinians and the neighboring Arab nations through negotiations and territorial compromises. The Right claims that the territories conquered by Israel in 1967 (the Six-Day War) are "liberated," not "occupied," and are, therefore, non-negotiable; peace will be attained only through military force and ideological fortitude. Social and economic problems were placed—both by Left and Right—at a lower priority, as derivatives of political gains and achievements. "Leftist issues," such as egalitarianism and equal rights for weak social groups, and "Right-wing issues," such as equity-based individual achievements and lessening the state's intervention in the economy, were presented in the 1990s as less pressing and to be attained when peace is achieved. Similarly, the rift between Left and Right regarding state-religion relations was accorded lower prominence. While the Left emphasizes the need to separate state and religion in order to provide a secular constitution, and the Right tends to maintain the existing status quo (in which all family matters are conducted in religious courts of law), both have declared willingness to compromise their positions in order to obtain support from at least some of the religious parties, and thus to attain more pressing goals (see also Kimmerling, 1993; Levy, Levinsohn, and Katz, 1993).

Moore (1996) shows that attitudinal changes seem to have occurred since Gottlieb and Yuchtman-Yaar (1985) published their findings, claiming that a strengthening of postmaterialist values and the formation of clearer attitudinal structures can be seen. The findings in Moore's (1996) study seem to indicate that attaining national security and a high and stable economic level are not an absolute or universal precondition for a shift from materialistic to postmaterialistic values. A shift toward postmaterialistic ideas and values is also possible in less advanced and less secure societies, of which Israel is but an example: the data seem to show that the young, secular, and highly educated in Israel have indeed entered the postmaterialist era. Moreover, the analysis seems to indicate that in different socio-cultural contexts certain postmaterialistic ideas are more "absorbable" than others: the "democratic" dimension of the postmaterialistic attitudes was transferred to Israel with more success than the ecological one. Thus, unlike the materialistic-postmaterialistic structures depicted by Inglehart's and Flanagan's theories, the structure of attitudes in Israel has two types of materialism as well as two types of postmaterialism. Materialists are subdivided into those who accord highest priority to economic issues and to those who accord highest priority to national and physical security (and the two are not related). Postmaterialists are subdivided into those who perceive socio-ecological issues as the most important and those who see democratic issues as the most important. These trends seem to have become more prominent in the 2006 Knesset elections, as well as in the 2008 municipal elections, in which specific groups focused on designated issues (like animal rights, quality of life, or privileges for the elderly).

Applying Flanagan's differentiation between Old and New politics to the Left-Right distinction (rather than to social classes), it is clear that each of the Inglehart-based measures occupies a different cell, explained by different factors (see Table 5.1). Old Politics in Israel focuses on economic issues and their social implications. New Politics focuses on political issues, especially foreign policy concerns, such as defining the territories in Judea, Samaria and Gaza as "occupied" or "liberated" by Israel in 1967, and, in consequence, whether to use the territories to negotiate for peace or not.

The Old Left (and especially its harbinger, the Labor Party) has undergone major changes since it ruled in the first 30 years of Israel's existence (1948-1977). In the formative years, its dominant socialist ideology meant centralization of both economic resources and socio-political apparatuses in order to contend with the absorption of mass immigration. Today, the Old Left seems to maintain its socialist ideology mainly at the economic level. It focuses on returning society to a more caring, less individualistic nature, as it was in its rather egalitarian past, and to decrease the enormous inequality that exists today.

Table 5.1. Left-Right, Old-New Politics in Israel

	Left	Right
Old Politics	Postmaterialist Socio-ecology	Materialist Economy
New Politics	Postmaterialist Democracy	Materialist Security

Source: Moore (1995a) Attitude (In)congruence: Sociopolitical Orientation and the Gendered Division of Labor. Sociological Imagination, 32, 143-163.

The Old Right adheres to capitalism. In fact, adopting this ideology is the only factor explaining adherence to economic (MAT) issues such as preserving high economic growth, maintaining a stable economy, and fighting inflation. Like the Old Left, this ideology is less prevalent among the younger and educated respondents in the present sample, but may still be prevalent among older cohorts.

The impact of the New Left and the egalitarian ideology upon political life was minor in the 1980s, but this changed in the early 1990s when the New Left "Meretz" party joined the ruling coalition formed by the Labor Party. The main concern of the united New Left in the 1992 elections was a foreign policy issue: making peace with Palestinians and the surrounding nations through negotiations and territorial compromises.

Social and economic problems (like egalitarianism, equal rights for weak social groups, and tolerance of minorities) that were among their topmost concerns throughout the years of their existence were placed at a lower priority. Though still very important to the New Left, they are now presented as derivatives of political gains and achievements. The New Left now claims that some of these problems will be solved when peace is attained and Palestinians obtain autonomous self-rule, and that other problems are less pressing than the chance to secure a peaceful resolution of the Israeli-Arab conflict.

Similarly, though very high on the New Left's political agenda, their strong emphasis on the need to separate state and religion in order to provide a secular constitution and religious freedom was not implemented. Abandoning this fight was presented as unavoidable and necessary in order to enable some of the religious parties to join—and strengthen—the coalition so that the more pressing and immediate goal of peace negotiations may be attained.

New Right ideology has also removed economic issues from the focus of the Old Right's agenda, emphasizing, instead, an uncompromising political stance vis-à-vis the increasing Arab militant movements. It advocates pouring social and financial aid into Jewish settlements in the occupied territories in order to strengthen Israel's power position. Social and economic policy issues of the New Right are less well-formed and accorded lower priority. Its basic capitalistic ideology emphasizes minimizing state intervention in economic processes, except where questions of national security are involved.

The religious orientation of the New Right is mixed. Some of the parties are strongly supportive of religious ideology; others are less so. The more religious parties maintain that religious rules should be the nation's code of law, and they base their claim for territorial annexation on historical-religious birthright claims ("Israel is the Biblical land of the Jews"); the less religious claim that annexation is an existential need that would ensure physical security. Though their ideology and justifications differ, these parties collaborate where security questions are concerned in order to increase their political influence.

In summation, whereas Gottlieb and Yuchtman-Yaar (1985) find few differences between materialists and postmaterialists regarding social and economic attitudes, Moore (1996) shows that Israel has two types of materialism as well as two types of postmaterialism. Materialists are subdivided into those who accord highest priority to economic issues and those who accord highest priority to national and physical security. Postmaterialists are subdivided into those who perceive socio-ecological issues as the most important social issues and those who see democratic issues as the most important ones.

Moore's (1996) analysis also showed that Left-Right placement is of great importance in the Israeli formation of materialist-postmaterialist ideologies. Whereas postmaterialists tend strongly to the Left, materialists tend just as strongly to the Right. People seem to have congruent political ideas influenced by their Left-Right orientations, but this congruence does not necessarily extend to attitudes and values that relate to different areas such as gender and the division of labor between the sexes.

Concurrently, a shift in gender division of labor has also occurred (Epstein, 1987), and the relationship between the two sets of attitudes is highly relevant to the change in the status of women in Israeli society. These changes are discussed later in the chapter.

3. Changes in Economic Processes

Significant changes occurred in economic processes during the last decades in Israel: the standard has changed from labor-intensive industry and agriculture to a post-industrial society with an emphasis on high-tech and services, and from mostly state-ownership to intense privatization. As in most advanced Western societies, three sectors have grown in Israel: high-tech industries (computers, biotechnology), finances/sales (banking, insurance and

financing; wholesale and retail trade), and services (health, welfare and social work; community, social, and personal services; business activities; accommodation services and restaurants; services for households; education;
public administration; transport and communications). In contrast, agriculture, manufacturing and construction are shrinking constantly. In 1998, for
example, these shrinking sectors included 27.4% of all the labor force, but
in 2007, only 23.1% of all workers were in these sectors. The rest moved to
services, high-tech, or sales. Global processes enabled Israeli corporations
to move their production to third-world countries (amongst them the Gaza
Strip, Jordan, and China), where the cost of labor is much cheaper than it is
in Israel.

This led to additional significant processes of change in the Israeli economy
that are relevant to the change in the situation of women: the weakening of the
"Histadrut" (Israel's amalgamation of labor unions),[4] the slowing of growth
of GNP (and its derivatives) in comparison with other Western societies,
the rising of education, and the changing of labor market composition (see
Table 5.2).

Table 5.2. Countries of the World: Gross National Product (GNP) per capita—2005

Rank	Country	GNP per capita (dollars)
1	Luxembourg	65 602
2	Norway	59 768
3	Switzerland	54 925
4	Denmark	47 363
5	Iceland	46 655
6	United States	43 743
7	Bermuda	41 875
8	Sweden	41 042
9	Ireland	40 232
10	Liechtenstein	39 412
11	Japan	38 984
12	Great Britain	37 632
13	Finland	37 471
14	Austria	36 912
15	Netherlands	36 600
16	France	35 854
17	Belgium	35 712
18	Germany	34 577
19	Canada	32 546
20	Australia	32 170
21	Isle of Man	31 200
22	Monaco	30 606

Rank	Country	GNP per capita (dollars)
23	Italy	29 999
24	Singapore	27 842
25	New Zealand	25 942
26	Spain	25 358
27	United Arab Emirates	24 213
28	Kuwait	23 423
29	Brunei	21 675
30	Greenland	20 702
31	Cayman Islands	20 667
32	Jersey & Guernsey	20 000
33	Aruba	19 800
34	Greece	19 687
35	Israel	18 624
36	U.S. Virgin Islands	18 609
37	French Polynesia	18 521
38	Qatar	18 212
39	Gibraltar	17 500
40	Andorra	17 468
41	Slovenia	17 352
42	Cyprus	17 081
43	Taiwan	16 764
44	Portugal	16 164
45	Macau	15 413
46	Bahamas	15 232
47	Martinique	15 063
48	San Marino	15 000
49	Bahrain	14 187
50	New Caledonia	13 889
51	Malta	13 589
52	Netherlands Antilles	13 552
53	Falkland Islands	13 333
54	British Virgin Islands	13 043
55	Puerto Rico	12 221
56	Nauru	12 143
57	Faroe Islands	12 083
58	Saudi Arabia	11 764
59	Korea (N + S)	10 975
60	Antigua and Barbuda	10 854
61	Czech Rep.	10 674
62	Trinidad and Tobago	10 444
63	Guam	10 118
64	Hungary	10 034
65	Niue	10 000
65	Tokelau	10 000
67	Barbados	9 741

Rank	Country	GNP per capita (dollars)
68	Guadeloupe	9 183
69	Estonia	9 107
70	Oman	8 999
71	French Guiana	8 836
72	Saint Kitts & Nevis	8 298
73	Seychelles	8 235
74	American Samoa	8 103
75	Croatia	8 064
76	Slovakia	7 955
77	Reunion	7 752
78	Anguilla	7 692
79	Palau	7 500
80	Mexico	7 154
81	Turks and Caicos Islands	7 143
82	Saint Pierre and Miquelon	7 143
83	Poland	7 112
84	Lithuania	7 041
85	Latvia	6 757
86	Montserrat	6 667
87	Lebanon	6 186
88	Chile	5 865
89	Libya	5 527
90	Mauritius	5 265
91	Botswana	5 178
92	Gabon	5 007
93	Cook Islands	5 000
93	Saint Helena	5 000
95	Malaysia	4 963
96	South Africa	4 959
97	Venezuela	4 807
98	Saint Lucia	4 731
99	Turkey	4 704
100	Panama	4 626
101	Costa Rica	4 589
102	Russia	4 466
103	Argentina	4 466
104	Uruguay	4 359
105	Wallis and Futuna	4 000
106	Grenada	3 925
107	Romania	3 834
108	Dominica	3 750
109	Saint Vincent	3 613
110	Belize	3 493
111	Bulgaria	3 473
112	Brazil	3 455

Rank	Country	GNP per capita (dollars)
113	Jamaica	3 396
114	Yugoslavia	3 291
115	Fiji	3 278
116	Thailand	3 065
117	Marshall Islands	3 016
118	Namibia	2 986
119	Kazakhstan	2 942
120	Tunisia	2 889
121	Macedonia	2 826
122	Mayotte	2 809
123	Iran	2 771
124	Belarus	2 760
125	Algeria	2 727
126	Ecuador	2 628
127	Peru	2 612
128	Albania	2 578
129	Suriname	2 539
130	Tuvalu	2 500
131	Bosnia	2 446
132	El Salvador	2 445
133	Jordan	2 426
134	Guatemala	2 403
135	Maldives	2 401
136	Dominican Rep.	2 370
137	Colombia	2 292
138	Northern Mariana Islands	2 289
139	Micronesia	2 252
140	Tonga	2 157
141	Western Samoa	2 108
142	Myanmar	2 039
143	Swaziland	1 934
144	Cape Verde	1 874
145	China	1 736
146	Morocco	1 694
147	Vanuatu	1 611
148	Ukraine	1 516
149	Armenia	1 473
150	Kiribati	1 414
151	Syria	1 384
152	Turkmenistan	1 371
153	Georgia	1 346
154	Philippines	1 304
155	Indonesia	1 279
156	Paraguay	1 275
157	Egypt	1 255

Rank	Country	GNP per capita (dollars)
158	Azerbaijan	1 241
159	Honduras	1 192
160	Sri Lanka	1 162
161	Angola	1 078
162	Equatorial Guinea	1 052
163	Djibouti	1 020
164	Guyana	1 011
165	Bolivia	1 009
166	Cameroon	1 009
167	Cuba	996
168	Lesotho	958
169	Congo	948
170	Nicaragua	906
171	Bhutan	871
172	Ivory Coast	843
173	Moldova	754
174	East Timor	749
175	India	724
176	Senegal	708
177	Mongolia	690
178	Pakistan	689
179	Papua New Guinea	657
180	Comoros	650
181	Sudan	643
182	Viet Nam	623
183	Yemen	604
184	Iraq	599
185	Nigeria	564
186	Mauritania	560
187	Kenya	527
188	Benin	514
189	Uzbekistan	508
190	Solomon	507
191	Zambia	486
192	Bangladesh	467
193	Haiti	455
194	Ghana	452
195	Kyrgyzstan	445
196	Laos	442
197	Chad	396
198	Burkina Faso	396
199	Sao Tome and Principe	385
200	Cambodia	380
201	Mali	379
202	Guinea	373

Rank	Country	GNP per capita (dollars)
203	Togo	352
204	Tanzania	350
205	Central African Rep.	347
206	Zimbabwe	343
207	Tajikistan	335
208	Mozambique	310
209	Gambia	290
210	Madagascar	289
211	Uganda	276
212	Nepal	268
213	Niger	240
214	Rwanda	230
215	Afghanistan	222
216	Sierra Leone	218
217	Eritrea	193
218	Guinea-Bissau	177
219	Malawi	161
220	Ethiopia	156
221	Somalia	136
222	Liberia	135
223	Dem. Rep. of Congo	120
224	Burundi	96

Source: http://www.studentsoftheworld.info/infopays/rank/PNBH2.html (Downloaded: February 21, 09.)

The weakening of the "Histadrut" became noticeable ever since the Likud came into power in 1977, when the alignment of the "Histadrut" and the government (which until then was headed by the Labor party) was broken. However, its power declined more rapidly in the 1980s when processes of privatization "forced" the "Histadrut" to divest itself of its assets and to sell its great concerns that dominated Israel's economy. In 1994, the Labor party lost its political hold on the "Histadrut," thus weakening its power even further. Today, few of its institutions still exist, among them the Women's Union (NAAMAT).

However, the post-industrial shift did not make Israel as highly developed as Western post-industrial societies. Israel has become one of the leading countries in electronics, software, communications, medical equipment, military developments and so forth. Despite these developments, Israel is still far below most other developed countries when diverse comparative measures are used.

Examination of the Human Development Index (HDI [UNDP, 2008]), for example, indicates that Israel is ranked 23 (of the 177 evaluated countries). HDI includes, in addition to GDP,[5] life expectancy at birth, adult (ages 15 and over) literacy rate, and the rate of enrollment in primary, secondary and tertiary education. The measure provides a broader understanding of economic processes in a country than the economic measure alone (see Table 5.3).[6]

Table 5.3. Human Development Report HDI rankings 2007/2008

High Human Development	Medium Human Development	Low Human Development
1. Iceland	71. Dominica	156. Senegal
2. Norway	72. Saint Lucia	157. Eritrea
3. Australia	73. Kazakhstan	158. Nigeria
4. Canada	74. Venezuela	159. Guinea
5. Ireland	75. Colombia	160. Rwanda
6. Sweden	76. Ukraine	161. Angola
7. Switzerland	77. Samoa	162. Benin
8. Japan	78. Thailand	163. Malawi
9. Netherlands	79. Dominican Republic	164. Zambia
10. France	80. Belize	165. Côte d'Ivoire
11. Finland	81. China	166. Burundi
12. United States	82. Grenada	167. Congo,
13. Spain	83. Armenia	168. Ethiopia
14. Denmark	84. Turkey	169. Chad
15. Austria	85. Suriname	170. Central African Republic
16. United Kingdom	86. Jordan	171. Mozambique
17. Belgium	87. Peru	172. Mali
18. Luxembourg	88. Lebanon	173. Niger
19. New Zealand	89. Ecuador	174. Guinea-Bissau
20. Italy	90. Philippines	175. Burkina Faso
21. Hong Kong, China (SAR)	91. Tunisia	176. Sierra Leone
22. Germany	92. Saint Vincent and the Grenadines	
23. Israel	93. Fiji	
24. Greece	94. Iran, Islamic Rep. of	
25. Singapore	95. Paraguay	
26. Korea, Rep. of	96. Georgia	
27. Slovenia	97. Guyana	
28. Cyprus	98. Azerbaijan	
29. Portugal	99. Sri Lanka	
30. Brunei Darussalam	100. Maldives	
31. Barbados	101. Jamaica	
32. Czech Republic	102. Cape Verde	
33. Kuwait	103. El Salvador	
34. Malta	104. Algeria	
35. Qatar	105. Viet Nam	
36. Hungary	106. Palestinian Territories	

High Human Development	Medium Human Development	Low Human Development
37. Poland	107. Indonesia	
38. Argentina	108. Syrian Arab Republic	
39. United Arab Emirates	109. Turkmenistan	
40. Chile	110. Nicaragua	
41. Bahrain	111. Moldova	
42. Slovakia	112. Egypt	
43. Lithuania	113. Uzbekistan	
44. Estonia	114. Mongolia	
45. Latvia	115. Honduras	
46. Uruguay	116. Kyrgyzstan	
47. Croatia	117. Bolivia	
48. Costa Rica	118. Guatemala	
49. Bahamas	119. Gabon	
50. Seychelles	120. Vanuatu	
51. Cuba	121. South Africa	
52. Mexico	122. Tajikistan	
53. Bulgaria	123. São Tomé & Príncipe	
54. Saint Kitts and Nevis	124. Botswana	
55. Tonga	125. Namibia	
56. Libyan Arab Jamahiriya	126. Morocco	
57. Antigua and Barbuda	127. Equatorial Guinea	
58. Oman	128. India	
59. Trinidad and Tobago	129. Solomon Islands	
60. Romania	130. Laos, People's Rep.	
61. Saudi Arabia	131. Cambodia	
62. Panama	132. Myanmar	
63. Malaysia	133. Bhutan	
64. Belarus	134. Comoros	
65. Mauritius	135. Ghana	
66. Bosnia and Herzegovina	136. Pakistan	
67. Russian Federation	137. Mauritania	
68. Albania	138. Lesotho	
69. Macedonia	139. Congo	
70. Brazil	140. Bangladesh	
	141. Swaziland	
	142. Nepal	
	143. Madagascar	
	144. Cameroon	
	145. Papua New Guinea	
	146. Haiti	
	147. Sudan	
	148. Kenya	
	149. Djibouti	
	150. Timor-Leste	
	151. Zimbabwe	

High Human Development	Medium Human Development	Low Human Development
	152. Togo	
	153. Yemen	
	154. Uganda	
	155. Gambia Low Human Development	

Source: http://hdr.undp.org/en/statistics/

One of the reasons for Israel's relatively low rank is a comparatively low rate of labor market participation. In contrast with countries like Norway, where 76% of the men and 68% of the women work, or Canada, where 73% of the men and 62% of the women work, only 61% of Israeli men and 50% of the women are in the labor force (Central Bureau of Statistics, 2008 [see Table 5.4]). These figures are partially due to low employment rates among Arabs and the Ultra-Orthodox: only 22% of Israeli Arab women work, because of a high birth rate and because few employment options exist in Arab towns and villages. Low rates are found among Arab men as well (44.8%), because they work mainly in unskilled, physically demanding jobs and tend to retire at an earlier age than Jewish men. Low rates of employment (44.3%) are found among Ultra-Orthodox men as well, because many of them are studying in "Yeshivas"[7] (Central Bureau of Statistics, 2005).

Table 5.4. Israel's Human Development Index 2005 (in comparison with a few other countries)

HDI value	Life expectancy at birth (years)	Adult literacy rate (% ages 15 and older)	Combined primary, secondary and tertiary gross enrolment ratio (%)	GDP per capita (PPP US$)
1. Iceland (0.968)	1. Japan (82.3)	1. Georgia (100.0)	1. Australia (113.0)	1. Luxembourg (60,228)
21. Hong Kong, (0.937)	8. Italy (80.3)	26. Romania (97.3)	26. Portugal (89.8)	24. Spain (27,169)
22. Germany (0.935)	9. Canada (80.3)	27. Argentina (97.2)	27. Argentina (89.7)	25. Kuwait (26,321)
23. Israel (0.932)	10. Israel (80.3)	28. Israel (97.1)	28. Israel (89.6)	26. Israel (25,864)
24. Greece (0.926)	11. France (80.2)	29. Cyprus (96.8)	29. Hungary (89.3)	27. United Arab Emirates (25,514)
25. Singapore (0.922)	12. Norway (79.8)	30. Uruguay (96.8)	30. Uruguay (88.9)	28. New Zealand (24,996)
177. Sierra Leone (0.336)	177. Zambia (40.5)	139. Burkina Faso (23.6)	172. Niger (22.7)	174. Malawi (667)

From: UNDP 2007/2008 Human Development Report http://hdrstats.undp.org/countries/country_fact_sheets/cty_fs_ISR.html

On the basis of HDI, UNDP developed several measures indicating the standard of living in a country. The most relevant for this context is the Gender-related Development Index (GDI) which takes into account gender differences in life expectancy, education (the adult literacy rate and the combined primary to tertiary gross enrollment ratio), and the estimated earned income (in USD). This measure shows that Israel has gone down two ranks and was ranked 23 of the 177 evaluated countries (overtaken by Luxembourg and Hong Kong) in 2008 (see Table 5.5). This indicates that gender inequality has increased, worsening the situation of women in Israel. The decline is attributed mainly to the maintaining of the wage gap (which in most Western societies has somewhat contracted, but in Israel remains almost constant at 40%). Hence, the forces that hinder Israel's development also reinforce gender inequality. This, of course, may have a detrimental impact on women's ability to be considered main breadwinners, and may influence women's desire to join the labor force.

Table 5.5. Gender-related Development Index (GDI) rank - UNDP 2007/2008 Report

HDI Rank in 2008	Country	HDI Rank in 2005	HDI Rank in 2008	Country	HDI Rank in 2005
1	Iceland	1	21	Hong Kong, China	22
2	Norway	3	22	Germany	20
3	Australia	2	23	Israel	21
4	Canada	4	24	Greece	24
5	Ireland	15	25	Singapore	–
6	Sweden	5	26	Korea (Republic of)	26
7	Switzerland	9	27	Slovenia	25
8	Japan	13	28	Cyprus	27
9	Netherlands	6	29	Portugal	28
10	France	7	30	Brunei Darussalam	31
11	Finland	8	31	Barbados	30
12	United States	16	32	Czech Republic	29
13	Spain	12	33	Kuwait	32
14	Denmark	11	34	Malta	33
15	Austria	19	35	Qatar	37
16	United Kingdom	10	36	Hungary	34
17	Belgium	14	37	Poland	35
18	Luxembourg	23	38	Argentina	36
19	New Zealand	18	39	United Arab Emirates	43
20	Italy	17			

HDI Rank in 2008	Country	HDI Rank in 2005	HDI Rank in 2008	Country	HDI Rank in 2005
40	Chile	40	75	Colombia	65
41	Bahrain	42	76	Ukraine	68
42	Slovakia	39	77	Samoa	71
43	Lithuania	38	78	Thailand	70
44	Estonia	41	79	Dominican Republic	73
45	Latvia	44	80	Belize	–
46	Uruguay	45	81	China	72
47	Croatia	46	82	Grenada	–
48	Costa Rica	47	83	Armenia	74
49	Bahamas	48	84	Turkey	78
50	Seychelles	–	85	Suriname	77
51	Cuba	49	86	Jordan	79
52	Mexico	51	87	Peru	75
53	Bulgaria	50	88	Lebanon	80
54	Saint Kitts and Nevis	–	89	Ecuador	–
55	Tonga	52	90	Philippines	76
56	Libyan Arab Jamahiriya	61	91	Tunisia	82
			92	Fiji	81
57	Antigua and Barbuda	–	93	Saint Vincent	–
58	Oman	66	94	Iran	83
59	Trinidad and Tobago	55	95	Paraguay	85
60	Romania	53	96	Georgia	–
61	Saudi Arabia	69	97	Guyana	87
62	Panama	54	98	Azerbaijan	86
63	Malaysia	57	99	Sri Lanka	88
64	Belarus	56	100	Maldives	84
65	Mauritius	62	101	Jamaica	89
66	Bosnia and Herzegovina	–	102	Cape Verde	92
67	Russian Federation	58	103	El Salvador	91
68	Albania	60	104	Algeria	94
69	Macedonia (TFYR)	63	105	Viet Nam	90
70	Brazil	59	106	Occupied Palestinian	–
71	Dominica	–	107	Indonesia	93
72	Saint Lucia	–	108	Syrian Arab Republic	95
73	Kazakhstan	64	109	Turkmenistan	–
74	Venezuela	67	110	Nicaragua	98

HDI Rank in 2008	Country	HDI Rank in 2005
111	Moldova	96
112	Egypt	–
113	Uzbekistan	97
114	Mongolia	99
115	Honduras	100
116	Kyrgyzstan	101
117	Bolivia	102
118	Guatemala	103
119	Gabon	104
120	Vanuatu	–
121	South Africa	106
122	Tajikistan	105
123	Sao Tome and Principe	109
124	Botswana	108
125	Namibia	107
126	Morocco	111
127	Equatorial Guinea	110
128	India	112
129	Solomon Islands	–
130	Laos	114
131	Cambodia	113
132	Myanmar	–
133	Bhutan	–
134	Comoros	115
135	Ghana	116
136	Pakistan	124
137	Mauritania	117
138	Lesotho	118
139	Congo	119
140	Bangladesh	120
141	Swaziland	122
142	Nepal	127
143	Madagascar	121
144	Cameroon	125
145	Papua New Guinea	123
146	Haiti	–

HDI Rank in 2008	Country	HDI Rank in 2005
147	Sudan	130
148	Kenya	126
149	Djibouti	128
150	Timor-Leste	..
151	Zimbabwe	129
152	Togo	133
153	Yemen	135
154	Uganda	131
155	Gambia	132
156	Senegal	134
157	Eritrea	136
158	Nigeria	138
159	Tanzania	137
160	Guinea	140
161	Rwanda	139
162	Angola	141
163	Benin	144
164	Malawi	142
165	Zambia	143
166	Côte d'Ivoire	145
167	Burundi	146
168	Congo	147
169	Ethiopia	148
170	Chad	151
171	Central African Republic	152
172	Mozambique	149
173	Mali	150
174	Niger	154
175	Guinea-Bissau	155
176	Burkina Faso	153
177	Sierra Leone	156

http://hdrstats.undp.org/indicators/268.html

Another indication of the shift toward a post-industrial society is the rising level of education: there were about 50,000 students in the six Israeli universities in the mid-1980s, and now there are over 250,000 students in those universities and the many (over 20) academic colleges that sprang up in the 1990s and were accorded recognition by the Higher Education Authority. This dramatic increase reflects both the availability of academic institutions and the desire of individuals to improve their lives and their wages. This had a significant impact on the employability of individuals, and the rate of unemployment decreased (especially among those with academic education).[8]

In the mid-1980s, female students became the majority (57%) of all undergraduate students, and in the mid-1990s they became the majority of the graduate students as well. Similar trends can be seen in Europe and North America (see Figure 5.1 and Figure 5.2). Still, most female students turn to the humanities (where they constitute 67% of all students), education (83% of all students), nursing (79%), and social sciences (61%). They are still the minority in mathematics and computers (where they comprise 31% of all students), physics (37%), and engineering (25%). This, of course, contributes to the maintaining of occupational sex segregation (see Table 6).

Figure 5.1. Female Students in Higher Education in Selected Countries (2000/1)

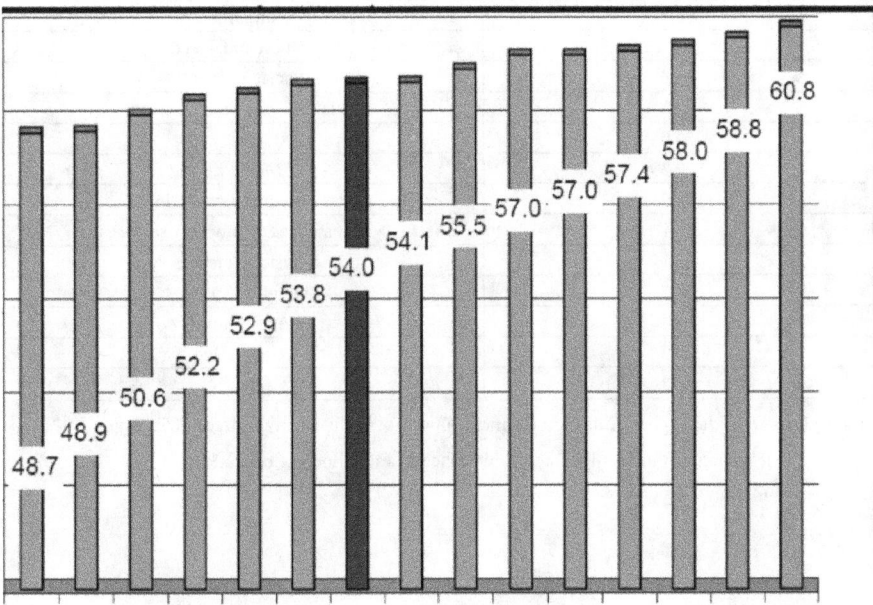

From: Trends in Europe and North America (Table 3.6), The Statistical Yearbook of the Economic Commission for Europe 2003

Figure 5.2. Education 1976-2007[1] - Students in Universities and Colleges

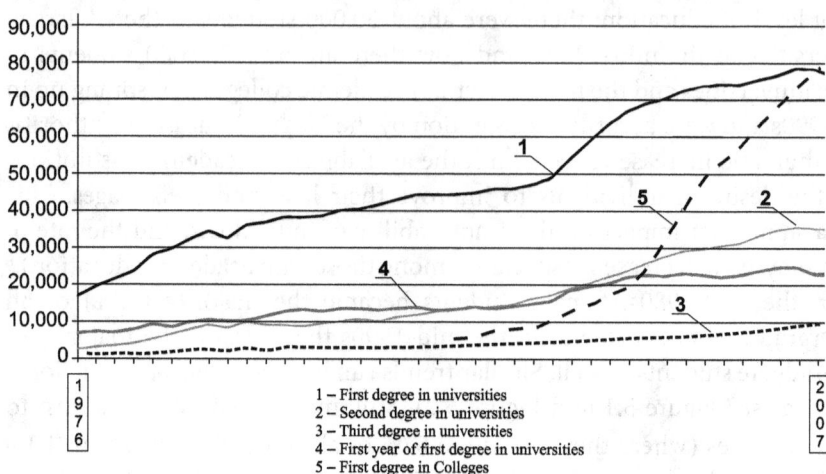

1 – First degree in universities
2 – Second degree in universities
3 – Third degree in universities
4 – First year of first degree in universities
5 – First degree in Colleges

[1]   Israeli Bureau of Statistics. (2006). Students in Universities and other Institutions of Higher Education, Jerusalem (p. 42, Figure B)

Table 5.6. Proportion of Women in Diverse Fields, in All Academic Institutions*

Percent women	Field of Study
66.5	Humanities
83.1	Education and Teaching
61.3	Social Sciences
49.1	Business and Management
50.0	Law
52.3	Medicine
79.3	Para-Medical occupations
31.4	Mathematics & Computer sciences
37.1	Physical Sciences
61.7	Biological Sciences
58.4	Agriculture
25.3	Engineering
56.2	Total

Source: Data from the Higher Education Council, 2004, sent to the Central Bureau of Statistics.

* Data include students in universities, academic colleges, and schools of education.

Occupational Sex Segregation

The aforementioned processes of transformation in the economic sphere have led to changes in labor force composition: the data shows that although the proportion of women is almost equal to the proportion of men in the labor force (48% and 52%, respectively in 2008, Central Bureau of Statistics, 2008), the gap between them is steadily closing so that the employment rate of the genders is expected to equalize in 2015 (Natanson, Tzameret, and Cohen, 2004). Yet sex segregation is still the dominant pattern, and breaking its barriers, especially in the lower-status occupations, is still slow (see Table 7).

Table 5.7. Occupational Sex Segregation[9]

	Employed Persons, By Occupation (minor group - two digits), Total population, 2005	Thousands			Percent Females	
Code	Occupation	Total	Females	Males	1980	2005
	Total	**2,573.6**	**1,190.0**	**1,383.6**	**41**	**46**
0	ACADEMIC PROFESSIONALS	358.0	174.4	183.6	38	49
00	Biologists, Pharmacologists and related professionals	6.3	4.1	2.3	40	65
01	Chemists, Physicists, Mathematicians and related professionals	25.7	8.8	16.9	20	34
02	Engineers and Architects	80.8	17.2	63.6	11	21
03	Medical Doctors, Pharmacists and Veterinarians	46.2	25.6	20.6	38	55
04	Judges and Lawyers	32.2	14.7	17.5	36	46
05	Economists, Psychologists, Accountants and related professionals	55.5	30.4	25.1	41	55
06	Humanities professionals	14.2	9.6	4.6	69	68
07	University and higher education teaching professionals	20.0	10.0	10.0	38	50
08	Post-secondary and post-primary teaching professionals	75.8	53.9	22.0	61	71
09	Religious sciences professionals	(1.2)	0	(1.2)	0	0
1	ASSOCIATE PROFESSIONALS AND TECHNICIANS	402.3	236.8	165.5	62	59
10	Natural sciences technicians and associate professionals	4.0	2.3	(1.7)	62	57
11	Civil engineering technicians and associate professionals	7.8	2.2	5.6	15	28
12	Electrical, electronic, mechanical and other engineering technicians and associate professionals	36.6	6.5	30.1	—	18
13	Practical computer engineers and technicians	67.1	18.5	48.6	21	28
14	Communications and medical equipment operators and photographers	10.3	3.0	7.3	—	29

Code	Employed Persons, By Occupation (minor group - two digits), Total population, 2005	Thousands			Percent Females	
	Occupation	Total	Females	Males	1980	2005
15	Medical laboratory workers, nurses and other paramedical professions	59.3	49.4	10.0	87	83
16	Teaching associate professionals in primary schools and in kindergartens, and social counselors	149.1	120.6	28.5	87	81
17	Journalists, and workers in arts and sports	55.8	30.7	25.1	36	55
18	Auditors and Accountants	7.5	3.5	3.9	17	47
19	Religious associate professionals	3.7	0	3.7	0	0
1X	Engineering technicians	(0.9)	0	(0.9)	0	0
2	MANAGERS	156.2	45.1	111.1	9	29
3	CLERICAL WORKERS	407.8	305.3	102.5	60	75
4	AGENTS, SALES WORKERS AND SERVICE WORKERS	513.9	283.2	230.7	40	55
5	SKILLED AGRICULTURAL WORKERS	32.9	3.0	29.9	14	9
6-8	MANUFACTURING, CONSTRUCTION & SKILLED WORKERS	466.7	48.7	418.0	11	10
9	UNSKILLED WORKERS	205.9	84.1	121.8	19	41

The majority of women joining the labor market still enter female-typed occupations. As indicated in Chapter Two, female-typed occupations (such as secretarial work, teaching, and domestic work) are those in which women are the majority of all workers in the occupation (over 60%). Consequently, many occupations are still sex-typed in the sense that one sex group enters them more than the other (see Chapter Two). While engineering and management remain male-typed (with 21% and 29% women in them, respectively), other occupations remain female-typed (e.g., biologists (65% women), nurses (83%), and clerical workers (75% [Central Bureau of Statistics, 2006]).

Most working women curtail their work roles by taking on part-time occupations and/or time-flexible jobs (Bergman, 1992; Cinamon, 2006). Such employment is more easily found in female-typed occupations (Moore, 1992). Because they rely mostly on women, female-typed occupations tend to be more "woman-friendly" in terms of flexibility, compulsory overtime, and adjusting working hours than male-typed occupations (Moore and Gobi, 1995). Most of these occupations pay lower wages than other occupations that demand the same levels of education (Moore, 1999), status enhancement in them is more difficult to attain, and the jobs generally require more routine tasks and less work commitment. Consequently, women who espouse this strategy tend to remain economically dependent on their spouses even when they work full-time jobs (Izraeli, 1993; Stier and Lewin Epstein, 2000).

However, women in that time span did enter many of the higher education and higher status occupations, turning many of them into mixed-type occupations, or at least diminishing the male majority in them in comparison with the 1980s. E.g., the rates of female auditors and accountants rose from 17% in 1980 to 47% in 2005, the rates of chemists and physicists rose from 20% to 34%, and the rates of doctors and pharmacists from 38% to 50%.

Though even now the distribution is far from equal, this growing tendency should not be disparaged, as women are becoming a substantial group within these occupations, and that brings about greater occupational and economic opportunities for women. The importance of these changes is discussed later in the chapter.

Changes in the Role of Religion

While changes in the economic, political and social spheres contributed to improvement in the status of women in Israel, religion and religiosity remain among the main forces that impede egalitarian trends. As Chapter Two shows, the inhibiting force of religion stems from an emphasis on the traditional-domestic role of women, which curbs both their employment aspirations and their potential independence and limits their roles in the public sphere: religious parties do not have female representatives; women cannot serve as judges in religious courts of law or act in any official capacity in religious institutions; and religious leaders create and/or support laws that strengthen gender inequality (or they oppose legislation that will increase such equality). Moreover, as women are barred from taking active roles in any of the religious institutions, they still cannot serve as role models for women in the public sphere.

Furthermore, forces against equality have become stronger in the past decades. In 2002, the Central Bureau of Statistics (CBS) began collecting data concerning religiosity (beforehand, data on religiosity were collected only by individual researchers for diverse purposes). According to CBS surveys (Central Bureau of Statistics, 2006), the proportion of Ultra-Orthodox Jews increased from 6% of the Jewish population in 2002 to 8% in 2004, religious Jews were 9%, "tradition-oriented"[10] were 12%, and observant[11] Jews were 27%. The proportion of secular Jews increased in the same period from 42%

to 44% of all Jews. Religiosity in Israel is strongly related to ethnicity. The Social Indicators Survey (Central Bureau of Statistics, 2006) shows that the majority of the religious and the "tradition-oriented" are Jews of African origin (17.1% and 32.1%, respectively) or of Asian origin (15.8% and 25.3%, respectively); among European Jews, only 6.4% are religious, and 6.5% are "tradition-oriented." Seculars, on the other hand, are of European origin (56.5%) but a much smaller proportion of Jews of African origin (12.6%) or Asian origin (19.1%) are secular.

In their survey, Levi, Levinsohn and Katz (2004) found that although 44% of the Jewish population in Israel defined itself as "non-religious," only 6-8% did not observe any of the religious decrees. About half of the secular Jews observe some of the religious decrees (e.g., fasting on Yom Kippur, celebrating Pesach, affixing a mezuzah to their doorpost, and/or performing a brit milah on their male sons). The remaining secular Jews maintain more of the Jewish traditions (e.g. eating kosher food, observing the Sabbath), though they still define themselves "secular." Hence, only about a quarter of all Jews in Israel may be considered truly secular. Moreover, 78% of the Jewish Israeli population prefers Israel to be a Jewish state (though not necessarily a religious state), according to that study. The rift between religious and secular Jews is growing, and many believe that the two categories of Jews are already engaged in a cultural war (Ben Yehuda, 2001).

Although in the past religious parties joined existing coalitions for the benefits that this joining provided, from 1990 onwards more than two thirds of the religious individuals were found to be right-wing, with decidedly hawkish foreign policy attitudes, much more extreme than those of their political leaders (Arian, 1998; Shamir and Arian, 1999). As a result, religious parties became increasingly more right-wing.[12] As many of the secular Jews tend to vote for center or left-wing parties, the rift is not only one of religiosity and culture but of political and social ideologies as well.

Becoming noticeably more right-wing increased the strength of religious parties (from twelve representatives in four separate parties in 1984 to twenty-seven, in three parties ("Shas," "Mafdal" and "Yahadut Hatora"), since 1999. There are, of course, additional religious Knesset members in non-religious parties, increasing the overall number of religious representatives to approximately forty, about a third of all Knesset members. Allocation of resources has also changed, with huge amounts of funds going to the educational, social and religious institutions supported by the diverse religious parties. This increased the power of religion in Israel, and contributed to the strengthening of religiosity among Israeli Jews, which, in turn, helped to curb the spreading of feminist and/or egalitarian ideologies.

While religiosity is strengthening, especially among Jews of Asian and African origin, the opposite trend may be seen among the secular segment of Israeli society, intensifying the gap between religious and secular. The secularism trend seems to be due to two very different forces: the ingrained secularity of the "Russian" immigrants and the growing visibility of non-Orthodox denominations in Israel.

The immigrants from the former Soviet bloc are mostly secular, and many among them came to Israel married to non-Jews, or as the descendants of Jewish men who were married to non-Jews (which makes them non-Jews according to Jewish law). Some of the immigrants knew nothing about Jewish religion and culture prior to their arrival. Consequently, the secularity of these immigrants is more pronounced than the secularity of veteran Israelis, who were brought up in the Jewish state where the basis of Jewish religion and culture are taught in all schools. Instead, the immigrants brought with them their socialist beliefs and a stronger desire for equality. As they are not as bound by the religious perceptions of gender roles as veteran Israelis, more among the immigrant women are employed, and many of them contribute to the family income as much as (or even more than) their husbands (and many among them who are single parents manage to provide for their children by themselves).

In addition, non-Orthodox forms of Judaism were "imported" to Israel, mainly from the USA, but also from England and Australia, where they are as widespread as the more Orthodox denominations. These denominations (e.g., Reform and Conservative Judaism) do not have official standing in Israel, and their rabbis can lead congregations, but cannot perform official ceremonies (like marriages). The Reform and Conservative denominations accord women official roles, and even ordain women as rabbis. Hence, Reform and Conservative women can serve as role models for other women and participate in determining the day-to-day aspects of their community life.

These two influences—that of the growing number of secular (mostly Russian) women and that of the religious but non-Orthodox women—cannot counter the growing power of institutionalized religion. Still, their impact on the traditional division of labor is noticeable, and in 2007 only 10% of men and women support the traditional division of labor, according to Moore (2007). The next chapter elaborates on these issues.

4. Changes in the Israeli Army

Since the 1980s, dramatic changes can be seen in the importance of the army in Israeli society in general, and in the status of women in military service. The army lost its position as the all-inclusive melting pot when the number of individuals choosing not to enlist grew to unprecedented proportions: 25% of the men do not enlist, and 17.5% of those who do enlist do not complete the full term. Thus, over 40% of those who should have enlisted did not fulfill their duty. Many explanations are provided for the decline, among them: the lack of consensus concerning the war in Lebanon; the growing individualism that decreased the desire to contribute to the common good; and the growing belief in the 1990s that the army is less important and that peace is an option (a belief that has declined since then because of the Intifada that began in 2000). Some blame it on the growing integration of women in combat units that were previously open to men only. The most relevant to our case are, of course, the changes that involve women.

Examining gender discourse in the Israeli military context from 1948 to 2000, Robbins and Ben-Eliezer (2000) link gender inequality in military service to Israel's founding as a "nation-in-arms." This reality turned Israel into an "enlisted society," and placed the army in the center of the collective conscience. They show that this situation had differential influence on women's military service in three distinct historical periods: the "social" roles of the 1950s, the "professional" roles of the 1970s, and the "quasi-combatant" roles of the 1990s. Their conclusion that this reality hindered the spreading of feminist ideologies in Israel is supported by many (e.g., Golan, Pazy, and Oron, 2001; Sasson-Levy 2003, Sasson-Levy and Amram-Katz, 2007).

The changes in the status of women in the Israeli army are similar to the transformation within the US army (Enloe, 1988, 1993). Until the 1980s, the military service of young women changed very little, and most of the drafted women were employed as clerks and secretaries. Some changes began in the 1980s when new positions as instructors of fighters in infantry and armored units were opened for women. They were also accepted as team leaders in boot camps (for male soldiers destined for the home front, and in technical roles, such as working as electricians or mechanics).

In the 1990s, pressure exerted by feminist and civil rights organizations led to more significant changes in the army. In 1994, Alice Miller, an officer in the air force, petitioned the Supreme Court to force the Israeli army to allow her to join the prestigious flight course. In response, in 1995 the Supreme Court ruled that the army must allow women to volunteer for the flight course like men do, and instructed the army to equalize the rights of men and women. The Alice Miller case constitutes an important precedent, as it defined the right to equality as part of the right to dignity and freedom, which is one of the basic laws in Israel (Greenberg, 1996; Maman, Ben-Ari, and Rosenhek, 2001).

One of the main consequences of these changes is the disbanding of the Women's Corps. Until 1997, all women belonged to a separate Women's Corps, and then assigned to other corps as needed, usually as clerks or secretaries. The disbanding meant that female soldiers were better integrated and became an integral part of the corps they were conscripted to (or volunteered to join).

In addition, in 2000 the security service law was changed according to the Supreme Court's ruling, and the conscription of women was changed: new operative and fighting roles were opened for women in almost all army units (some infantry and armor divisions still exclude women because of their weaker physical strength). A special advisor to the Chief of Staff was appointed to ensure that the more egalitarian policy is implemented and the rights of female soldiers are protected, and that they serve in an environment that is free of harassment and discrimination. Moreover, most of the courses—such as officers' training and specialized professional courses - were unified so that men and women trained together, and efforts were made to ease the advancement of women to senior positions in the service in "non-feminine" jobs. In 2007, about 1,500 women served as front line fighters.

However, Sasson-Levy and Amram-Katz (2007) show that the integration did not alter the cultural model of the army, and did not create an equal opportunity environment for women. Women soldiers in "masculine" roles were influenced by the hegemonic—masculine—model of the combat soldier, and distance themselves from traditional femininity. Thus, while they prove that women can perform masculine roles, they do so by denying their own femininity and collaborating with the military androcentric norms. To succeed and survive in these roles, they must internalize the military's masculine ideology and values and learn to identify with the patriarchal order of the army and the state. "This accounts for a pattern of 'limited inclusion' that reaffirms their marginalization, thus prohibiting them from developing a collective consciousness that would challenge the gendered structure of citizenship" (Sasson-Levy, 2003, p. 460).

In addition, women must overcome the sexual harassment that still prevails in the Israeli Army. Even in the beginning of the third millennium, such cases are still being brought in front of Israeli courts of law, usually by young low-ranking women who file suits against high-ranking superior officers (Barak-Erez, et al., 2007). Still, the proportion of women officers, even in high ranks (colonels, brigadier generals) rose sharply in recent years: data supplied by Army authorities show that in fight-support units, the proportion of women majors rose from 28% in 2000 to 37% in 2008, and the proportion of lieutenant colonels doubled in those years from 14% to 28%. In the Logistics Corps, for example, women are now 39% of all officers (Greenberg, 2009). They are still barred from the highest ranks by law, but this, too, may change in the near future through Knesset legislation which has already been announced.

There still are diverse jobs that are not available to women, especially combat roles. Today, women are allowed "front" activities, but not in combat roles (e.g., they may train soldiers [e.g., as tank instructors], but are not allowed to drive the tanks themselves during combat or training activity).

Moreover, it is still much easier for women to avoid military service altogether than it is for men. They only need to declare that they are religious and they will be exempt from service forthwith. Because of the increase in sexual harassment incidents,[13] many young women prefer to avoid the stressful atmosphere in both remote camps and the professional bases, limiting both women's enlisting and choice of available jobs. In "masculine" combat roles, women soldiers tend to trivialize incidents of sexual harassment, even take them for granted or as an affirmation of their femininity (Sasson-Levy, 2003).

In conclusion, although many changes in the army now make it possible for women to hold diverse jobs and positions that were previously reserved only for men, the organizational culture is still, in many cases, hostile, discriminating and/or humiliating for women (Golan, 1997; Klein, 2002). It may be that the process is still in primary changes and the culture will also change.

5. The Impact of the Combined Influences on Women

The social, ideological, political, economic, religious and military changes in recent decades have decreased both gender inequality on the one hand, and women's willingness to fight for greater equality on the other. Consequently, at the beginning of the new millennium young men and women in Israel encounter different opportunities and limitations then previous generations encountered.

6. Changes in Family Structure

Traditional family is losing its centrality in Israel, and families are less stable than in the past: fewer marriages, higher divorce rates, fewer children per woman, and a higher age at which women have their first child can be seen in Israel in the third millennium. This may reflect a considerable change in the attitudes, beliefs, and values of women, and may have a significant impact on women's work and on the solutions they find for combining family and work. Still, marriages in Israel are more prevalent than in other societies (see Figure 5.2). Table 5.8 shows that the decline in the proportion of marriages[14] continues to decrease (from 11.2 per 1000 individuals of all ages each year in the 1950s, to 9.6 in the 1970s, to 5.9 in 2006), and the proportion of divorces increases.

Table 5.8. Marriage and Divorce Rates: Israel 1950-2006

	Years*	Rate**
	1950-1954	11.2
	1955-1959	8.3
	1960-1964	7.5
	1970-1974	9.6
	1980-1984	7.3
Marriages	1985-1989	6.6
	1990-1994	6.1
	1995-1999	6.2
	2000-2004	5.9
	2005	5.8
	2006	6.1
	1960-1964	1.0
	1970-1974	0.9
	1980-1984	1.3
	1985-1989	1.3
Divorces	1990-1994	1.5
	1995-1999	1.8
	2000-2004	1.9
	2005	2.0
	2006	2.1

From: The Israeli Bureau of Statistics (2003). Statistical Yearbook, Table 3.1, and the Israeli Bureau of Statistics (2008), Press Release, August 14, 2008.
* Average number per year in the range
** Number per 1000 citizens.

Figure 5.3. Proportion of Marriages in Israel and some European Countries—1990 vs. 2000

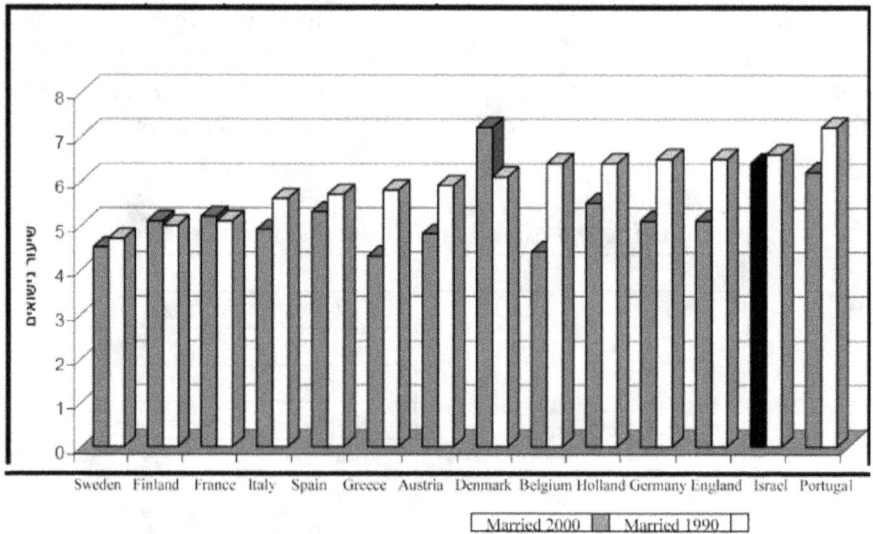

From: People in Europe 2, Families and births, (Table p. 87), Eurostat Yearbook 2003, European Communities

Though some of the decline may be explained by the same factors that influence other Western societies, some of the decline in Israel may be due to a growing number of individuals who choose alternative types of families: avoiding marriage altogether (the proportion of bachelors rose to 70% of individuals aged 20-24 in 2006, in comparison with 53% in 1986; 57% of individuals aged 25-29 in 2006, in comparison with 38% in 1986; and 6% of individuals aged 45-49 in 2006, in comparison with 3% in 1986), choosing cohabitation (living together without marriage of any kind; the proportion remains constant at around 3% of all couples in Israel. In comparison, 33% of all couples in Sweden where women are aged 30-34 cohabit, and 16% in Canada), or choosing single parenthood (the number of single mothers who were never married increased by 57% from 8,400 in 2000 to 13,200 in 2006). Choosing these alternatives indicates changes in the traditional structure of families, and modification of the autonomy of women (Women's Lobby, 2004).

One of the consequences of these changes is the decline in the number of children per family. The birth rate of Jewish women was 3.56 in 1955, 3.00 in 1975, and 2.79 in 1985, and it stabilized around 2.60 in the mid-1990s (Israeli Bureau of Statistics, 2006). The main causes of the decline, in addition to a marriage at a later age, are the rising education level, better employment opportunities, improved family planning and cultural changes (Women's Lobby, 2004). These factors both strengthen the changes and are strengthened by them: the fewer children a woman plans, the greater her tendency to invest more in human capital (education, on-the-job-training, and so forth), and thus increase her employability and rewards at work. Moreover, these multi-tiered changes appear in tandem with a growing diversity in the occupational structure. Hence, women's increased employability and the shift toward a service-oriented labor market provide women with a growing number of possible jobs and occupations, with better pay, greater advancement opportunities, and egalitarian legislation to ensure the implementation of their rights. The impact of these processes, together with the spreading awareness of their rights and the influence of diverse feminist ideologies, is discussed in the next chapter.

Changes in Social Action

The spreading of feminist ideas imported from Western societies and the accumulating knowledge of feminists' achievements in other countries, together with the less centralist nature of capitalism, has contributed to the creating of several feminist organizations in Israel in the mid-1980s (e.g., The Women's Lobby, Woman-to-Woman ["Isha Le-Isha"], Your Voice ["Kolech"]), and to the turning of complacent women's organizations (like NAAMAT) into more feminist organizations fighting for women's rights.

Until the 1980s, existing women's organizations fought for women's place in society without contesting the existing social order, avoiding direct conflict and the corresponding blame they would receive that their actions obstruct the welfare of society as a whole. Since the 1990s, even organizations like NAAMAT are more willing to act against the existing social order, and their influence on the status of women has become more noticeable. In the 2000s, these organizations have become more postmodernistic, and are now fighting for the rights of mothers and wives (like establishing shelters for battered women and their children and creating daycare centers within workplaces).

These organizations and associations often combine forces to either create or support initiatives that increase equality. They work with and contribute to diverse parliamentary committees, such as the committee for gender equality (in the Knesset) and the committee for equal work opportunities (in the Ministry of Commerce and Industry), and serve as advisors to the Prime Minister, the Chief of Staff, and diverse private sector organizations. Another indication of the change in the status of women in Israel is the proportion of female Knesset members. From nine (out of 120) women in the 1999 elections, the number of women at the Knesset reached seventeen elected members in both 2003 and 2006 (see Figure 5.4) and twenty-two members in 2010. More women are now included in important Knesset committees like the National Security Council and the Monetary Committee. Still, with the Knesset made up of only 14.3% women, Israeli women are under-represented in comparison to those of many other countries (see Table 5.9).

Figure 5.4. Number of Women in the Knesset (1949-2008)

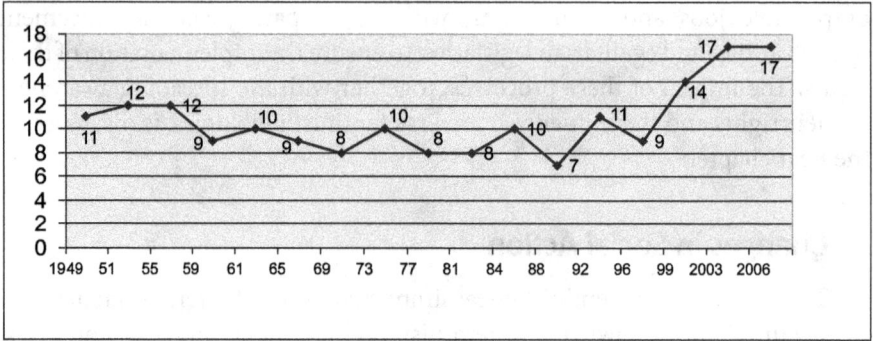

Source: www.knesset.gov.il

Table 5.9. Proportion of Women in Parliaments of Diverse Countries

Rank	Country	Proportion of women in parliament	Rank	Country	Proportion of women in parliament
1	Rwanda	48.8%	33	Australia	24.7%
2	Sweden	47.3%	37	Tunisia	22.8%
3	Costa Rica	38.6%	41	Ethiopia	21.9%
4	Finland	38%	44	Pakistan	21.3%
5	Norway	37.9%	47	Canada	20.8%
6	Denmark	36.9%	48	Poland	20.4%
7	Netherlands	36.7%	49	China	20.3%
8	Spain	36%	52	Dominican Republic	19.7%
8	Cuba	36%	52	Great Britain	19.7%
9	Argentina	35%	60	Sudan	17.8%
10	Mozambique	34.8%	66	U.S.A.	16.2%
11	Belgium	34.7%	76	Israel	14.3%
12	Island	33.3%	82	Greece	13%
14	Austria	32.2%	86	France	12.2%
17	Tanzania	30.4%	95	Hungary	10.4%
21	Belarus	29.1%	99	Georgia	9.4%
28	Iraq	25.5%	99	Japan	9.4%
28	Surinam	25.5%	126	Turkey	4.4%
31	Ecuador	25%	135	Egypt	2%
31	Switzerland	25%	138	Yemen	0.3%

Source: Inter-Parliamentary Union website, www.ipu.org/wmn-e/classif.htm, visited: January 31, 2007.

With their new awareness, the changed conditions in the country, and the spreading of post-industrial egalitarian ideas (Moore, 1995a), since the

1990s women seem to be more willing to fight for changes in their social and economic positions. Some initiatives in this direction were taken by female Knesset members elected at the end of 1992, so that political and institutional support for these efforts has been gained. When it comes to gender issues, female Knesset members from diverse parties join forces to attain feminist goals.[15] They work in concert to pass laws, such as equal pay for work of equal value, affirmative action in the public sector, and in selection of directors for government-owned companies. Also, much pressure was placed on Israel's Supreme Court to implement laws against the abuse of women (in rape or incest cases), and increase the punishment of offenders.

During the 1990s, the optimistic feelings accompanying the peace process in which Israel and its neighbors were involved reflected the belief that the state of war, which had existed between them for almost 50 years, was ending. This may have—directly or indirectly—contributed to the acceleration of the process of change in women's status by creating a socio-cultural legitimacy for women's rights movements: no longer in existential danger, Israelis were able to address matters of social inequality (Moore, 1996). Although hope of a "New Middle East" was quenched for most Israelis, the belief that social and cultural changes are possible—even necessary and unavoidable—did not die.

However slowly, the legitimacy accorded by ideological pluralism to feminist ideas has begun to filter to grassroots levels, and women's awareness of them has increased. This process provided a wider basis of support for feminist action groups. An attitude survey, performed by The Strategy Institute for Haaretz newspaper (Special Supplement, March 4, 1994), shows that 34% of the women in Israel defined themselves at that time as "feminists." (The definition of feminism was deliberately left open to individual interpretations to maximize responses.) A more recent study by Dahaf Research Institute (June 2007), used the same question and showed that the proportion has grown, and 48% of the women in Israel define themselves as "feminists" (vs. 39% of the men). When specific aspects of feminism are analyzed, support of both men and women is even stronger (over 50% for women and 40% for men; e.g., when asked about their support of equal opportunity for both genders, equal pay for work of equal worth, or the belief that women can perform jobs in different ways than men, but just as well).

In addition, women's fights for higher occupational status—especially in female-typed occupations—increased in the 1990s. In part, the justification for these fights derives from the liberal quest for lessening social inequality, but it also reflects post-industrial (or post-structural) feminism and emphasizes the unique merit of women's contributions.[16]

In conclusion, ideological pluralism allows diverse views to coexist so that socially differentiated categories may espouse different ideologies. It seems logical to expect the dominant social group to espouse the hegemonic ideology and the oppressed (or subordinate) group to espouse a different, seditious ideology. Ideological pluralism also indicates legitimacy of alternative views, and this is a necessary condition for the spreading of alternative ideologies to grassroots level. Only when alternative ideologies are widely supported do they become a motivating force for social action for the groups that espouse them (Tal, 1993).

Although gender equality is a basic value in Israel law, and the Scroll of Independence (the parchment on which Israel's Declaration of Independence was written in 1948) clearly proclaims no gender-based discrimination, several specific laws were defined since the late 1980s to ensure gender equality, especially in regard to the work sphere: the Law of Equal Employment Opportunities (1988), the Law of Equal Pay for Male and Female Workers (1996), the Law for Prevention of Sexual Harassment (1998), and the law that established the Authority for the Advancement of Women's Status (1998). The very necessity of these laws is an indication that the general decree of equality was insufficient, and did not prevent discrimination.

Women are still not equal citizens. Though to a lesser extent than in previous decades, discrimination can be seen in hiring, advancement, wages and work benefits, on-the-job training, and the retirement of women. Women still encounter sexual harassment in workplaces, and they often avoid taking their plight to court for fear of dismissal; women are still underrepresented in directorates of public and private corporations; working mothers' rights are not always protected, and women's status in the religious Courts of Law, in which all family matters are handled, is still inferior to men's. The next chapter focuses on some of these issues.

ENDNOTES

[1] Life expectancy at birth is the average number of years that a person born in a certain year is expected to live, given the death rates in the period.

[2] "Others" are either non-Jews married to Jews and therefore allowed to become citizens upon immigration, or the descendants of non-Jewish mothers in mixed marriages.

[3] Immigrants arrived since the 1980s from other countries as well, mainly from Ethiopia, but their much smaller numbers and their weaker social capital influenced Israeli society much less than imigrants from the former Soviet bloc.

[4] Created in 1920 as the all-inclusive labor union of all the workers in Israel, it also produced jobs for a multitude of workers. Its huge agricultural (e.g., "Tnuva"), construction (e.g., "Sollel Boneh"), transportation (e.g., "Shelev"), and

industrial (e.g., "Coor") concerns were dominant in Israeli economy and society, and enabled the "Histadrut" to provide many social services like health care (Kupat Holim), residences for the elderly (Mishaan), and education (Amal). It also created a women's division—NAAMAT—that addressed the specific work issues of women and in later years provided additional services for women like daycare centers, legal services and so forth.

5   GDP (Gross Domestic Product) represents the market value of all goods and services in a nation in a given year, measured in USD.

6   An example of such economic measure is GNP (Gross National Product). According to the World Bank report (2005), Israel is ranked 35 (of the 224 evaluated countries) with $18,624 per capita, which is lower than most Western societies. Even Greece (with $19,687 per capita) is ranked higher, so that Israel only supersedes European countries like Andorra, Cyprus, Portugal and Malta. This is the result of the intense intervention of governments in economic processes, which reduces production (e.g., the government controls all public services, owns the military industry, subsidizes industry, and owns or controls almost all the land [93% of the land], and so forth [Plesner, 1994]).

7   Yeshivas are non-academic religious schools of higher learning where individuals continue to study for 20 years or more. They grant no academic degrees, but provide the title "Rabbi."

8   Moreover, the increased demand for academic education left behind those ethnic groups in which high academic attainment is less common, like Jews from Asian and African origin, but the proliferation of academic institutions enabled them to attain relevant higher education and improve their occupational status.

9   Due to changes in the classification of occupations, some categories that appear in 2005 were not classified in 1980 (---).

10 Tradition-oriented are individuals who observe all the main religious decrees and many of the minor decrees.

11 Observant Jews are individuals who observe some of the main religious decrees, and decide which decrees they choose to observe, often seeing these decrees as part of the Jewish tradition rather than religion.

12 For example, until the 2003 elections, the religious leader of the Sephardic religious party (Rabbi Ovadia Yosef) supported withdrawal from the territories Israel conquered in 1967 (in accord with Leftist policy), but his party joined most coalitions (whether left- or right-wing). Its religious and political leaders were willing to compromise their standing on foreign policy issues to become coalition members and gain dominance over important ministries such as Internal Affairs, Education and Religion. In the coalition, they control the domestic scene and can advance issues that are on their agendas. Hence, their allegiance is granted to the party most willing to pass religious laws and to enforce the existing ones more forcefully (the reader should remember

that Israel has no constitution). Since then, the right-wing shift led to the announcement that they will only join a right-wing coalition.

13 The number of reported sexual harassment incidents has increased 78% in recent years, and a survey in the army shows that while one of five female soldiers is harassed, only a few complain. In most cases, the complaints are dealt with within the unit. Cases against high ranking officers were brought before the Israeli courts, some of them in recent years.

14 Marriages in Israel are only performed by religious authorities. Consequently, inter-religious marriages are totally impossible in Israel. Couples who belong to different religions, and couples who choose civil marriages, must leave the country and turn to other countries if they wish to marry. They may then register at the Home Office as married.

15 For example, the Commision for the Advancement of Women's Status was chaired by Naomi Blumental (from the Right-wing Likud), and included Yael Dayan (Labor) and Naomi Chazan (from the Left-wing "Meretz"). Heading its subcommittees were: Anat Maor ("Meretz"), Tamar Gozanski ("Hadash," the Jewish-Arab Party) and others.

16 The more radical approaches seem to have skipped Israel, and this may be due to several concurrent social processes. First, compulsory military service may have hindered women's willingness and ability to espouse ideologies that undermine and/or contradict patriarchal ideologies (Izraeli, 1993). Second, the earlier disappointment with socialist ideology made radical (especially the Marxist and Socialist) feminism less attractive in Israel. Third, some of the radical feminist approaches suggest common interests for gender, class, and ethnicity. However, the lower-income Asian-African Jews have turned away from socialist ideology and are now the majority among supporters of the right wing. Thus, gender, class and ethnicity-based social categorizations share no ideological concerns.

Chapter 6

Consequences for Women

The many macro-level demographic, economic, ideological and religious changes discussed in the previous chapter brought about significant transformations for women. This chapter deals with some of the consequences which Gutek (2001) reviews: topics that have disappeared over the past 20 years (e.g., the legitimacy of women's work); important topics that were not studied or could not be studied 20 years ago but are being studied now (e.g., women as leaders); previously neglected topics (e.g., stereotyping); and rapidly emerging topics (e.g., mentoring, effects of preferential selection, sexual harassment [Gutek, 2001, pp. 380-1]).

The prevalent consensus in Israel and most Western societies is that women should be equal to men, although equal treatment is not yet standard. Even those who do not consider themselves "feminists" tend to believe in equal opportunities and equal pay for both genders. Many also agree that although men and women may perform the same jobs in different ways, they may still carry them out equally well, and that the dissimilarity between them should not lead to inequality.

The impact of macro-level changes is not uniform across all groups and categories in each society, and egalitarian and equal-worth ideals are not spread evenly. In Israel, as in all Western societies, some segments maintain more traditional beliefs concerning the social roles of men and women and the division of labor between them, while others are more egalitarian. The main cultural areas in which changes may have occurred and which are examined in this chapter include self-attribution of traits and locus of control, gender identities, the gendered division of labor, perceptions of family and work roles, and stereotypes against women.

1. Self-Attribution of Traits

As Chapter Three shows, culture is instilled in members of society through socialization processes that begin in early childhood. These processes define for each social category, in each society, what traits, preferences, values, attitudes, beliefs and behaviors are considered "right" or "wrong," "proper" or "improper," for members of that society.

Though for many years personality traits were gendered, so that masculine traits (e.g., aggressiveness, dominance, competitiveness) were considered more appropriate for men and feminine traits (e.g., gentleness, affability, consideration) were considered more appropriate for women, repeated applications of Bem's (1981, 1987) Sex Role Inventory (BSRI) have shown that, in most studies, there are between five to eight trait factors, not only the two dimensions of femininity and masculinity. The strongest factors are usually the instrumental factor (including such traits as being analytical, decisive, leaderly and assertive) and the expressive factor (including such traits as being nurturing, understanding, sympathetic and loyal; e.g., Moore and Aweiss, 2003). In recent decades, research in Israel found greater variability in the personality traits that men and women attribute to themselves, allowing women to consider themselves assertive, competitive and ambitious without losing their femininity, while men may consider themselves warm, understanding and kind without feeling weak or unmanly (e.g., Moore, 2003).

Self-attribution of instrumental ("masculine") traits has been associated with more effective coping behaviors than self-attribution of expressive ("feminine") traits (Leung and Moore, 2003; Thompson, Sobolew-Shubin, Galbraith, Schwankovsky, and Cruzen, 1993). Therefore, it is not surprising that women in Israel and elsewhere tend to self-attribute instrumental traits more than men self-attribute expressive traits (Moore, 1999; Twenge 1999).

These issues are of special importance in societies where the proportion of women who turn to masculine organizations or occupations has increased in recent years (Gilbert, 1994; Goh, 1991; Jacobson, 1994; Jones and McNamara, 1991). Such trends in women's employment can be seen in Israel (Izraeli, 1993; Moore, 1992b). These changes are associated with normative changes in gender role attitudes and in the division of labor between men and women (Izraeli, 1993; Jackson, Hodge, and Ingram, 1994). It seems that changes in the gendered perceptions of traits may also be involved. If so, women may have to elaborate on the gender scheme to include traits that were hitherto considered masculine, especially when they work in masculine organizational settings (or jobs) in which such traits are required for job performance.

As more women enter jobs that were considered male-typed until a few decades ago (e.g., doctors, lawyers, and managers), their work environments should be examined to determine whether the organizational setting strengthens the self-attribution of some traits. Such an examination was carried out in 1999, in one of the most "masculine environments": the Israeli Police Force.[1]

A "masculine" organization was chosen because in most Western societies the pressure to espouse "masculine" traits is stronger than the pressure to espouse "feminine" traits: the former are more highly valued in these societies than the latter. In addition, in this specific masculine organization, occupational socialization is synonymous with organizational socialization, so that the process of occupational socialization is "tailored" to its specific organizational needs because of the monopoly that the police force has on all aspects of law enforcement in most Western societies.

Most police officers are male (McElhinny, 1994; Morgan, 1994). For women, joining the police force may be construed as "atypical" as they tend to be less power-oriented than men (Chasmir, 1982; Martin, 1990; Toch, 1991; Waddington, 1994).

In Israel, where army and police are interrelated and militarism has become an inseparable component of the civic culture (Kimmerling, 1993), women who join the police force may be even more disadvantaged than policewomen in other countries (Shadmi, 1993): military officers join the police force as ranking officers and are required to take only a short course in which their military skills are adapted to the civilian scene. Since more men become military officers than women, women hardly ever join the police force as officers (Hovav and Amir, 1979).

Despite the limitations, the number of women joining the Israeli Police Force has increased in recent years.[2] The salary increases and the social benefits (subsidized daycare, pension plans, etc.) that were offered to all police personnel (but especially to officers) in the 1980s served as an added incentive for people of both genders to join the force. In addition, a growing awareness of policy changes in Western countries regarding the integration of women in field jobs encouraged more women to turn to operative jobs and, at the same time, enhanced the system's willingness to accept them. In 1995, women constituted about 20% of the entire police force, and formed about 24% of all the officers (though only 2.7% of officers in the highest three ranks [Israeli Police, Annual Reports, 1995]). Still, their distribution among the specific units shows that women made up but 5% of the highest-risk units (like bombs disposal and detective squads). In contrast, they constituted 70% of the passport control units at the airport and over 80% of all administrative workers (Shadmi, 1993; McKenzie, 1993).

One explanation for the de-facto sex-segregation in organizations such as the police force is that the penetration of women into these organizations threatens their social order, weakening or "contaminating" the masculine unity (Oakley, 1993; Morgan, 1994). In addition, women who join such organizations have a dilemma: acting feminine, they may find their behavior labeled "inappropriate"; acting in accord with job requirements, they may find their behavior labeled "unfeminine" or "male-like" (Ashmore, Del Boca, and Wohlers, 1986). Choosing to maintain femininity, says Shadmi (1993), women in the police force will "pay" by not being promoted. Choosing to be "unfeminine," women may be considered gender-atypical or aggressive achievers and be rejected by their peers. Whether they choose the "feminine and inappropriate" strategy or the "unfeminine and atypical" one, women are forced to make decisions, choices and compromises that their male colleagues do not need to consider, and whichever their choice or decision, women— unlike men—have a "price" to pay (Morrow, 1993; Mueller and Wallace, 1992). Moreover, both these strategies force women to compromise the gender scheme. If, indeed, men and women are socialized into differentiated social roles (Bem, 1981, 1987; Cohen, 1991), men who join the police force operate in accord with the gender scheme but women do not (Strading, Crowe, and Touhy, 1993). This is, perhaps, one of the less discussed reason for sex-segregation and women's preference for female-typed jobs and organizations.

A third alternative with which women can minimize the negative consequences of such choices is enlarging the gender scheme to include—in addition to feminine traits—some of the less stereotypical characteristics, and/ or those "masculine" characteristics that are not in direct contrast with the basic feminine ones (e.g., being analytical, hard working and self confident). Thus, without renouncing their gender identity, these women are able to infuse this identity with new and context-relevant meaning (Coltrane, 1994; Hearn and Collinson, 1994; Lefkowitz, 1994). This is especially salient among women who participate in specialized organizational and/or occupational courses, and women whose tenure in the organization is longer, because these women will identify more strongly with the organization's goals and values.[3]

Analyzing the responses of 500 Israeli policemen and policewomen, Moore (1999) showed that women in the Israeli Police Force believed they were highly feminine and men believed they were highly masculine. Moreover, when self-attribution of the concrete traits "masculinity" and "femininity" were examined, most men and most women reported that only the gender-appropriate one applied to them. (I.e., men said they were masculine and women said they were feminine. The proportion of those who reported both as high or both as low is negligible.) However, when self-attribution of other traits is examined, the analysis shows that men and women in the police force report having similar traits. As hypothesized, both were similarly optimistic, independent, understanding, and assertive.

The similarity may be due to a tendency of people with certain traits to choose specific organizations whose requirements fit their traits and their value orientations or to organizational influences that reinforce some traits amongst its workers. The relationship between traits and context can also be considered simultaneous and dialectic in the sense that people with specific traits choose to work in organizational settings that fit their traits, but once in the organization, the environment strengthens the traits which are related to performing the required tasks.

Whether traits are context-induced or the choice of context is determined by existing traits, several interrelated conclusions may be drawn. First, the findings indicate that the gender scheme is more flexible and context-related than previously assumed. While it is true that men and women behave in gender-typical ways, the gender scheme is flexible and allows for variation for both sexes, and there is no reason to assume that the two groups employ diverse cognitive processes when forming their gender schemes. (See Moore, 1994). Thus, women in "masculine" organizational settings adapt their gender scheme and modify the definition of what it means to be "feminine." For them, there is no contrast between being feminine and being assertive, dominant and analytical. It seems that even when they are employed in female-typed jobs (like secretarial work), women in the police force are influenced by the organizational context.

In addition, the finding according to which women claimed to be highly feminine even when they espouse "masculine" traits may also mean that the femininity/masculinity distinction cannot be treated as a clear-cut dichotomy. It seems that "feminine" and "masculine" may have different meanings for different people, and they aggregate different traits under their personal definitions for "masculine" and "feminine." It may also be interpreted as indicating that the social construction of masculinity and femininity is weakening, and that there is a more flexible perception of these concepts that allows people to include in them components that were not hitherto considered consistent with the other gendered traits.

Another possible conclusion is that necessity may strengthen some traits and diminish others, though it does not alter the basic gender rendition. Being independent, analytical, assertive, dominant, and aggressive are usually considered "masculine" traits, but they are necessary characteristics for some aspects of performing police work. The data showed that women espoused them as much as men. Moreover, the levels of "feminine" traits like being shy, considerate, warm, soft-spoken and gullible—probable hindrances for police work—were as low among women as they were among men. Thus, traits, too, are perhaps not as immovable as usually depicted. When a specific trait is essential for task-performance, it may gain salience, so that when self-attributing traits, the individual will perceive that trait as more applicable and befitting him- or herself.

Still, gender differences in the police force do exist. Women tend to be segregated into specific jobs even when they attain high ranks (and the ranks of the sampled women are not lower than those of the men). The jobs they enter are distinct from men's jobs in the degree of femininity required (or tolerated) in them, in the authority levels they contain, and in the amount of influence on policy-making decisions they enable (Wright, Baxter and Birkelund, 1995).

In a more recent study (Moore, 2007), based on a representative sample (N=800) of the entire working population in Israel, a more significant shift was found. In this study, too, thirty-two of the BSRI traits were examined, half of which, according to Bem (1981), are "feminine" traits, and half of which are "masculine."[4] A principle component analysis shows that, as in previous studies, the traits create eight factors that explain 55% of the variance (see Table 6.1).

Table 6.1a. Personality Traits- 2007: Principle Component Analysis Matrix [a]

(Communalities and factor loadings, from Moore, 2007)

	Mean	S. D.	Extraction	1	2	3	4	5	6	7	8
Compassionate	6.31	.989	.594	.755	.111	.012	.017	.011	.041	-.030	.096
Sympathetic	6.16	1.145	.558	.706	.189	.060	.085	-.056	.063	.061	.049
Sensitive	6.26	1.126	.532	.701	.031	-.014	.042	-.014	.086	-.074	.160
Warm	6.10	1.202	.568	.669	.282	.154	.062	-.008	.026	.085	-.069
Understanding	6.36	.919	.515	.661	.224	.068	-.049	-.018	-.033	-.107	.091
Soft spoken	5.59	1.533	.429	.519	.212	.179	-.005	.120	.015	.219	-.142
Gentle	5.78	1.309	.518	.495	.042	.378	.110	-.226	.093	.221	-.094
Yielding	4.96	1.728	.521	.471	-.074	.231	-.345	.173	-.164	.213	-.137
Loyal	6.58	.892	.368	.464	.180	.129	.126	-.039	.063	-.250	-.142
Polite	6.19	1.108	.428	.461	.185	.287	.129	-.249	.104	.090	.020
Analytic	5.97	1.224	.345	.334	.271	-.165	.274	.102	.006	-.035	.215
Assertive	5.80	1.321	.630	.149	.736	-.038	.129	.103	.001	.193	-.024
Strong personality	5.89	1.267	.599	.195	.716	-.007	.171	.123	.047	-.035	.028
Independent	6.11	1.276	.529	.102	.686	-.019	.005	-.031	.051	-.190	.087
Decisive	5.70	1.328	.550	.276	.626	-.092	.118	.117	-.061	.115	.167
Cheerful	5.86	1.383	.449	.119	.568	.261	.028	-.172	-.026	.098	-.056
Leader	5.59	1.508	.578	.244	.560	-.110	.385	.193	-.036	.052	.065
Forceful	5.99	1.248	.477	.363	.465	-.046	.247	.110	.186	.124	-.051
Gullible	3.95	2.098	.586	.099	.037	.747	.011	.051	.112	-.019	-.014
Shy	4.25	1.928	.457	.148	-.052	.652	-.055	-.005	-.010	-.063	-.022
Childlike	3.20	2.071	.552	.046	-.106	.621	.145	.096	-.016	.146	.318

	Mean	S. D.	Extraction	1	2	3	4	5	6	7	8
Defend my beliefs	5.59	1.649	.480	.277	.291	.361	.059	.166	-.074	-.367	-.131
Ambitious	5.32	1.797	.681	.147	.272	.045	.757	.073	-.055	.040	.009
Competitive	4.62	1.956	.664	-.103	.143	.088	.730	.090	-.206	.127	.162
Flatterable	5.03	1.897	.479	.288	.078	.075	.464	.339	.120	.030	-.198
Aggressive	3.19	1.912	.713	-.093	.022	.080	.041	.830	-.005	.035	.070
Dominant	3.75	1.912	.568	-.039	.229	.017	.269	.645	.006	.047	.152
Feminine	4.88	2.319	.755	.214	.176	.162	-.051	.043	.801	.080	-.007
Masculine	4.09	2.334	.778	-.006	.103	.034	.098	.032	-.853	.148	.075
Athletic	4.09	2.028	.630	.046	.140	.056	.142	.063	-.063	.760	.010
Individualist	4.90	1.741	.585	.031	.024	.117	.068	.064	-.010	-.058	.747
Take risks	4.83	1.733	.505	.142	.262	-.074	.017	.173	-.152	.323	.504

Table 6.1b. Personality Traits- 2007: Total Variance Explained

Component	Extraction Sums of Squared Loadings (=Initial Eigenvalues)		
	Total	Variance %	Cumulative %
1	6.721	21.003	21.003
2	3.021	9.440	30.443
3	1.902	5.945	36.388
4	1.534	4.792	41.180
5	1.235	3.861	45.041
6	1.096	3.424	48.465
7	1.080	3.374	51.839
8	1.031	3.223	55.062

The analysis shows that eleven traits form the first—expressive—factor, explaining 21% of the variance (including ten of the originally "feminine" traits: compassionate, considerate, warm, sympathetic, sensitive, gentle, soft-spoken, yielding, loyal, and understanding; and one trait—analytic—that was previously considered "masculine"). Seven of the originally "masculine" traits form the second—instrumental—factor (assertive, strong personality, independent, decisive, cheerful, leader, and forceful; explaining 9.4% of the variance).[5] The differences indicate that the expressive dimension is more resilient and unchanged whereas the instrumental one is less so: it is weaker, and includes fewer traits than hypothesized. However, this is but a partial picture.

Examining the self-attribution of each trait separately (see Table 6.2) shows that gender differences exist in only nineteen of the thirty-two traits.

The self-attribution of the other thirteen traits (including traits like ambitious, individualist, shy, assertive, analytic, leader) was similar for men and women. Of the nineteen traits in which gender differences were found, sixteen traits were self-attributed by women more than by men; only three were self-attributed by men more than by women: competitive, athletic, and masculine. It is interesting to note that most (twelve) of the sixteen traits in which gender differences were found were originally "feminine" traits. The rest (four) were originally "masculine" and are now self-attributed by women more than by men: strong personality, independent, forceful, and defends own beliefs.

Table 6.2. Gender differences in self-attribution of traits
$(N_{(females)}=460, N_{(males)}= 340)$

	Trait	Sex1	Mean	S.D.	t
1	Compassionate	women	6.41	.892	3.430**
		men	6.17	1.093	
2	Sympathetic	women	6.30	1.049	4.102**
		men	5.97	1.241	
3	Sensitive	women	6.35	1.110	2.853**
		men	6.13	1.136	
4	Warm	women	6.21	1.155	3.273**
		men	5.94	1.246	
5	Understanding	women	6.46	.821	3.880**
		men	6.21	1.022	
6	Soft-spoken	women	5.73	1.432	3.078**
		men	5.39	1.644	
7	Gentle	women	5.88	1.282	2.588**
		men	5.64	1.334	
8	Yielding	women	4.92	1.794	-.745
		men	5.01	1.637	
9	Loyal	women	6.71	.737	5.005**
		men	6.40	1.041	
10	Polite	women	6.33	.975	4.093**
		men	6.01	1.245	
11	Analytic	women	6.03	1.192	1.437
		men	5.90	1.263	
12	Assertive	women	5.87	1.300	1.668
		men	5.71	1.347	
13	Strong Personality	women	6.01	1.255	2.921**
		men	5.74	1.269	
14	Independent	women	6.25	1.210	3.512**
		men	5.93	1.342	
15	Decisive	women	5.70	1.381	-.011
		men	5.70	1.255	

	Trait	Sex1	Mean	S.D.	t
16	Cheerful	women	5.90	1.347	1.068
		men	5.80	1.430	
17	Leader	women	5.62	1.528	.626
		men	5.55	1.481	
18	Forceful	women	6.17	1.143	4.994**
		men	5.73	1.338	
19	Gullible	women	4.12	2.129	2.665**
		men	3.72	2.036	
20	Shy	women	4.29	1.992	.813
		men	4.18	1.838	
21	Childlike	women	3.13	2.138	-1.147
		men	3.30	1.976	
22	Defend My Beliefs	women	5.80	1.574	4.258**
		men	5.31	1.707	
23	Ambitious	women	5.27	1.872	-.905
		men	5.39	1.690	
24	Competitive	women	4.36	2.008	-4.431**
		men	4.98	1.828	
25	Flatterable	women	5.16	1.944	2.255*
		men	4.85	1.817	
26	Aggressive	women	3.29	1.972	1.674
		men	3.06	1.822	
27	Dominant	women	3.84	1.954	1.568
		men	3.63	1.849	
28	Feminine	women	6.17	1.208	25.093**
		men	3.02	2.275	
29	Masculine	women	2.83	2.093	-23.058**
		men	5.83	1.310	
30	Athletic	women	3.88	2.071	-3.418**
		men	4.38	1.935	
31	Individualist	women	4.86	1.769	-.785
		men	4.96	1.703	
32	Take Risks	women	4.76	1.801	-1.1217
		men	4.91	1.633	

In summation, the gender schema has changed. Instrumental traits are now mostly gender-neutral, and men and women self-attribute them equally. The expressive traits remain mostly "feminine" and women self-attribute them more than men, though men self-attribute some of them more than they self-attribute some of the hitherto "masculine" traits (sympathetic, sensitive and polite, for example, are attributed by men more than traits like decisive, assertive, and forceful). This may indicate that men value these traits and consider them more desirable than some of the "masculine" traits.

These findings seem to indicate that the social construction of masculinity and femininity has changed. Instead of the clear-cut distinction between "feminine" and "masculine" traits, there is today a more flexible perception of these concepts (i.e., androgyny) that allows people to include in their gender schema components that were not hitherto considered consistent with other gendered traits. Women today may see themselves as highly feminine but also as ambitious, decisive, and independent, whereas men may see themselves as highly masculine but also as loyal, sensitive, and considerate (Lengua and Stormshak, 2000; Moore, 2007). Table 6.3 shows that androgyny is the prevalent type for women, while the undifferentiated is the most common for men. Neither the "feminine" (for women) nor the "masculine" (for men) types are prevalent.

Table 6.3. Bem's personality types by Gender

Personality Types		Gender		Total
		Women	Men	
Undifferentiated	Count	78	91	169
	%	25.7%	34.3%	29.7%
Feminine	Count	76	39	115
	%	25.0%	14.7%	20.2%
Masculine	Count	46	70	116
	%	15.1%	26.4%	20.4%
Androgynous	Count	104	65	169
	%	34.2%	24.5%	29.7%
Total	Count	304	265	569
	%	100%	100%	100%

Cramer's v = .207, p≤ .000

The combination of instrumental and expressive traits is advantageous for two reasons. First, it denotes individuals who are more flexible and adaptable than those who are either masculine or feminine (Smith, Ellis, and Benson, 2001; Woodhill and Samuels, 2003). Second, it incorporates two routes for attaining an internal locus of control—the instrumental and the expressive means of attaining control.

2. Locus of Control

The traditional approach to locus of control refers to assumed internal states that explain why certain people actively and willingly try to deal with difficult circumstances (internal control), whereas others do not (external control [Lewis, Ross, and Mirowsky, 1999]). This approach to locus of control assumes that internal control is based on stable personality traits, such as information seeking (Lefcourt and Davidson-Katz, 1991), alertness (Lefcourt, 1983), and decision making (Hawk, 1990), all of which are instrumental characteristics (Mirowsky, Ross, and Willigen, 1996). In contrast, individuals who lack internal control see life situations as dependent upon luck, God, the situation, or the behaviors of other individuals.

The existing measures of locus of control do not take into account the possibility of alternative methods that individuals may apply to attain mastery or control. The alternative approach suggested by Moore (2003) is that other stable—expressive—traits like empathy, or the ability to rely on friends to attain one's goals, are an alternative means of attaining control. Thus, expressive individuals may increase their control over life events (i.e., internal locus of control) through their control over social relations. This is an innovative viewpoint according to which the locus of control approach that distinguishes between internal and external control should be elaborated upon and modified. It indicates that individuals who lack instrumental internal locus of control, may still have expressive internal control, i.e., they may attain internal control by using alternative means. Though the study was conducted in Israel, it is logical to assume that its findings are relevant to other societies as well.

The ability to "tap" both instrumental and expressive sources of control is possible for individuals who adopt both types of traits. This enables individuals to shift from one source to the other according to context rather than losing control, or being compelled to use the same type of control even when it is less appropriate or productive (Sharpe, Heppner, and Dixon, 1995). If rational, instrumental actions do not lead to desired consequences, androgyny (i.e., the type of personality that is high on both instrumental and expressive traits) enables individuals to turn to expressive means to attain the same end rather than developing a sense of lack of control (Moore, 1998). Moore's findings in Israel show that instrumental control is not the only means of attaining and maintaining self-efficacy.[6] Moore and Aweiss (2003) indicate that in Israel, instrumental control is not the only means of attaining and maintaining self-efficacy. Expressive control was just as prevalent, and the two mechanisms are not mutually exclusive. Members of both genders add expressive means of control to their repertoire of tools without relinquishing instrumental control, but men use expressive control as a means to attain life satisfaction more than women, which may indicate that the use of such non-conventional behavior is accorded greater legitimacy among the already advantaged men than among the less advantaged women. For women, choosing such means is still perceived as "acting according to their nature," i.e., not the rational, objective, practical way. Still, as more women now include instrumental traits in their gender schema together with expressive ones, and these traits are associated with stronger internal control, women seem to aspire to greater control over their lives, being less willing to settle for a dependant role. This is in accord with the growing numbers of women who join the labor market, searching for meaningful careers.

The fact that expressive means of attaining control are possible and socially sanctioned may indicate that a change has already occurred, and it will become legitimate for women as well. This may even provide women with an advantage in the future.

3. Gender Roles

Although the extent and prevalence of the gendered division of labor vary from one society to another, the general pattern according to which men are considered the major breadwinners and women the major homemakers exists across societies. In Israel, the family and domestic roles of women are still highly traditional, placing motherhood at the core of women's lives and aspirations (Moore, 1998), but financial necessity often forces them to seek employment. Women's and mothers' participation in the labor market needs justification, because being employed outside the home distracts women from their primary familial obligations and detracts from their ability to fulfill them (Izraeli and Talmud, 1998).

The growing participation of women in the Israeli labor force enabled more women to discover the benefits of work: economic independence, self-actualization, a source of identity and interest, control over their lives, and wider, more diversified social networks. Women often want "the best of both worlds," namely a family with children and a job or career. Consequently, women's perceptions and preferences concerning work outside the home and its relationships with family life have changed significantly. More women now attach high value to their jobs than before (Moore and Toren, 1998). As noted earlier, this change occurred in Israel somewhat later and at a slower rate than in other Western countries, mainly because of the persistence of traditional family values, the result of which is that the great majority of women are not willing to give up marriage and/or having children.

However, researchers show that gender-role attitudes have changed in the past decades, especially among working women. Women espouse egalitarian gender attitudes today more than in the past,[7] and the change is more noticeable among women than among men (Crosby and Ropp, 2002). In addition, the studies show that working women are more egalitarian than nonworking women (McCall, 2000). The evidence regarding changes in men's gender-role attitudes and their participation in domestic responsibilities is less clear (Netz and Haveman, 1999; Noonan, 2001), but they, too, seem to be changing. Moore (1996b) shows that in Israel, both men and women see men's family roles as men's most important roles, even more important than their work roles. Hence, family roles are now considered of the same importance for both men and women (see also Harpaz, 1992). Though they agree on the importance of family roles, men and women still differ when they evaluate work roles: whereas women tend to accord these roles great importance for both genders, men tend to see them as important for men, but far less important for women.

On the whole, men's perceptions of the time they devote to domestic obligations are similar to women's. However, men claim that they spend more time taking care of their spouses and paying bills, while women invest more time in child-care and education. As child-care is usually more urgent and inflexible, women's perceived burden is still greater than men's.

Moreover, as the traditional division is weakening, new patterns emerge. Some people—both men and women—seem to be "family-oriented" in the sense that they accord high importance to the family roles and lower importance to the work roles of both genders. Others—both men and women—seem to be "work-oriented," i.e., they accord high importance to the work roles of both genders and a lower importance to the family roles. Still others rank all roles as of high or low importance. Explanations of differences in gender roles' perceptions focus either on differences in traits (Richmond-Abbott, 1992; Ridgeway, 1993), or on diverse structural limitations on work flexibility that constrain the emphasis on family roles (Andersen, 1993; Moore, 1994; Rothausen, 1994; Silver and Goldscheider, 1994). Although men still tend to perceive women's domestic roles as more important than their work roles (as the traditional division of labor predicts), they perceive their own roles as more balanced (i.e., similar importance is attributed to both roles).

Because the home-work dichotomization is weakening, people have a wider variety of traits, roles, beliefs, attitudes, and behaviors to choose from (Jacobs and Gerson, 2004). This flexibility of choice can be seen in changes in both the domestic and the work spheres (e.g., more women enter male-typed occupations and/or full-time careers, and men seem to contribute more to the domestic sphere than in the past (Adler, 2002; Williams, 2000).

Moore and Toren (1998) addressed the importance women ascribe to work and family as representing four distinct types: "Traditionals," who emphasize only the family (34.2%), "Careerists," who emphasize only work (4.5%), "Combiners," who emphasize both (50.7%), and "Personals," who emphasize neither family nor work (10.7% [see Table 6.4]).

The study, based on a representative sample of 3,000 working women, showed that the large group of "combiners," women who attribute high importance to family and work, was more work-oriented and committed than could generally be expected in a family and child-centered society such as Israel. As mentioned before, Israel is a latecomer regarding changes and innovations of traditional family formations which have been reported earlier in other modern countries (e.g., Moen and Wethington, 1992).

Table 6.4. Typology - Importance of Family and Work

		FAMILY		Total
		Not Important	Important	
Work	Not Important	Personal 10.7%	Traditional 34.2%	44.9%
		N=311	N=994	N=1,305
	Important	Careerist 4.5%	Combiner 50.7%	55.1%
		N=130	N=1474	N=1,604
Total		15.2%	84.8%	100.0%
		N=441	N=2,468	N=2,909

There were also significant differences among the four types in almost all the variables and measures Moore and Toren (1998) examined. The "traditionals" had more children than all other groups (with "combiners" as close second), and more among them were married. They were also older than other women. Moreover, they worked in lower status jobs, fewer among them held positions of authority, they worked fewer hours, and more among them were in female-typed occupations. Still, their wages were highest (though the differences among "types" was not statistically significant) because of the Israeli taxing system.

The group most different from the "traditionals" is the "personals," not the "careerists," as could perhaps be expected. The "personals" had fewest children, fewer among them were married, they were younger than all other groups, and their education was higher. The data also showed that their seniority (in terms of years in the labor market) was lowest, their occupational SES was highest, and their wage per hour was higher than most, even though fewer among them had children.

Moore and Toren (1998) concluded that working women are divided according to their emphasis on family roles: on the one hand, those who value family highly—the "combiners" and "traditional"—and on the other hand, those who do not ascribe high importance to family, namely the "careerist" and "personal" (self-focused). The emphasis on the work role seems to act as a second tier of dissimilarity. These differences have a significant influence on the perception of role combination as conflictual or beneficial, with "combiners" seeing the existence of diverse roles as multiple sources of satisfaction rather than causing conflict.

4. Role Combination

As seen in Chapter Three, conceptualizing the family-work relationship as conflictual has dominated research literature as well as popular opinion and discourse for several decades (for example, Goode, 1960; Snoek, 1966; Coser and Rokoff, 1971). This conflict, it was argued, mainly afflicts working mothers who have to allocate scarce resources, such as commitment, time and energy, between their family and work obligations.[8]

But there is contradictory empirical evidence regarding the impact of a heavier load on role conflict. Some research shows that role conflict is stronger for working mothers (Ruble, Cohen and Ruble, 1984), while other research arrives at the opposite conclusion (Crosby, 1987; Epstein, 1988; Kulman, 1986). Several factors were offered as explanations for the inconsistent findings: historical changes (Ross, Mirowsky, and Huber, 1983), spouse participation at home (Epstein, 1988), and developing strategies for reducing time pressure (Thoits, 1987). However, even the greater family burden does not necessarily result in role conflict. To the contrary—combining diverse roles is often perceived by these women as beneficial (Crosby, 1987).

When dealing with the predicaments of working mothers, most studies focus on time limitations, assuming that when work demands and family obligations are incompatible, women tend to give priority to their children and families over their work and careers (Hochschild, 1997). However, this is true mostly in emergencies. Under regular conditions, this can no longer be taken for granted for all working women. Since the feminist movement and the significant increase of women and mothers of young children in the labor market in the 1970s and 1980s, the perception of "the ideal mother" has greatly changed: the traditional motherhood role is no longer sacrosanct (Gerson, 1985) and a good mother is not necessarily one who "sacrifices" herself for her children, or "has all the time and care to give" (Williams, 2000). Moreover, many now believe that children's wellbeing is not hurt by the fact that a mother works outside the home.

In modern, developed countries, these normative changes are manifest in demographic shifts. Marriage rates have dropped, divorce rates are up, women have fewer children and at a later age, more among them are single mothers, and they tend to participate in the labor market for longer periods of their lives. It is important to note that recent ideological and actual transformations took place not only in the United States and Western Europe, but have reached more traditional societies too, such as Italy and Spain, where a growing number of women delay childbearing, and fertility rates have dropped dramatically [Garcia Martin, 2001]).

As seen in Chapter Five, similar processes are taking place in Israel, changing the involvement of women in the family, and increasing their investments in education and occupational careers. These processes are slower than those in Western countries because Israel is a family-oriented and child-centered society due to its particular historical, religious and cultural traditions. Giving up motherhood for an occupational career is still not an endorsed lifestyle choice among large parts of Israeli female society, as compared to several countries where the childless "career woman" is more common and normatively accepted.

These changes in women's attitudes, beliefs and behaviors led some researchers (e.g., Crosby, 1991; Epstein, 1988; Kirchmeyer, 1992; Moore and Gobi, 1995; Rothbard, 2001) to question the taken-for-granted notion of competition and conflict and to suggest that the combination of multiple roles not only causes stress, strain and fatigue, but may have positive effects, such as expansion and accumulation of resources, enhancement of self- confidence, meaning and identity, satisfaction, and multiple success (Tiedge, Wortman, Downey, Emmons, Biernat, and Lang, 1990).

Consequently, in contrast with "scarcity" or "depletion" perspectives, the "enrichment" or "enhancement" models were introduced. The main argument of the enhancement approach is that people's resources are not fixed and that engagement in multiple roles may expand existing resources and even create additional ones. A multiplicity of roles, rather than being a detrimental burden, can be an enriching benefit to the individual. Sieber (1974), one of the first to articulate this proposition from a sociological-psychological viewpoint, distinguishes four enrichment processes of role "accumulation": (1) increasing role privileges, (2) attaining overall status security, (3) obtaining resources for status enhancement, and (4) enriching women's personalities and ego gratification. The benefits of multiple-role engagement are reflected in diverse measures of wellbeing (Barnett and Gareis, 2006; Bielby, 1992), and they have positive effects, such as increasing self-confidence, satisfaction, and multiple sources for success (Hill, 2005). Similar findings were obtained in Israel as well (Moore, 2007).

Current approaches tend to view combining family and work as beneficial and enriching rather than conflict-producing. According to these approaches (e.g., Moore and Toren, 1998), women who ascribe high importance to both family and work (the "combiners") will report stronger satisfaction with their lives than will women for whom only one life domain is highly salient.

Recent studies show that the subjective experience of a growing number of working women and mothers is no longer that of conflict. Combining family obligations and work roles can be viewed as a coping strategy of women in an era of societal transition, "offering women a new scenario of options and opportunities" (Hakim, 2002).

An example of the positive effects of role combination may be seen in Calandra's (2002) research dealing with the problem of combining research and teaching in academia, according to which female university professors who balance teaching and research enjoy more rewards than women in "traditional" jobs, and which further notes that the secret to getting both family and work roles done is to have a lot of energy and commitment, a desire to perform both roles, and a lot of support both at home and at work. Calandra (2002) concludes that women who want children and also aspire to develop an occupational career will be happier and more successful doing both than foregoing one for the other. Crosby (1991) describes a woman who had a family as well as a demanding job: "This woman…enjoyed and felt invigorated by the challenges of contemporary role combination" (Crosby, 1991, p. 61). Juggling gave her a sense of accomplishment.

Additional evidence for the advantages of engagement in multiple roles comes from a study of Israeli faculty women that shows that the most productive researchers were also the mothers of the largest number of children (Toren, 1988, 2000). This seemingly counterintuitive finding shows that such combinations may produce beneficial consequences and enhanced balance. Toren (2000) claimed that her interviewees declared that being out on maternity leave actually helped them in their research work and that their family gave them strength. In fact, these women express the enrichment or enhancement point of view that participation in non-work roles can actually "support, facilitate, or enhance work life" (Crouter, 1984, p. 430). A very similar conclusion is reached in a study of American professional women, according to which "…workers' activities and responsibilities in non-work domains may actually energize them for work and enhance work attitudes" (Kirchmeyer, 1992, p. 776).

Another Israeli study of mothers who turn to higher education (universities and colleges) after their youngest children go to school shows that rather than expressing feelings of guilt, respondents said that studying makes them better mothers, and being mothers makes them more attentive students (Pessetta-Schubert, 1999). In the same vein, research on women in management positions found that respondents felt that non-work role experiences (child-rearing and -caring) provided opportunities to enrich their interpersonal skills at work (Ruderman, Ohlcott, Panzer, and King, 2002). Put another way, skills and resources obtained in one role can be applied to fulfill tasks in other role-areas.

In a mixed and dynamic socio-cultural environment in which individuals receive ambiguous messages as to life roles' salience, curtailing career or family may constitute a coping and balancing strategy, and the combination of both may constitute an alternative strategy.[9] Assigning importance to both domains is regarded here as an adaptive coping mechanism to changing circumstances on the economic-occupational and ideological-cultural levels.

Examining whether both genders today see role combination as possible, even beneficial, rather than conflictual, Moore (2007) asked a representative sample of over 800 men and women the following question: "There is a lasting debate concerning women's ability to combine family and a career successfully. Here are five often-heard claims. With which of them do you agree? 1 - There is no problem today in combing family and career—many women do it successfully (19%); 2 - It is possible to combine family and career—each woman finds her own solutions if she encounters difficulties (36%); 3—Women with both careers and families have to deal with unending pressures (21%); 4—It is very difficult to combine family and careers. Women can develop careers until they have children, but when they become mothers, they must limit their work obligations (19%); 5—It is impossible to combine the two—the idea that, like men, women can develop careers when they have families is an illusion (6%)."

Though the difference between men and women in the mean response to this question is not significant (see Table 6.5), there is some difference in the distribution, with more women emphasizing the pressures that women encounter when they combine family and work, and men divided into those who see benefits in role combination, and those who consider it difficult or impossible.

Table 6.5. Perceptions of Role Combinations

		Gender		Total
		Women	Men	
1 - There is no problem today in combing family and career—many women do it successfully		16.6%	22.5%	19.1%
2 - It is possible to combine family and career—each woman finds her own solutions if she encounters difficulties		34.9%	36.7%	35.6%
3 - Women with both careers and families have to deal with unending pressures		25.5%	14.2%	20.7%
4- It is very difficult to combine family and careers. Women can develop careers until they have children, but when they become mothers they must limit their work obligations		18.1%	20.1%	18.9%
5- It is impossible to combine the two—the idea that, like men, women can develop careers when they have families is an illusion		5.0%	6.5%	5.6%
		Mean	s.d.	
t-test	**Women**	2.60	1.112	T=n.s.
	Men	2.51	1.223	

Though it may be beneficial, the dual commitment is not an easy lifestyle choice, and the question is,—how do women cope with the complications and ambiguous messages? How do they resolve the problems or reduce the inherent strains? What characteristics enhance their ability to combine the two worlds?

A large part of family-work studies examine practical coping strategies, such as working part-time, choosing less demanding jobs, and hiring help for child-care and housework, or, on the other hand, delaying marriage and childbearing, having fewer children, and so on (Moore and Gobi, 1995). Both strategies are examples of cutting back time or tasks in one role-domain so as to be able to invest more resources in the other.

Turning to female-typed occupations as a strategy to limit their work involvement (See Chapters Three and Five) is one of the main solutions that women used to choose. This type of solution implies that women believe that work contributes more to creating pressures, although in reality, domestic responsibilities account for a greater part of the strain. But the number of women who choose an alternative strategy—that of limiting their domestic obligations in order to devote more time to their work roles—is increasing. Women who choose this strategy are less home-oriented and attribute less importance to their traditional feminine roles (Kessler-Harris, 1990; Ollenburger and Moore, 1992). This strategy, and the perceptions of gender roles that accompany it, are more prevalent among women who work in gender-atypical occupations that require academic education (Moore, 1996a,b).

Moore (1995b) examined the sources of stress when combining the two roles in a study that compared university professors in five nations: Australia, Bulgaria, Israel, The Netherlands, and the United States.[10] University professors were chosen for several reasons. First, this is one of the high-status male-typed occupations women are now turning to in growing numbers. Second, although cultural differences exist, the job characteristics of university professors in diverse societies are comparable. Third, since this is a high-status occupation associated with liberal attitudes, Moore (1995b) assumed that less gendered division of labor would be found, so that both men and women would attribute similar importance to their work and family roles. Finally, this occupation is comparable (at least in domain) to one of the major female-typed occupations: school-teachers, in which a large proportion of the total female work force is employed (a sample of school-teachers was drawn for comparison).

Analyzing samples from diverse societies showed that cultural differences influence the perceptions of role conflict, burden and gender roles of women in these societies. The study also showed that in all examined societies the home burden contributed to role conflict more than the work burden. For women who work in male-typed occupations, where working hours are more numerous and less flexible, domestic obligations seem to be the major source of role conflict even though they devote less time to these duties. This finding indicates that either the meaning of work as the main cause of role conflict (Merton, 1957) changed in the 1990s, or it was misplaced in the first place. Blaming work for creating role conflict may be traced to several, mostly non-egalitarian, social expectations: 1. the traditional division of labor that would lead people to expect domestic responsibilities to be women's primary roles, so that any obligation that detracts from their ability to perform their primary roles is seen as causing role conflict; 2. the lack of social and technical facilities (such as day-care centers, domestic help, and lighter domestic work loads) in a less industrialized world) that created a then-justified basis for these beliefs regarding women's work; 3. a paternalistic interpretation of women's work behaviors and needs; and 4. actuarial bias, according to which most women are pressed for time, having to juggle their responsibilities (e.g., Okin, 1979).

Thus, it may be the occupation type they choose (and the characteristics and preferences that led to these choices), not some gendered predisposition, that facilitates role conflict. It seems logical to assume that as more women enter male-typed occupations, and the division of labor becomes more egalitarian, the emphasis on work as creating conflict will decrease even further, diminishing the actuarial basis of the stereotypical perceptions of women's work.

The findings for the male-typed occupation (and the one sample of school-teachers) also indicated that there may be differences in the basic dispositions or attitudes of workers who turn to male-typed occupations and those who turn to female-typed ones. Occupational choice is not random, so that those who enter female-typed occupations and those who enter male-typed ones may have different predisposing characteristics. Workers in female-typed occupations seem to choose a "limited work role" strategy, while workers in the male-typed occupations seem to choose a "limited family role" strategy.

Whereas individuals with different characteristics self-select themselves for different occupations, occupations also shape the behaviors of those who enter them. If predispositions determine the time allocation strategy that will be employed, then women with different characteristics will turn to different occupation types, and the strategy they espouse will reflect their preferences. If, on the other hand, the occupation imposes the strategy, then women have less freedom to choose the strategy and are "forced" into certain occupations in which they can implement the strategy that fits their needs. The different strategies may also be due to a combination of the two, so that workers with a certain disposition turn to occupations in which a specific time allocation strategy is required, while workers with different dispositions turn to occupations in which a different strategy is more prevalent.

It may also be that work in male-typed occupations is adjusted to the traditional division of labor that attributes greater importance to men's work roles than to their family roles, and therefore, all workers in them are forced to follow the "limited family role" strategy. In contrast, female-typed occupations have no inherent or predetermined strategy, and therefore workers in them can prefer to emphasize either the family sphere or the work domain. In either case, women cannot be treated as a homogeneous group, for whom a single and specific strategy is applicable.

Moore and Toren (1998) analyzed the work-family intersection (whether conflictual or beneficial) as perceived and felt by women and examined women's subjective orientations, preferences, and attitudes to family and work. Their study, based on 3,000 Israeli working women in 2000, focused on work-family orientation as the degree of importance that individuals attribute to their engagement in each domain, assuming that the subjective dimensions affect the objective accommodations and tradeoffs that women make to multiple role obligations in their lives (see also Hakim, 2002; Carlson and Kacmar, 2002).

They hypothesized that if one adopts the scarcity-conflict approach in reference to the family-work problematic, then the logical coping strategies to overload and conflict would be the avoiding or curtailing of certain roles and tasks, role articulation, role contraction, priority scaling, compromise, balancing, sequencing, etc. This would force women to choose to limit either their work involvement or their family involvement (Moore and Gobi, 1995). According to the "curtailing" model, combining roles provides no benefits and the sense of pressure and conflicting demands may even hinder a woman's performance.

If, on the other hand, one accepts the enrichment or enhancement perspective, which views a multiplicity of roles, though not stress-free, as potentially beneficial, then combining career and family roles could be a better solution than avoiding one of them. According to this view, these two important life areas may enrich each other, and their combination has positive results, even if either or both roles are limited (e.g., Marks and McDermid, 1996). Those who choose to engage in both roles will see themselves as benefiting from both, so that the one augments and contributes to the other. Thus, even when fulfilling tasks that are related to one role, the other role enriches the way women perform those tasks, etc. Put in another way, spillover from one domain to another can actually be advantageous, and "[m]oreover, the enrichment argument assumes that the benefits of multiple roles outweighs the costs associated with them, leading to net gratification rather than strain" (Rothbard, 2001, p. 657).

Moore and Toren (1998) concluded that women's positive attitudes toward both family and work should signal to employers that married women, with or without children, are not necessarily less motivated or committed to their jobs than single women who are supposedly not hindered by family duties and demands (e.g., Bielby and Bielby, 1984; Mannheim, 1993).

Moreover, these findings are compatible with the enhancement model (Sieber, 1974; Marks, 1977; Ruderman, Ohlcott, Panzer, and King, 2002; Rothbard, 2001): women for whom both family and work are highly important and valuable find the combination to provide an enriching experience. It increases their self-worth, broadens and diversifies their social networks and empowers their position in the family. In addition, that study showed that "combiners" adhere to more gender-egalitarian values pertaining to work-roles in general, and they are more willing to make tradeoffs at work to accommodate their family needs.

Since both family and work are sanctioned and endorsed in the socio-cultural context, engaging in both roles and regarding them as highly important appears to be a functional coping mechanism in a complex and changing environment where old and new norms coincide. Moreover, this combination may also be regarded as an integrating mechanism linking family and work through individuals who fulfill roles in both domains.

This is not to say that this kind of combination is easy to implement in practice by individual women and families. It does, however, mean that employers do not have to worry about women's work involvement, nor about their familial responsibility and commitment, but rather should aim to establish legal, institutional, and organizational arrangements that will make the combination of family and work more rewarding for women, as it is for men.

5. Are the Stereotypes Changing?

As shown in Chapter Three, sex-based stereotypes, like all stereotypes, result from the cognitive process of categorizing social groups, and although they are often clear and obvious, they may also be hidden or implied, turning blatant stereotypes into more difficult-to-detect prejudicial behaviors. "Benevolent sexism" (i.e., "a subjectively favorable, chivalrous ideology that offers protection and affection to women who embrace conventional roles" Glick and Fiske, 2001, p. 110), is an example of such stereotypes, which lead to gender inequality. Women often endorse benevolent sexism (especially in the most sexist cultures), and are rewarded for conforming to the patriarchal status quo (Krefting, 2003).

As stereotypes derive from cultural values, attitudes and norms, they may change when society changes (Heilman, 1995). The stereotypes in work settings are expressed in selection decisions, interpretation of actions, and performance evaluations, and they reinforce stereotypic expectations, fortifying them against information that may challenge or discredit them. The result is self-limiting behaviors by women (Pleck, 1997).

The gendered traits and the division of roles discussed earlier in this chapter are often associated with—and strengthened by—stereotypes and gender ideology: that is, perceptions, expectations and beliefs concerning the appropriate roles of women and men in family and society (Auster, 2001). If traits are becoming less gendered, and gender roles are changing to allow men and women a more egalitarian division of labor, are the salient stereotypes against working women changing as well? This issue is of grave importance for socialization processes as well as for women who make atypical life choices that may compel them to go against the norms or social expectations (Cleveland, Stockdale, and Murphy, 2000).

If the stereotypes are not weakening as quickly as the behaviors of individuals are, unconventional behavior will not be sanctioned or legitimized. As Davies Netzley (2002) shows, the feminine personality is still considered more suitable to female-typed occupations, whereas the masculine personality is still considered more suitable to male-typed occupations. She states that gender stereotypes are still used to justify the gendered hierarchy of occupations, so that other things being equal, male-typed occupations have higher prestige.

Stereotypes are among the previously "neglected topics," according to Gutek (2001). Research in the last decades provides mixed findings concerning changes in stereotypes, with most studies showing that there is no change or even a strengthening of gender stereotypes (so that even new domains like virtual service providers on the Internet suffer from the same gender stereotyping seen in actual customer services, thus reinforcing the existing gender divisions [Gustavsson, 2005]). Others studies show a reduction in stereotypic attitudes and perceptions. Valentine (1998) found that it is mostly men with low scores on self-esteem who tend to believe negative stereotypes and oppose the employment of women, while men with high self-esteem scores tended to approve of women working. It is logical to assume that the opposition to women will be even stronger against women in managerial or male-typed jobs.

Most studies examine work-related stereotypes; fewer studies focus on stereotypes concerning women's family roles (Antecol, 2001). Research of work-related stereotypes focus mostly on male-typed or managerial jobs (Pelham, Hetts, and Stratton, 2001). Powell, Butterfield, and Parent (2002) claim that there has been no significant change in the emphasis that men and women place on stereotypical masculine characteristics of managers, and show that although managerial stereotypes place less emphasis on masculine characteristics than in earlier studies, a "good manager" is still perceived as predominantly masculine.

Stereotypes concerning women in these jobs deal with two issues: the necessary characteristics of managers or workers in male-typed jobs, and whether women have them; and the debate as to whether women perform this type of job differently from men, and the devaluation of their work investments if different performance is assumed. Rutherford (2001), for example, maintains that these two issues may explain women's lack of progress to the tops of organizations, and claims that men seem to be able to hold on to the most powerful positions in organizations because the stereotypes favor them. Moreover, she argues that having a large number of women in management positions does not lead to a more feminized management style. "Stereotypes of women still act against their acceptance into positions of power, while men's ability to adopt traditionally feminine skills of communication means that women's supposed advantage may have been leapfrogged" (Rutherford, 2001, p. 344). This finding concurs with Moore's (2007) finding according to which although women self-attribute masculine traits more than men self-attribute feminine ones, men use feminine traits as an alternative means of attaining control over life situations more than women, for whom these means are not considered legitimate (at least in Israeli society).

Beck and Davis (2005) also investigated why women at diverse managerial levels in an Australian organization did not advance rapidly despite equal employment opportunity policies. They claim that gender inequality persists because of stereotyped perceptions embedded within organizational cultures. Similar findings were found for Poland in Tomkiewicz, Frankel, Adeyemi-Bello, and Sagan's (2004) study, in which they compared attitudes toward female managers in Poland and in the United States. Their results suggest that Polish women encounter stereotypic barriers when they aspire to managerial careers and that Polish males express more stereotypic attitudes toward female managers than do American males. Similarly, Owen, Scherer, Sincoff, and Cordano (2003) compared the stereotypic perceptions of female managers in the United States and Chile and found that men in both cultures had more stereotypic and negative perceptions of women managers than did women, and that in the United States both males and females had less stereotypic perceptions of women managers than Chileans.

Examining women's performance in situations in which the stereotypes lead to an expectation of poor performance, Sekaquaptewa and Thompson (2003) show that this was indeed detrimental to women's performance. Men's performance was not affected by such expectations, and this may act as a self-fulfilling prophecy. Even when they work in similar jobs, men and women still employ different strategies because of stereotypes, claim Millward and Freeman (2002), who tested the hypothesis that role expectations may constrain or facilitate innovation. They found that innovative solutions were attributed more often to a male than a female manager, whereas adaptive solutions were attributed more often to a female than a male manager, and attributed the differences to women's tendency to avoid risk of failure or mistake, the risk of criticism, and the risk of not receiving credit for ideas.

Moreover, Krefting (2003) shows that women find it difficult to prove they have the skills to "play the game" according to men's rules and politics, while men presume that they themselves do have the skills. Consequently, women remain on the margins of high-power hierarchies. A similar finding was reported by Toren and Moore (1997), showing that academic institutions do not take into account "potential for success" when they contemplate the advancement of women, but they do when considering men's advancement: women have to provide proof of their ability to succeed in academia, while men need only prove they have the potential to succeed, and the "burden of proof" is, therefore, harsher for women than for men.

Another category of studies reveals that women's family roles may still be a major cause for devaluing their skills. Cuddy, Fiske, and Glick (2004), for example, claimed that even at the beginning of the new century, one of the reasons women fail to advance is that when working women become mothers, they are ascribed greater warmth and their "homemaker" stereotyping strengthens, but their perceived competence as "professionals" declines. In contrast, working men who become fathers gained perceived warmth without losing their perceived competence. Moreover, these stereotypic perceptions had a significant impact on the hiring of, promoting, and investing in working mothers relative to working fathers or childless employees. Similarly, Mueller and Yoder (1997) showed that women employed in gender atypical occupations were stereotypically considered less expressive and more socially distanced than those employed in typical occupations.

Other studies place the blame for inequality—at least in part—on women. Examining why women are underrepresented in international management, Fischlmayr (2002), acknowledges that the main factors are the companies' reluctance to send women abroad because of the stereotypical views of decisionmakers, the prejudices women are expected to face abroad, the career demands of their spouses, and the small number of women in top management. However, she also adds as a factor "women's own fault for not being selected" (Fischlmayr, 2002, p. 773), claiming that they lack self-confidence, exhibit stereotypical behavior, and underestimate their abilities. She concludes that women themselves contribute to their underrepresentation in international management. Feminist studies, however, contest these explanations (Crosby, Williams, and Biernat, 2004).

Attempting to refute the stereotypes, some studies provide evidence that they lack substance. Hayes, Allinson, and Armstrong (2004), for example, found no support for stereotypic characterization of women managers and women in general as being more intuitive than their male equivalents. They even show that female non-managers are more analytical and less intuitive than male non-managers, and more analytical than female managers. Similarly, Gottfried, Gottfried, Bathurst, and Killian (1999) claim those working mothers who retain most of the family burden still invest as much as men in their work, and Moore (2009) shows that men and women place the same importance on both their family and work roles.

Other studies that challenge the influence of stereotypes deal with the impact of family on women's work. Gottfried, et al. (1999), for example, contend that maternal employment appears to have no adverse consequences on child development. Indeed, the children of employed mothers seem to benefit from their mothers' employment in many ways (e.g., they tend to be more independent and self-confident), and they tend to have less stereotyped attitudes about gender roles than do children whose mothers are unemployed. Their mothers are not as overstressed or dissatisfied as the stereotypes previously assumed, assert Crosby and Jaskar (1993), no matter how many children they have (Mueller and Yoder, 1997). Prior findings denigrating single-child mothers and glorifying eight-child mothers were not replicated, though childless women were still evaluated less favorably.

The varied findings concerning these stereotypes may indicate that in advanced Western societies, some of them are changing. Not as fast as gender roles and traits, perhaps, but ideological change can be seen and has the potential to legitimize even further changes.

Even in a traditional society like Israel, examination of the stereotypes in 2007 shows changes. Nine prevalent stereotypes were analyzed: 1. working women are not as good mothers as non-working women; 2. working women are not as good spouses as non-working women; 3. raising children hinders women's careers, but not men's; 4. for most women, having a family is more important than a professional career; 5. men are the main breadwinners for their families; 6. men get most of their satisfaction in life from their work, and less from their family; 7. men are more loyal to the workplace than women because they must provide for their families; 8. for most men, a successful careerist woman is a less desirable spouse; and 9. it is justified that men's salaries are higher than women's when in similar work (see Table 6.6).

Respondents were asked to indicate how strongly they agreed or disagreed with each stereotype on a scale from 1 (totally disagree) to 6 (totally agree). Principle component factor analysis shows that these stereotypes form two factors. The first includes the two stereotypes comparing the motherhood and spousal relations of working and non-working mothers (items 1 and 2). These stereotypes are not strongly supported by either men or women (the means for women are 1.97 and 1.84, respectively; for men, 2.21 and 2.12), indicating that Israelis do not think that working women are worse mothers or spouses than non-working women. The rejection of these stereotypes is stronger among women than among men (t = -2.65 and -3.15, respectively).

The second factor relates to the seven more general stereotypes concerning gender roles and preferences. Responses to these items show that Israelis support most of them, but not all. In most cases, women are more stereotypic than men. They believe, for example, that "raising children hinders women's careers, but not men's" more than men believe that. Their belief may be due to their firsthand knowledge of the price they pay when they become mothers: a heavier burden, more time pressure, expectations that women will shift the centers of their lives to their homes when they become mothers, and so forth (see also Cuddy, Fiske, and Glick, 2004; Mueller and Yoder, 1997).

Table 6.6. Gender Differences in perception of Stereotypes (T-Test)

		Gender	N	Mean	Std. Deviation	t
1	Working women are not as good mothers as non-working women	women	461	1.97	1.259	-2.651**
		men	340	2.21	1.302	
2	Working women are not as good spouses as non-working women	women	461	1.84	1.143	-3.149**
		men	339	2.12	1.332	
3	Raising children hinders women's careers, not men's	women	457	4.39	1.468	4.781**
		men	340	3.87	1.543	
4	For most women having a family is more important than a professional career	women	455	4.15	1.419	.497
		men	329	4.10	1.442	
5	Men are the main breadwinners for their families	women	461	3.73	1.757	.070
		men	337	3.72	1.635	
6	Men get most of their satisfaction in life from their work, less from their family	women	451	3.29	1.542	5.299**
		men	334	2.72	1.442	
7	Men are more loyal to the workplace than women because they must provide for their families	women	461	3.28	1.756	.044
		men	337	3.27	1.685	
8	For most men, a successful careerist woman is a less desirable spouse	women	446	2.86	1.510	1.831
		men	335	2.66	1.508	
9	It is justified that men's salaries are higher than women's when in similar work	women	459	1.89	1.355	-3.612**
		men	340	2.26	1.510	
	stereotypes1 (1 & 2) (Cronbach α = .79)	women	460	1.9065	1.09860	-3.146**
		men	338	2.1627	1.18666	
	stereotypes2 (3—9) (Cronbach α = .68)	women	427	3.6417	.96828	3.716**
		men	314	3.3790	.93802	

* p≤ .05
** p≤ .01

Women also believe that "men get most of their satisfaction in life from their work" more than men, indicating, perhaps, that women have not yet realized the change that men's responses seem to indicate: family is of great importance for them today (see p. 26), and is now considered a legitimate source of satisfaction.

Both men and women still see men as the "main breadwinners for their families," and perhaps this is the reason why they both believe that "men are more loyal to the work place than women." There are no gender differences concerning these issues, but despite these beliefs, women still reject the claim that "men should earn more than women" more strongly than men. Hence, they seem to be indicating that although the burden of breadwinning is still mostly men's burden, as domestic responsibilities are mainly women's burden, when they do the same type of work, they should earn equal wages.

Though most of the examined stereotypes are still held by both men and women, and in some of them women are even more stereotypic, some of them are weakening. But is that true for all segments of Israeli society?

Examination of the 2007 data shows that there are no differences between religious and secular Israelis regarding the stereotypes concerning the motherhood and partnership of working and non-working women (see Table 6.7), and the stereotypes are rather weak. However, there are some interesting differences between them in the more general stereotypes.

Table 6.7. Stereotype differences between religious and secular men and women (ANOVA)[a]

		women		men		Main effects		gender X religiosity interaction
		Secular (N-207)	Religious (N=164)	Secular (N=195)	Religious (109)	gender	religiosity	
1	Working women are not as good mothers as non-working women	1.83	1.88	1.98	2.30	7.058**	2.874	1.960
2	Working women are not as good spouses as non-working women	1.79	1.72	1.94	2.15	7.460**	.307	2.010
3	Raising children hinders women's careers, not men's	2.90	2.83	2.52	2.78	4.539**	.386	1.842
4	For most women having a family is more important than a professional career	2.96	3.03	3.00	3.26	.796	.504	1.259
5	Men are the main breadwinners for their families	4.09	3.96	3.86	4.33	.003	1.158	6.556**
6	Men get most of their satisfaction in life from work, less from their family	3.28	2.93	2.50	2.61	27.822**	1.755	3.790*

		women		men		Main effects		gender X religiosity interaction
		Secular (N-207)	Religious (N=164)	Secular (N=195)	Religious (109)	gender	religiosity	
7	Men are more loyal to the workplace than women	4.50	4.27	3.76	3.74	30.829**	1.404	.698
8	For most men, a successful careerist woman is less desirable	3.51	3.43	3.42	3.81	.551	.763	3.086*
9	It is justified that men's salaries are higher than women's when in similar work	1.66	1.91	2.00	2.44	15.880**	9.719**	.791
10	stereo1 (1 and 2)	1.78	1.79	1.94	2.18	8.481**	1.632	1.933
11	Stereo2 (3 to 9)	3.55	3.42	3.15	3.39	11.619**	.157	6.184**

[a]   Averages are not exactly the same because of missing values in religiosity.

Religious men believe in the "men the breadwinner" stereotype more than all other groups, and they find "career women" the least desirable. Secular men, on the other hand, agree that men get their satisfaction from work, not from their families, less than all other groups, while secular women think so more than all other groups. Collectively, these findings seem to indicate that the more traditional segments of Israeli society have changed less than the less traditional, secular segments. However, a closer look at the data shows that religious women seem to be less supportive of the stereotypes than their secular counterparts! Hence, it may be assumed that some changes in the traditional segments of society are occurring, led by women.

Still, findings from a previous study (Moore, 2006) show that religious women work fewer hours and more among them are in part-time jobs than secular women, their accumulated number of years in the labor market and their tenure in current jobs are lower, fewer among them are in positions of authority, they are in lower-status jobs, and they work closer to home so that the time they spend traveling to work is shorter than that of secular women. Their work patters seem to reflect a belief that women should choose occupations and jobs that will minimize role conflict and take family considerations and responsibilities into account (the "minimizing work role" strategy—see Moore and Gobi, 1995). They seem to think that women should enter jobs in which skills do not deteriorate in order to enable them to leave work when family obligations necessitate it (e.g., when their children are young or when their work interferes with that of their spouse).

It is not surprising, therefore, that religious women retain negative beliefs and work-related stereotypes more than secular women. They also accept the negative stereotypes against working women, according to which they are but secondary providers and cannot invest in their careers as much as men do or they will risk being poorer mothers and wives. Moreover, researchers show that the impact of religion is unchanged by women, no matter what they do (Sered, 1997), and its impact is even strengthening among diverse groups (like those who go through religious fortification, especially among adolescent girls [Rapoport and Garb, 1998] and new immigrants from the United States [Sands and Roer-Strier, 2004]). Even when religious women attain higher education than their mothers, and this provides them with greater freedom, it is men who define what women will learn, how much they can learn and in which institutions (El-Or, 1993).

However, Blumen (2002) claims that among Ultra-Orthodox women, exposure to modern values of work and gender leads to discontent, which is suggestive of private resistance and the modification of women's personal values. Still, as these women are very religious, a dent in the armor is but a slight lessening in traditional divisions.

Conclusions

As the former chapters indicated, structural, macro-level factors (e.g., education level, the degree of sex-segregation in the labor market, availability of childcare facilities, tax exemptions for working mothers or dual-worker families, and other measures of industrialization) should be included in the analysis of changes in the lives of women as they contribute to our understanding of differences among societies.

The changes are difficult to attain. Women must first become aware that they are discriminated against and deprived of equal status as a group, and identify with the group despite the possible differences between them. Second, women must realize that their inferior position in patriarchal societies is the result of a structuration process dominated by men, and that the process can be influenced by collective action (e.g., joint women's activities for the attainment of common interests and the establishment of organized women's movements or pressure groups).

Also, analysis of the Israeli socio-historical processes seems to indicate that attempts to advance women's issues through activity in male-dominated social movements are futile (as Chafetz, Lorence and Larosa [1993] claimed). Joining such movements, in which women are forced to depend on the good will of mostly-male policy- and decision-makers did not increase equality for Israeli women in a significant manner. Although some laws were passed in their favor, the socio-cultural changes they brought were minimal.

Women's organizations that espoused derivative ideologies (rather than competing ideologies), like NAAMAT and WIZO did in their earlier days, had but limited freedom of action, and provided superficial and marginal changes in women's life conditions. They may have also bound women's actions, and confined them to activities that did not jeopardize the social systems created and maintained by male-dominated ideologies. Only when competing (mostly feminist) ideologies appeared in Israel and were espoused by both existing and new women's organizations were women able to denounce the structuration processes and fight for change in the patriarchal social structure.

Thus, the dissatisfaction with social systems directs the structuration processes away from reproducing the existing socio-cultural systems and toward social change. The gendered division of labor is weakening, so that women not only join the labor force, they may also opt for careers in male-typed occupations that demand intense involvement and investment of time and energy.

Some of the noteworthy consequences of these changes include the emergent legitimacy for a growing flexibility in the gender schema of men and women, the increased egalitarianism in gender roles, and the weakening of the gender stereotypes that limited the behaviors of both genders. The less rigid gender schemas allow men and women to join occupations that require behaviors that were considered typical of one gender and not the other (e.g., female managers and male kindergarten teachers). Most men and women still choose gender typical occupations, but the variety of options for both genders has somewhat increased. It also changed the division of roles between men and women. Though men are still considered the main breadwinners and women the homemakers, the balance has somewhat changed between the 1980s and the beginning of the new millennium, a trend that seems to have continued and even gained momentum in the first decade of the twenty-first century (see elaboration in Chapter Seven).

The change is slower in the more traditional segments of society, and religious women still adhere to the traditional gender roles more than secular women. But for them, too, some changes have occurred, and their support for the division of roles is weakening so that they are less stereotypic than religious men.

Although in many Western societies stereotypes against working women and their ability to successfully combine family responsibilities and work obligations are less relevant today than they were in the past, these stereotypes are still prevalent (Diekman and Murnen, 2004; Lyness and Terrazas, 2006), especially among the more tradition-oriented segments in societies. It seemed logical to assume that as more women entered male-typed occupations, and the division of labor became more egalitarian, the stereotypes would weaken, diminishing the actuarial basis of the stereotypical perceptions of women's work. The change is rather slow (Diekman and Murnen, 2004; Mueller and Yoder, 1997), and diverse explanations were suggested for their perseverance (e.g., Cleveland, Stockdale, and Murphy, 2000; Eckes, 2002).

Many of the explanations present the tendency to accept the traditional division of labor as the basis for agreement with the stereotypes against working women and the devaluation of their work investments, especially against women who are mothers and wives (Hill, 2005; Spence and Buckner, 2000). Orthodox women tend to support libertarian, egalitarian ideologies less than secular and nontraditional women (Moore, 1996; Poloma and Pendleton, 1990). Such women who strongly support the traditional gendered division of labor tend to have heavier family responsibilities than women who do not support it (i.e., the former marry more, and have more children than the latter [Reynolds and Aletraris, 2007]). Because accepting the stereotype means lowering expectations regarding a woman's ability to succeed at work, those who accept the stereotypes tend to believe that it is still difficult (or even impossible) for women to successfully combine family and career. This belief is expected to hinder the ability of women to succeed in the labor market. In contrast, women who do not accept the stereotypes are expected to believe that role combination is possible, and as a result will express greater life satisfaction. This is expected to be most salient among women in female-typed occupations as they are in jobs that enable them to combine the roles more easily.

In this view, gender stereotypes are ideological and prescriptive rather than simply descriptive. Their influence on women's employment is unlikely to diminish simply with the passage of time or the accumulating of evidence on women's capabilities. While insightful, alone this framing leads to the pessimistic view that ambivalent attitudes toward women are intractable.

As a result, today Israeli women face all the problems which women in other achievement-oriented societies have to face, but their plight is aggravated by the complexity of Israel's immigrant society and its religiosity. Hence, the growing possibilities of joining atypical occupations call for a re-examination of the stereotypes concerning women and their work, the formation of models for imitation and identification, and a more thorough examination of the factors involved in the structuring of labor markets. These issues are discussed in the next chapter.

ENDNOTES

[1] The "masculinity" of an organization is determined by three factors: the proportion of men employed in it; the type of tasks required in the majority of its jobs; and the characteristics required for performing the work. The Israeli Police Force is a masculine organization according to all three criteria: men constitute 80% of all its workers; the tasks defined by its charter include high risk, high responsibility, protection of civilians and their rights, the use of physical force, and field (operative) work. The characteristics necessary to perform this work are also considered masculine (i.e., authority, forcefulness, dominance).

[2] Until the early 1960s, very few women were employed by the Israeli Police Force, and they too were all in female-typed jobs (such as secretarial and typing work). The growing need for police workers in the 1960s-1970s led to some policy changes that enabled women to join a variety of hitherto male-typed jobs, and women were encouraged to join the force. These women were only partly integrated, as just a few of them were given field jobs while the majority was still placed in administrative jobs at headquarters. Thus, the policy change was not implemented: in 1976, for example, women constituted only 7% of the officers (see also Jones, 1986; Pitman and Orthner, 1988).

[3] The courses available in the Israeli Police Force are many and diverse. Some of them are compulsory, like the basic course, which all new recruits must participate in within six months of entering the organization. In these courses policemen and -women are introduced to the organization's methods of operation, techniques and procedures, and to its ideology and norms. Other courses which are more specific and professional, like courses for detectives, forensic technicians or high-ranking officers, are voluntary, and are based on individuals' abilities and commanding officers' recommendation.

[4] Bem's whole list was examined in previous studies in Israel (e.g., Moore, 1995, 1996). Based on item-to-total correlations, all gender-neutral traits were removed and only relevant items were retained. See Chapter Three.

[5] Less variance is explained by the other six factors, which include one to three traits in each. These factors represent the negative "feminine" traits (gullible, shy, childlike, explaining about 6% of the variance); "personal attainment" (ambitious, competitive, flatterable, explaining less than 5% of the variance); negative "masculine" traits (aggressive and dominant, explaining less than 4% of the variance); gender identification (feminine and masculine, explaining about 3% of the variance); and separateness from the collective (individualism and risk-taking, explaining about 3% of the variance).

6   Even Western approaches, according to which rational and assertive behaviors are the basis of perceived control, seem to accept that in other societies where less equitable practices may dominate individuals may turn to non-instrumental means to attain control (Lefcourt, 1981, 1983).

7   Egalitarian attitudes mean "accepting of both women exhibiting traditional male role behaviors and men exhibiting female role behaviors. Therefore, an egalitarian individual would not be prone to gender bias, whether the attitude object is male or female" (King et al., 1994, p. 340).

8   Recent analyses of the work-family interface have again turned to focus on the issue of time, i.e., working hours, time bind, time squeeze, time allocation, meaning of time, etc. (Hochchild, 1997; Jacobs and Gerson, 2001; Thompson and Bunderson, 2001).

9   A similar hypothesis was advanced by Marks and McDermit (1996): "People with more balanced role systems will report less role strain, more role ease, greater wellbeing, and more positive role-specific experience than people with less balanced role systems."

10   Israeli school-teachers were used as a comparative baseline because they are in a traditionally female-typed occupation, and in the more traditional of the examined societies.

Chapter 7

Where to? Conclusions and Extrapolations

The structuration processes that societies go through lead to changes in social relations across space and time (Giddens, 1984). We should, therefore, expect changes over time in gender relations, division of gender roles, even the perception of gender itself. Historical examination of these issues confirms that this is actually the case. The accumulated changes throughout the years are highly visible in profound transformations in gender relations and the life experiences of men and women in Israel, as they are in many other societies.

Moreover, in the technological age, with its widely accessible communications, globalization, and mass media that reach almost all societies, such changes spread more rapidly from one society to another than ever before. The radical changes also brought about shifts in the issues that gender researchers and social researchers in general focus on. According to Gutek (2001), since the 1980s a significant shift can be seen in the studies of women: some of the issues that interest or trouble women and gender researchers today were not examined in the 1980s because they were almost nonexistent. For example, the lack of studies of single, unwed mothers: their proportion in Israel was so small until the mid-1980s that they were not defined as a social category and data were not collected by the Israeli Central Bureau of Statistics until then. Another example is that of women in managerial positions: there were too few of them, so no studies of these women were carried out. Other gender issues, such as stereotypes concerning professional women, were more or less ignored (though studies of stereotypes were conducted from the 1930s) because it was easier—even socially required—to deny their existence and the fact that women may carry out the same jobs, equally well, but in different ways than men. Other issues were settled during that period, so that they are no longer debated (like "Should women work?," or "Is the option not to marry, or not to bear children, a socially legitimate choice for women?").

Though it is difficult to predict what forms these issues will acquire in the future, some near-future trends may be extrapolated from the current processes, enabling the description of possible changes in gender relations and in the social roles of men and women. One of the more meaningful structuration principles that can be seen in the third millennium is that there is no solitary direction of development and change, but a wide variety of options that are open to men and women, making them freer than earlier generations to choose desired preferences. If this trend persists in the coming decades, the number of options would increase.

Even today, young members of society are free to choose from a growing variety of life-styles according to individual preferences or group membership. The weakening hold of traditional values and norms in some segments of society seems to strengthen this trend and legitimize more options for more individuals. Some of the alternatives that exist today tend to be applicable to specific social classes, categories, and groups more than to others (like gay/lesbian marriages, which are more prevalent among non-religious individuals), but with time they may become available to others.

Moreover, these preferences seem to represent, at least in some cases, contradictory trends. Thus for example, in Israel the spreading values that support the choice of intensive motherhood and require minimizing work involvement are in opposition to the legitimization and encouragement of women's high-tech or managerial careers. These careers require extensive traveling, which entails minimizing domestic involvement, finding substitutes for mothers, and enlisting the help of partners and family.

This chapter examines how the trends and lifestyles that exist in societies today may shape future structuration processes. Actions always lead to consequences (or reactions) and, therefore, the actions of today lead to consequences for tomorrow. Some of these consequences are planned and intended, but others – perhaps the more interesting ones—are unintended. These consequences can change the initial conditions that lead to future actions both on the micro and the macro level (Giddens, 1976, 1979; see Chapter One).

For example, second-wave activist feminists (see Chapter Four) fought for women's right to receive pay when they leave work after childbirth. The fight was won in many societies, which was the intended consequence of the actions women took, with each country defining the duration of paid "maternity leave" (the name later changed to "family leave" to enable men to temporarily leave their jobs when they become fathers).[1] The legal changes also provided normative support for women who left their work to bear and raise children.

Simultaneously (as a consequence of actions taken in different spheres like medical research), doctors and nurses increased the pressure on women to breastfeed, telling women that if they were going to be home for several months anyway, why not fulfill their most basic—instinctive—role in life and breastfeed. Being legitimately free from the labor market, but still needing to justify their "absence" if they decided to prolong their maternity leave, many women chose to breastfeed for at least the period in which they were on leave. Thus, a new trend has begun, which was probably an unintended consequence of paid leave: urging women to breastfeed for a longer period and providing ideological support for prolonged breastfeeding (Liedloff's [1977] "continuum concept," for example).

The choice to breastfeed has diverse consequences that were not foreseen, planned or intended by the fighters for maternity leave, and may even be contrary to their intention: finding life as "stay-at-home" moms less stressful, many women take an extended maternity leave and do not return to their jobs. These new trends gained theoretical support by some of the third-wave feminist approaches that support reintroducing the traditional division of labor. Consequently, more women leave their workplaces after giving birth and return to an economic dependence on their partners, which is contrary to the aims of second-wave feminism. These trends are spreading and becoming more acceptable (like Hattery's [2001] "intensive motherhood")

The chapter focuses on the trends that are already visible and are expected to grow and spread in three areas: for men, for women, and for the interactions both in the family sphere and in the work-related organizational sphere. (The analyses deal only with changes that are relevant to topics discussed in previous chapters). As we have seen in Chapter Four, changes in Western societies appear in Israel a few years after they are assimilated and become "normative" in the societies where they were created. Hence, the chapter describes some trends that are noticeable in Europe and/or the United States, but have only recently appeared in Israel and, therefore, have not been thoroughly studied in the Israeli context.

1. Trends for Men

Changing Masculinity

Traditional masculinity was defined by Levant (1995, p. 11) as "avoidance of femininity; restricted emotions; sex disconnected from intimacy; pursuit of achievement and status; self-reliance; strength and aggression; and homophobia." Masculinity is always defined not only as different from femininity but also as superior to it (Connell, 1995; Gray, 1992).

This pattern is becoming less prevalent, acceptable, or even self-serving for men. The most important shift in masculinity is that avoidance of all that is feminine has lessened. Therefore, young, well-off, urban men today are able to embrace some of the customs and attitudes once perceived as the province of women (Anderson, 2005). Levant (1995) claims that the social restriction of men's emotions is weakening and the search for intimacy rather than detached sex is growing. Similarly, the pursuit of achievement and status has become less important to men than it used to be.

Although the concept of "femininity" has become more elaborate, and women today embrace characteristics that were previously considered "masculine" without violating social norms and risking negative sanctions, this trend is much weaker for men, and "feminine" behaviors are less acceptable for them (see Chapter 6). However, the representation of "traditional" masculinity became more restricted, and the cultural changes compelled men to curb extremely masculine behaviors: aggression among children is reprimanded, fierce individuality is frowned upon, and extremely patriarchal attitudes are delegitimized. It is not surprising, therefore, that slowly and hesitantly men begin to include alternative characteristics in their repertoire of traits and self-presentations. Espousing feminine traits among men is still not considered appropriate in all segments of society, and even when it is normative, feminine traits are transformed by men to assume a masculine interpretation. Thus, for example, exhibiting warmth and understanding are legitimate behaviors for men in intimate relations in many societies, and are not seen as a sign of weakness; however, such behaviors are less positively viewed in work relations (Moore, 2009).

The social and cultural changes have extended to socialization processes for boys and girls as well. Parents, pre-school teachers and school-teachers tolerate a wider variety of behaviors for both genders, and even legitimize "uncharacteristic" behaviors more than they used to. Though a totally "feminine" behavior is still prevented or repressed in young boys, and it is still not considered appropriate for young boys to dress up in women's clothes or to be "femininely cute," totally "masculine" behaviors (like aggressive bullying and domineering behaviors) are also not tolerated, and all socialization agents are attempting to curb them or tone them down. Thus, young men in the twenty-first century are raised according to a more balanced behavioral model in which characteristics like warmth, understanding and sensitivity are as highly valued as assertiveness, rationality, and leadership (Anderson, 2005).

Studies show that men today use these expressive ("feminine") traits to enrich their experiences and their life-satisfaction (see Chapter Six). They even use these traits as an additional means of increasing their sense of control (even though this is still not considered a legitimate option for women (Moore, 2007). Thus, men may "switch" from an instrumental to an expressive type of internal control in order to maximize their benefits.

Consequently, a growing tendency to self-attribute a complex and elaborate combination of traits is evident today, strengthening the tendency to develop new androgynous or undifferentiated gender schemas. In some social categories, men and women self-attribute traits regardless of their gender-appropriateness so that many positive traits became gender-neutral (such as optimistic, loyal, and ambitious). So far, the process was more noticeable among women than among men. Their spreading is not uniform, and they are slower and less inclusive within the more traditional categories. Still, their effects are noticeable, indicating that in modern society, no social category is entirely closed and isolated from outside influences (Ehrensaft, 1990).

Such changes in men can already be seen in the representation of the metrosexual. The representation is rather new,[2] not sufficiently studied or well-defined. Sampson (2002) describes the metrosexual as follows: "The typical metrosexual is a young man with money to spend, living in or within easy reach of a metropolis—because that's where all the best shops, clubs, gyms and hairdressers are. He might be officially gay, straight or bisexual, but this is utterly immaterial because he has clearly taken himself as his own love object and pleasure as his sexual preference." Although they are seen more often in particular jobs, working, for example, as highly visible media celebrities, models, and pop and sports stars, they serve as role models, and their presence is becoming noticeable among young men in many high-status professions (such as lawyers, financial analysts, and businessmen).

But the presentation of metrosexuals as narcissistic, pleasure-seeking individuals addresses only part of what defines them: they are also interested in improving their relationships with others (especially women), enhancing their careers without feeling chained by conventions, and increasing their general wellbeing by fulfilling diverse aspects of their potential (Anderson, 2005).

Metrosexuals only made their appearance after cultural transformations led to changes in views on masculinity. Perhaps metrosexuality is a reaction against the more constricting "masculine" schema that occurred when diverse traits became acceptable for both genders; it may also be due to the shift that led some men to feel too confined within the gender roles (Williams, 1995). It may also be attributed to the reduction of cultural, institutional, and organizational homophobia, and the re-socialization of men into gender integration. Whatever the cause, metrosexuality may be considered a means of establishing greater equality between the sexes (Coad, 2008; Datta, 2005).

"Domestic Men"

No longer considered "effeminate," men who acknowledge their emotional side, and do not consider free expression of sentiments threatening, are also able to relate better to their children. "New fatherhood" is becoming a well-known term. It refers to involved, caring fathering, which generally leads to stronger bonds between men and their children (Parke, 1996). The importance attributed to the issue in the last decade is apparent in the many studies published in books, journals, conferences and websites (e.g., Doherty, 1998; Tamis-LeMonda and Cabrera, 2002).

The intensive parenting norm that became apparent at the beginning of the twentieth century affected fathers as well as mothers, and researchers (e.g., Griswold, 1997; Stearns, 2003) have increasingly asserted that fathers need to spend more time parenting. Evidence that men are aware of this norm is evident in both the increase in the amount of time that fathers spend with their children (Jacobs and Gerson, 2004) and the fact that fathers more than mothers report feeling that they do not spend enough time with their children (Milkie, Mattingly, Nomaguchi, Bianchi and Robinson, 2004; Pleck and Pleck, 1996).

"New fatherhood" is based on the many studies that show how important fathers are in the lives of their children. Infants form attachments to those who regularly take care of them and their needs, claim attachment theorists (Lamb, 2002a,b). The sensitivity of caregivers varies, and individual differences (which transcend gender boundaries) in sensitivity and responsiveness affect the quality of the attachment relationships (DeWolff and van Ijzendoorn, 1997). Moreover, fathers are as competent to care for their children as mothers are, given opportunity and experience, even when the children are young (Lamb, 1997).

Furthermore, researchers have clearly demonstrated that, on average, children benefit from being raised in two-parent families rather than in separated, divorced, or never-married single-parent households (Clarke-Stewart, Vandell, McCartney, Owen, and Booth, 2000). Children who are deprived of meaningful relationships with one of their parents are at greater risk psycho-socially, even when they are able to maintain relationships with their other parent (Amato, 2000).[3]

Children growing up in fatherless families are disadvantaged relative to those growing up in two-parent families with respect to psycho-social adjustment, behavior and achievement at school, educational attainment, employment trajectories, income generation, involvement in antisocial and even criminal behavior, and the ability to establish and maintain intimate relationships. Stated differently, there is substantial evidence that children are more likely to attain their psychological potential when they are able to develop and maintain meaningful relationships with both of their parents (Hetherington and Kelly, 2002; Kelly, 2000).

United States President Barack Obama's speech on fatherhood (given on January 24th, 2009), launching his new fatherhood program, emphasizes these themes:

Of all the rocks upon which we build our lives, we are reminded today that family is the most important. And we are called to recognize and honor how critical every father is to that foundation. They are teachers and coaches. They are mentors and role models. They are examples of success and the men who constantly push us toward it.

But if we are honest with ourselves, we'll admit that what too many fathers also are is missing — missing from too many lives and too many homes. They have abandoned their responsibilities, acting like boys instead of men. And the foundations of our families are weaker because of it.

As fathers and parents, we've got to spend more time with them, and help them with their homework, and replace the video game or the remote control with a book once in a while.

We should be making it easier for fathers who make responsible choices and harder for those who avoid them. We should reward fathers who pay that child support with job training and job opportunities and a larger Earned Income Tax Credit that can help them pay the bills.

The involvement of fathers in the raising of their children has, indeed, increased significantly. Fathers worldwide still contribute far less time to direct care of children than do women, but fathers' participation in caring for their children is increasing. Although there are significant variations across societies, studies from diverse settings find that, on average, fathers contribute about one-third more time to direct childcare as they did a few decades ago (especially in Europe and North America [Barker, 2009]). For example, in the US, in the 1960s, fathers participated in caring for their children about 25% as much as mothers—by the late 1990s that had risen to between 55 and 70%. In Canada, the increase between 1986 and 1996 was from 50 to 65% (Fatherhood Institute, 2005). In the UK, fathers now provide about a third of the parental childcare, according to the Equal Opportunities Commission (Engle, 1997). Also, after divorce, non-custodial fathers now spend substantially more time with their children than they did in earlier decades. According to recent studies (e.g., Hetherington, 1999), 35 to 40% of children have weekly contact with their fathers, and there are fewer occurrences of fathers' absence or shirking of responsibility than in previous decades (Hetherington and Kelly, 2002). Engle (1997) claims that men still control most of the family resources, and when they are more involved in raising their children, there is more money, time, food and caring directed to children's needs.[4]

Moreover, studies in the past decade confirm that men, too, benefit from involved fatherhood. For example, research shows that men's psychological well-being is higher the more time they spend caring for a child: they are more relaxed, report greater life-satisfaction, and so forth (Haas, 2006). In addition to the obvious gains for themselves and the apparent benefits for their children, fathers' involvement has societal advantages as well. Storey, et al., (2000), claims that highly involved fathers-to-be show changes in hormonal levels (decreased levels of testosterone and increased levels of prolactin) around the birth of their infants, and this may somewhat decrease the levels of aggression in society. The advantages for women of a more equally-shared family burden are obvious. However, it seems that not all women are thrilled to see their men spend more time at home. This issue and its consequences are elaborated upon later in the chapter.

Future Trends for Men

Now that homosexual couples, divorced or separated men, and metrosexuals have acceptable "legitimization" for their need to leave work early several times a week, and they appear happy with their lives, married "straight" men who work very long hours seem to be re-examining their situation. Until recently, women were the only ones leaving early, and men found it easy to claim that women have different needs and different desires, some even going as far as claiming that "Women are from Venus; Men are from Mars" (Gray, 1992). When men, too, began working shorter hours, leaving work to be with their children, these hard-working married men realized that they are the only category with no justification for demanding greater flexibility in working hours. They lack the ability to claim time for their families or themselves, and they only have their work as a source to directly derive satisfaction from. Of course, they enjoy their families too, but as a "second-hand" pleasure, since they only contribute indirectly to the functioning of the family (they contribute funds and status, perhaps, but not direct influence on its activities, based on intimate acquaintance with each family member's needs and preferences). The fact that women—and now some men too—want to leave work early seems to have led these men to ask themselves: "What am I missing? What do these men and women who leave work early gain?"

Moreover, married work-oriented men carry most (if not all) the financial burden of their families, a load which often leads to anxiety and stress: the expectation that they will create the resources to cover debts, mortgage, medical expenses, good schools and the like may be overwhelming for some men, especially when they are the sole providers for their families. On the other hand, the partners of these men, especially the partners of career-oriented men, in jobs that provide high status and income, and advancement opportunities, seem to enjoy the highest levels of freedom: they do not share the burden of providing for their families, they can buy domestic services (cleaning, cooking, baby-sitting) and daycare for their children, and they have time to enrich themselves and to devote their free time to things they like to do (whether these things generate income or not).

Those men and women who work fewer hours do so either out of necessity (family requirements, for example) or by choice, and they often have an added burden due to demands made by the two roles they fulfill, but they also have an additional source of satisfaction. In the past, work-oriented married men seemed happy to leave most domestic obligations to their partners, but this seems to be changing in many societies. As more men will realize the benefits of close relations with their children, and the satisfaction derived from contributing to the shaping of their development, the desire to limit working hours may continue to spread.

The growing desire of some women to develop their own careers may strengthen this tendency in men: because work opportunities have grown for women, and self-fulfillment through work is legitimate for them, women who choose this path will encourage their partners to work fewer hours, to share both the financial and the domestic burden more equally, and support them when they change their preferences. Thus, dual-career couples today may decide on the particular days when one partner comes home early from work to be with the children, and the days in which the other partner does so (Dew, 2009). This type of arrangement, which is currently rarely seen among married couples but appears to be on the rise among young, educated, less traditional, egalitarian, urban couples, will enable both partners to develop meaningful careers as well as to enjoy the benefits of close ties with their children, and lead to a stronger sense of sharing and companionship.

The main opposition to this budding trend comes from employers and work places. When it was only (or mostly) women who wanted to work fewer hours or demanded time-flexibility, employers conceded, but at a price: they paid lower wages to part-time workers, because they considered these workers less committed to their jobs (Moore, 1995b). Now that men, too, are demanding flexibility in working hours, employers will have to reconsider their policies and values or risk losing some of their workers to organizations which are more responsive to workers' needs and demands. This may act as an additional egalitarian force that will—indirectly—assist women in attaining equal wages and opportunities.

We may also assume that men in the near future will begin to take into account additional considerations that hitherto only women were concerned with, like working closer to home, avoiding a move to another country (or state) if this would break up the family, preferring less satisfying work in more time-flexible jobs, and so forth.

However, a counter-trend may is also apparent: women often push men away from home and pressure them into harder, more time-consuming work. Examples of such behaviors can be seen as the result of intensive motherhood and prolonged breast-feeding, both of which render men dispensable in the domestic sphere, delegitimizing their attempts to become significant care-givers. Also, protecting their territory, many women become over-critical of their partners, thus driving them away: by offering constant advice, critiquing their methods of parenting, or demanding specific ways of caring for a child, these women strengthen men's insecurities concerning child-care, especially among men who assume that women are instinctively able to care for infants. These issues are discussed in the next section of this chapter.

2. Trends for Women

As the previous chapters indicate, recent decades brought about significant changes in women's lives, and society has become more open and accepting of diverse lifestyles, legitimizing the varied attitudes associates with these lifestyles. If, in the past, women had to compromise, usually giving up their careers once they had children, their options today are more varied and numerous. In addition to the acceptable, familiar and prevalent option of combining family and work, there are new—socially legitimate—alternatives available to women today. These new choices may be grouped into three major categories: 1. returning home; 2. intensive careering; 3. self-centered individual development ("the power to be whatever I want").

Returning Home

There were always women who chose not to work, or to work part-time, or women who chose jobs that allowed them to focus on their domestic and family roles. There were also women who could not join the workforce because there were no social arrangements available to care for their children while they worked.

An ideological change can be seen accompanying the return home in recent years, especially among young career women: armed with third-wave feminist ideologies, and fully aware of the opportunities that the labor market has to offer, some successful high achievers choose to return home once they become mothers (Arendell, 2000). Some of the third-wave feminist trends, as well as cultural norms, cherish motherhood and consider it the proof of femininity. Motherhood has become part of the feminist notions of fulfilling what it means to be a woman, as separate and different from what it means to be a man (Hays, 1996).

Consequently, when a working woman, especially one who successfully attained a high rank in her chosen profession, decides to stop working after childbirth to become a "full-time mom," she tends to embrace an ideology that supports her decision, even hails her as "doing the right thing" for her child and family. Even the cultural terminology has changed and instead of "housewives," these women are now referred to as "stay-at-home moms," emphasizing their mother role rather than their domestic responsibilities (McDonald, Bradley, and Guthrie, 2005). Several social processes and cultural rationalizations facilitate the transition from full-time careers to full-time motherhood:

a. **Maternity Leave Policies**—As the previous chapters show, women in all Western societies are allowed to leave their workplaces for several weeks or months (each country defines a different length of leave and the pay while away from work. In Israel, "maternity leave" was extended from twelve to fourteen weeks in 2008). In addition, employers in many of these societies must reserve the position the woman vacated for several months, often up to a year, to enable her to return if she so desires (though they are not required to pay for this extended leave). In that period, women often learn to enjoy the freedom from pressure and competition; they enjoy the ability to perform all their responsibilities with maximal flexibility, so that despite the burden of childcare and domestic obligations, life becomes simpler than when work concerns are added.

b. **"Only Mom Can"** - Once they become mothers, women are exposed to beliefs, norms, and ideologies concerning motherhood that they may have been aware of earlier in their lives, but not at the same intensity. Western societies tend to define a good mother as one who is always available to her children, putting their needs before her own, constantly there for them until they are ready for school (age 5 in most societies), and responsible for them at all times (McDonald, Bradley, and Guthrie, 2005). Thus, although mothering is a low-status undertaking (almost every woman can become a mother), it should be considered so important and intrinsically rewarding as to outweigh the lack of financial rewards (Wearing, 1984).

These beliefs are, of course, normative constructs, not evidence-based scientific conclusions. Still, they influence women's decisions regarding staying at home or returning to work. The degree of influence these beliefs have on women's decisions depends on their preferences and sex role ideology (Hakim, 2000), as well as on their social class, education and income (Pfau-Effinger, 1999). Should a woman believe that she is the best possible caregiver for her children or that employing a substitute or placing her children in child care will have long-term harmful effects, and she can financially refrain from working, she is likely to choose to stay home with her children rather than return to work (McDonald et al, 2005). Crompton and Harris (1999) claim that these beliefs serve to control women more than to benefit their children.

c. **The Pressure to Breastfeed**—Most Western societies recommend a minimum required breastfeeding. In Israel, the recommendation (since 2009) is four months of only breastfeeding, followed by a slow introduction of other foods with continued breastfeeding, adding dairy products to infants' diets only at the age of nine months (Gal, 2009). The UK and United States governments, as well as the World Health Organization (WHO), advocate exclusive breastfeeding for the first six months of life and then supplemented breastfeeding for at least one year (World Health Organization, 2003). Some doctors recommend that breastfeeding should be prolonged for as long as the baby desires.

The insistence on breastfeeding is formalized and strong, and most pediatricians and nurses participate in exerting pressure on women to do so. Hospitals in most Western societies employ breastfeeding consultants to teach women how to perform this function successfully, hoping that they will continue to do so when they return home with their infants. The number of women who choose to continue breastfeeding significantly longer than the prescribed period is slowly growing so that even when their children grow up and eat solid foods women continue breastfeeding for the comfort, solace, and bonding it allows both baby and mother (Dettwyler, 1995).

Breastfeeding has gained such wide social support that in most Western societies, breastfeeding in public is culturally sanctioned, and laws passed in these societies enable women to do so in all public places. Many are still uncomfortable with it, and mothers often hesitate to breastfeed in public for fear of people's reactions and criticism (Riordan, 2005).

However, 90% of women in the UK, according to Lee (2008), feed their babies formula milk, wholly or partially. "Is Breast Really Best?," asks Wolf (2007), and her answer is that the advantages of breastfeeding are often propaganda: "When the science supporting public health campaigns is assumed to be unequivocal, the result can be sensational messages that neglect basic ethical principles concerning evidence quality, message framing, and cultural sensitivity. The NBAC was based on research that is inconsistent, lacks strong associations.... It capitalized on public misunderstanding of risk and risk assessment... And it was insufficiently attentive to the psychological, socioeconomic, and political concerns of its intended audience" (ibid, p. 623).

d. **The "Child in the Center" Ideology**—and its derivatives (the "Continuum Concept" [Liedloff, 1977], "Intensive Motherhood" [Hays, 1996; Lee, 2008]).

Another socio-cultural trend that facilitates women's choice to leave work after childbirth is seen in the child-centeredness of Western societies. Seeing mothers as primarily responsible for childrearing, whether the child has an additional parent or not, is in vogue (this value system has existed in Germany, Austria, Switzerland and even the Netherlands for many years). The ideology defines a child-centered process (i.e., the child's needs before the mother's) that necessitates expertise (i.e., because of their immense importance for the development of children, mothers need to perfect their skills and learn how to be good mothers, and experts guidance is essential), unconditional emotional absorption (i.e., requiring great emotional involvement in the child-rearing process, concessions in all life domains, and the ability to stop any other activity in order to respond to the child's needs), and financially expensive (i.e., prioritizing family expenditure so that child's needs are fully met [Hays, 1996]). *Intensive motherhood* appears to be the normative motherhood (Douglas and Michaels, 2004), and Arendell (2000) claims that it has become synonymous with good mothering, regardless of social class. Hence, women who must work (for economic reasons) often feel guilty because they cannot provide their children with the care and stability they need.

The importance of mothering in a child-centered society, and the required expert guidance for mothers, paved the way for society's intervention in the process. Doctors, nurses, teachers, consultants, policy-makers and others tell mothers what risks to avoid (even before the child is born!), how to manage their lives, what to do (or not do) so that their child will grow up "properly," whom to consult on every issue, and so forth (Reece, 2006).

One of the better-known derivatives of these principles is the *continuum concept* (Liedloff, 1977). The concept is based on the notion that babies need constant physical contact with their mothers to achieve optimal physical, mental, and emotional development. To attain that, she recommends that babies sleep in their parents' bed; be in constant physical contact, carried in arms, until they choose to separate from parents; be breastfed in response to their signals; and that parents should immediately respond to every signal without judgment, displeasure, or invalidation of the baby's needs (Liedloff, 1998).

Attachment Parenting[5] is a related concept, named by William Sears (1995, 2002), which presents parenting philosophy based on the principles of the Attachment Theory. According to the theory, the emotional bond with caregivers that a child forms has lifelong consequences. The ability to form a secure attachment style is dependent on sensitive and emotionally available parents (especially mothers) and leads to a child's socio-emotional development and well being, preventing insecure attachment styles that may lead to mental health problems.

e. **Motherhood as Identity** –the final social process that facilitates the transition from full-time careers to full-time motherhood discussed in this chapter is the one by which women on maternity leave who consider prolonging their stay at home often turn their motherhood into a major identity source, so that most of their identity revolves around "being Mom." Motherhood defines such a woman's schedule, her activities, and the essence—even justification—of their existence. This is often a byproduct of the other factors cited above: prolonged breastfeeding, intensive mothering, the belief that only she understands and can care for her child, and the socio-cultural pressure to raise well-adjusted, happy, successful children.

However, the whole process by which feminist trends and cultural norms turned motherhood into proof of femininity, and thus into women's major identity, in fact led to diverse negative consequences for women, claim Arendell (2000), Hays (1996), Lee (2008), and others.

Women who give up full-time careers for full-time motherhood often feel frustrated after a while. Women's level of education is rising worldwide, as we have seen in earlier chapters, and many of the full-time moms indeed have high academic educations, which enable them to develop powerful careers prior to giving birth. Hence, lacking professional adult conversations, interactions with peers, and even the pressure to prove her professional self may become irritating and upsetting after a while, and the ex-career woman misses her job and its demands (Warner, 2005). These women may also feel guilt for dodging their share in the obligation to financially provide for the family, placing the entire burden on their partners' shoulders. Moreover, this culture of total motherhood has led to an "age of anxiety" for mothers in modern society, contends Warner (2005), in the sense that fear of failure has become the prevalent concern of all mothers, especially full-time moms. The unrealistic obligations that intensive mothering creates also contribute to women's anxiety. Actual failure, and a realization that their efforts were to no avail despite their many concessions, sacrifices and compromises, together with feelings of missing out on the professional sphere, may lead to frustration or even total breakdown, argues Hays (1996).

Moreover, staying at home means that the "end-product" should justify the effort, the sacrifice, and the loss of income she may have brought to the family, and the "burden-of-proof" is entirely on her. Alas, the criteria for success as a parent are ambiguous and imprecise, so women cannot devise clear strategies or measure whether they reached their goals and whether their children have reached the standards they could not define. If the children turn out problematic or unhappy, or are unsuccessful in school or society, full-time mothers who were the sole or major care-taker find it more difficult to pin the failure on an outside force and tend to blame themselves. "I didn't do enough"; "I haven't sacrificed enough"; "There were times when I acted selfishly because I was too tired, or busy, or impatient"—these are but a few of the things that women may blame themselves for. If motherhood has indeed become their major role in life, and they fail in that role, they have no alternative sources from which to draw pleasure, status or confirmation.

To avoid such failures, full-time moms might invest too much, do too much, have difficulty setting boundaries for their children, or smother their independence. Full-time motherhood can be very strenuous and demanding on both mothers and their children (Warner, 2005). Not knowing how to do the "right thing," or what is the right thing to do, often leads mothers to over-doing or under-doing (Liedloff, 1998). Consequently, at times, full-time moms create the conditions for their subsequent failures, which are then attributed to them alone. A strong supporting family and social network may counter some of these negative consequences (Sears, Sears, and Pantley, 2002).

The pressure is so intense and so unrewarding, claim Krueger, Kahneman, Fischler, Schkade, Schwarz, and Stone (2009), that performing childcare is ranked in the 19th place (out of 21) of all the pleasant and unpleasant states in life (an unpleasant state is defined as an episode in which the most intense emotion is negative). Thus, in the United States, exercising, making love, reading, praying, watching TV, and even preparing food and doing housework are rated higher than childcare. (In France, it is ranked after most but not all of these states, so childcare should be considered less unpleasant.) The responses probably refer to taking care of young children, and is not necessarily related to the love that parents feel toward their children. Still, it is a revealing finding, indicating that for most parents childcare is a not a pleasant chore.

In summation, the transition from full-time careers to full-time motherhood has its benefits for women, but it also demands a heavy price that women must pay. Moreover, there is no conclusive or convincing body of research that shows that full-time mothering is in any way superior to part-time loving parenting carried out by both parents. It limits the father's role to that of breadwinner, without encouraging him to actively participate in raising the children and shaping their future. Still, it has become one of the main forces that curbs women's work-related ambitions and career aspirations.

Intensive Careering

Some women choose the route of intensive careering rather than intensive motherhood. Though this choice is more popular among unmarried women, a growing number of women who are mothers often choose this option in the twenty-first century, as can be seen in the previous chapter. The ideological change that supports this trend is based on the escalating legal demands for equality and the expanding cultural insistence on maintaining appropriate ("politically correct") representation of gender, race, age, disability and so forth. Although this trend is not as strong as the one that has accompanied the tendency of some women to become full-time moms, there is a radicalization of previous attitudes. Women who choose this alternative or support it believe that combining family and work is enriching rather than a source of conflict, something they desire and feel is rightfully within their options, so that they are as entitled to their career aspirations as men. The change in values, beliefs and norms (see Chapter Four) makes these aspirations acceptable socially, though not all segments of society equally support them.

Throughout Western society, career-oriented women often have to give up on family life and remain single, or to postpone marriage and children until they have attained higher education and professional status (Blossfeld and Huinink, 1991). The married ones among them are also twice as likely to initiate divorce procedures as women with less education, especially when they are high-earners (Wilson, 2006).

Though some claims that men prefer women who are less educated and successful than themselves, the proportion of women obtaining graduate degrees is growing, and they receive more than 50% of all master's degrees. They are less afraid of the myth, spread in the 1980s, that "40-year-old women have as much chance of marrying as they do of being killed by a terrorist," and seem to be choosing careers despite the odds.

In the 1990s, DINK ("Dual Income, No Kids"[6]) families proliferated, especially among white middle class Americans, claim Marsh, Darity, Cohen, Casper, and Salters (2007). In this family structure, both partners opt to advance their careers and incomes, and decide not to have children so as not to encumber either partner with the burden of taking care of them. Women who opt for this family pattern often regret their choice at a more advanced age, especially if their partners decide they do want children. For men, changing their minds when they are 40 or over is possible; for women, it is much more difficult (Gottfried Eskeles, Gottfried, Bathurst, and Killian, 1999; LeMaster,

Marcus-Newhall, Casad, and Silverman, 2005). In Europe, the option is more often DIOKs ("Dual Income, One Kid"), and the couple postpones having that child until both of them are well established in their careers.

In a nationwide survey, Hewlett (2002) found that 33% of high earning career women ages forty to fifty-five were childless. The proportion is even higher in corporate jobs, where 42% of the career women of the same ages are childless. The survey shows that only 19% of the men in the same job category were childless. Most of the women reported that they had wanted children: "By and large, these highly achieving women have not chosen to be childless. The vast majority yearn for children. Indeed, many have gone to the ends of the world to find a baby, expending huge amounts of time, energy and money" (p. 34). Only 14% of the surveyed women said they had not wanted children.

Many reasons may be given for the childlessness of these women. Some claim that many of them cared more about their careers than about marriage and children, and now they are paying the price. A more plausible explanation was provided by Hewlett (2002), according to which only 57% of the women over 40 in highly paying corporate jobs are married, compared with 83% of male high achievers. Moreover, she claims that the high achievers either married early (and then divorced before they had children) or never married, and the primary reason so many career women don't have children is that they don't have spouses. It seems that between the ages of thirty and forty, career-oriented women find it more difficult to find partners. Later, if and when they do want to have children, and are willing to do so even without a partner, they find it more difficult to get pregnant and/or have children.

Why is it difficult for these women to find spouses? Some of the obstacles are related to women's choices; others are men's. Young women born in the 1980s were brought up believing that they could "have it all"—loving spouse, perfect children, nice home, high level of education, fulfilling career—and still have time to work out, meet friends, enjoy vacations and so forth. Most of it is possible when they begin the route towards "having it all"—they get their education (more women than men nowadays obtain graduate degrees), they enter the labor market (many join demanding, time-consuming, highly rewarding, fast-moving careers), they meet the perfect partner (who is both loving and supportive, and shares the burdens of caring for the home they make for themselves together), and even find time to enjoy vacations with that perfect partner, work out, and go out with friends.

But after a while, having children becomes an issue. Because stable dyadic relationships are still considered normative, preferable, and desired, women begin, when they turn thirty, to feel the pressure to enter such a relationship as a prelude to having children. If they are highly educated and with corporate careers, the task is often more difficult than they were led to expect (Roxburgh, 2006).

One reason for the difficulty is that the "perfect partners" seem less willing to make long-term commitments than their parents did, and many choose to remain single far longer than the previous generation (Marsh, Darity, Cohen, Casper, and Salters, 2007). Many among them are certainly not willing to participate in raising their children. Despite the many role changes, most men still consider women the main caretakers of children, and, therefore, incapable of continuing their work if they want children. It seems that they still believe that their own career demands (and their usually higher wages) make it impossible for them to contribute much to the domestic sphere. Hence, if men want children, they often prefer women in more "traditional," less demanding jobs, or in professions that will enable them to devote enough time to their children (Gottfried Eskeles, et al., 1999).

Another difficulty has to do with the growing complications related to maternal age. The older the woman, the more problematic it is to get pregnant and carry the pregnancy to term. Often, women who postpone having children find getting pregnant a grueling task, requiring painful, complex and expensive medical intervention (Haelyon, 2006).

Combining Family and Career

Although the percentage of mothers in the labor force increased from 45% in 1965 to an astonishing 78% in 2000 (Bianchi, Robinson, and Milkie, 2006), most mothers still work part-time, and even when they work full-time they work fewer hours than men (mothers spend thirty-seven hours per week in paid labor, compared with forty-four hours of paid work for fathers [Milkie, Raley, and Bianchi, 2009]). These studies also show that mothers who work full-time and have young children do significantly more housework and childcare than fathers (mothers spend fifteen hours on child care and twenty-one hours on housework per week; fathers who are married to women who work full-time spend only nine hours on child care and fifteen hours on housework per week). This may explain why about 41% of U.S. married mothers of preschoolers are homemakers and only 15% of married mothers of small children work full-time (Bianchi, and Robinson, 2010).

The data may be hiding even larger differences. Mothers who maintain full-time high status careers when their children are young tend to keep in touch with their family more than men (Milkie, Raley, and Bianchi, 2009). They call home more often, and are more accessible, than fathers. They reveal an ability to juggle several responsibilities at the same time, and many of them seem to have highly creative skills, great efficiency, the ability to foresee problems, derive satisfaction even from routine management, and sustain open links with diverse aspects and people they work with. It may be said that their management style is an extension of the lessons that motherhood has taught them (see Chapter Six).

These skills and abilities, however, create a "feminine" management style that is applicable to lower levels of management, claims Rutherford (2001). They become irrelevant or even detrimental to the advancement of women to higher positions. Her conclusion is supported by Wahl's (1998) study of five multinational corporations, which showed that style was dependent on the organizational position of the manager, not his or her gender (see also Rutherford, 2001; Wajcman, 1998). Hence, a "masculine" style[7] (i.e., a controlling approach, executed in an impersonal professional manner, with an emphasis on performance) will be used by both men and women in higher management levels, and a "feminine" style (i.e., a more communicative, caring approach to management with an emphasis on people skills like listening), may be used by both men and women in lower management level (though women tend to choose this style more than men). These findings seem to indicate that while men do not change their management style when they attain higher positions, women are forced to change theirs.

In recent years, as men turned more empathic and women more instrumental, and understanding emotions at the workplace became more important, women's suitability for managerial jobs grew significantly, and it has become more difficult to consider management "a male preserve." Still, these changes did not lead to a major increase in the numbers of women reaching senior levels (Thomson, 1998). Although there is little evidence that women's skills are required in senior management, men's tendency to open up to such skills may indicate that it may be an alternative route to such positions (Moore, 2007; Still, 1994). However, this route may still be viable for men more than for women, who risk being viewed as acting according to stereotypes.

Some researchers (e.g., Powell, 1988) attribute the failure of women to make a radical breakthrough into the senior ranks of management to their failure to adopt the masculine style of management. According to this explanation, a specific (masculine) style is necessary for top management, so that only those who use that style and have the related traits and abilities will attain these positions, regardless of gender. This means that "empathic" (expressive) men find it as difficult to advance to such positions as do women, while women who choose the instrumental style have a better chance. Schein (1994) suggests that women's absence from senior management positions is due to the devaluation of women's qualifications. Hence, even though women have changed, the preconceptions, the discriminatory practices by which managers are promoted, and the preference of men to work with people who are similar to them (i.e., men) still continues.

This seems to be an impossible game to win. Emphasizing the similarities between men and women makes it difficult for women to compete with men on men's terms (Kanter, 1977); emphasizing the differences accentuates women's disadvantages (Cockburn, 1991).

If a growing number of men and women develop more complex management styles, the gender distinction will diminish, and it will become even more difficult to hinder women's upward mobility, or for women to consider management unsuitable for their traits, styles, beliefs and needs. Hence, it seems that if the trend of later marriage, fewer children per woman and higher career aspirations is maintained, more women will choose the option to emphasize work rather than family, and will thus serve as role models.

Self-centered Individual Development

One of the most obvious developments among young women today is that there is no "mainstream." "Be what you want," "choose your style," "you can become anything you wish"—these are some of the claims often heard in the media aimed at teen-aged girls. They are encouraged to do their own thing and be themselves not only by the media, but also by a more egalitarian culture that includes their parents, teachers, trend-setters, pop stars and so forth. Their movies and cultural icons present them with confident, self-reliant, tough, intelligent, independent female lead characters. The coherent messages from such diverse sources seem to have had an impact on the identities and behaviors of young women, but they created a more salient individuation among the girls: there is no specific and unified image of the right way to be, no definitions of a "right" way to act or behave. Hence, there can be no convergence of concerns to attain a common goal.

Moreover, the individualized messages are not necessarily feminist (or perhaps the actions and behaviors they lead to are not easily defined as feminist). Women today often lack feminist awareness or refrain from labeling themselves "feminist," but they act in ways that second-wave feminists would define as feminist (e.g., the strong manager who assertively negotiates salary and benefits, based on her recognition of her unique contributions to the organization and the job, which she does not consider "feminine"); other women may consider themselves feminist, but they act in ways that are undifferentiated from traditional women (e.g., the activities and behaviors of "traditional housewives," who accept the conventional division of roles, are not distinguishable from those of full-time moms whose actions are based on a feminist ideology).

Young women today decide for themselves whether they consider themselves feminist or not, how to be feminists, and what feminism means in their lives, claims McRobbie (2008), developing a new type of feminism which she calls "popular feminism." They refer to the previous feminist ideologies as anachronistic, believing that previous generations have already won the battle for them, attaining equality and freedom of choice. Instead, they develop their own rough language (McRobbie, 2004), often choosing to behave like the boys of their age, to the dismay of older feminists. However:

It is not enough to write this off as girls simply becoming like boys. Even if they are playing at what it is like to be a lad, this in itself is an interesting phenomenon. Our own surprise at the apparent pleasure young women seem to get from subjecting men and boys to the kind of treatment they have come to expect, by virtue of being a girl, is a mark of just how unexpected this kind of response is. One young woman recently described to Women's Realm how "we sit in a café on the quayside eying the male runners as they pass by. For years men have talked about women as though they're pieces of meat. Now we say 'look at the state of this bum, two out of ten,' or 'get a load of this crumpet.'" This kind of reverse sexism can also be seen as a riposte to an older generation of feminist whom younger women now see as weary, white and middle class, academic and professional, and certainly not spunky, vulgar or aggressive. Coming across as loutish and laddish is a provocation to a generation of feminists now established as figures of authority... To these young women official feminism is something that belongs to their mothers' generation (McRobbie, 1999, p. 126).

McRobbie (1999, 2004) refers to this type of "popular feminism" as a cultural shift, which includes the mainstream mass media, the school system and even government agencies, so that popular feminism reaches a much wider audience. As such, it has the potential to transform society in new ways that were not apparent in earlier periods: in informal, unorganized, less ideological, less dictating ways, in which each woman defines her own ways of being valued as a person. Since they have wider cultural support, they may achieve greater equality than previous feminists, even though they do not work as a group to attain their goals. This shift was largely ignored by feminists of earlier generations, because they could not see the effectiveness of the non-ideological individual actions.

In summation, both men and women are changing, so that many aspects of their lives are changing: their traits, attitudes, beliefs, values, preferences, and behaviors. Consequently, the binary division of "male" and "female" identities seems to be less applicable today than it used to be. Diverse and more complex identities (e.g., lesbian, gay, bisexual and transgender) become more noticeable, and, although they are still under-represented in the mainstream media, television shows, magazines, and movies now offer "regular" audiences the chance to get acquainted with the alternatives. Tolerance of sexual diversity is slowly growing in society. This may lead to a wider change in the relations between genders. No longer rigidly defined, the roles men and women play and their ways of interaction may also change to accommodate the new flexibility.

3. The Impact of these Trends on Family Life and Organizational Practices

The many changes that men and women went through had a major impact on both family and work spheres. Some of the changes in these spheres can be clearly seen today; others are just beginning, and are more apparent among trend-setters (e.g., media icons, political figures, social leaders), and are generally legitimized by mass media. Therefore, we should expect the trend to strengthen and become more widespread, reaching broader populations in the near future.

Changing Families

Statistics throughout the Western world show a decline in the proportion of "traditional" families, so that married heterosexuals (mother and father) and their biological children are but a single variation on what a family is. Single parenthood, cohabitation (with or without children), divorced parents having joint custody, gay/lesbian families, and remarried individuals raising children from previous marriages are but a few of the better known alternative patterns that are becoming viable and legally recognized family options in many societies (Lixia, Weston, and de Vaus, 2009).

In Western society, but also in many third-world countries where necessity (rather than liberal, feminist or related ideologies) is the force that leads to change, a wide spectrum of allocations of domestic and work burdens is now legitimized, from the traditional division to the reversal of roles, with all the variations in between. It is, of course, socially acceptable for a couple to choose the "full-time mom" and "breadwinning dad" option, and in some segments of society, it is even considered the best option, as we have seen earlier in the chapter. The "New Families," however, need a different division of roles, and that, too, is legitimized by society. It seems that common to most types of new families is a more egalitarian division of labor (when there is more than one adult in the household), with much more reliance on negotiations as the means to decide who does what and when (Joyner, 2009).

Cohabiting couples, young individuals, and gay and lesbian couples report a stronger desire for equality in family and work responsibilities, with a greater flexibility in the shaping of their lives than their parents had (but see Lindsay, 1999). Men seem less afraid of social stigma if they assume greater responsibility for the domestic sphere than their partners, and they do not tend to consider having a partner who earns more a threat to their masculinity as previous generations tended to feel (Deklyen, Brooks-Gunn, Mclanahan, and Knab, 2006). Likewise, women are not considered "bad partners" if they do less at home but shoulder more of the financial burden.

The question now becomes: how do couples decide how to divide the domestic and work responsibilities? In a recent study (Moore, In Process), respondents in a representative sample of 800 working and non-working men and women in Israel were asked to choose one of three answers to the following question: In your opinion, how should a couple divide family and work responsibilities between them? (1) Most of the work responsibilities should be a man's, most of the family responsibilities should be a woman's; (2) both should contribute equally to family and work responsibilities; (3) both should decide together which division suits them best, and if it suits them that the woman should work and the man will take care of the home, that's fine. Their answers show an interesting pattern: about 70% of the women chose "equality" (option 2) and about 60% of the men chose "joint decision" (option 3), with very few women (about 10%) and men (17%) choosing the "traditional division" (option 1).

Having no theoretical explanation for the different choices of the two gender groups, a focus group was created (comprised of young female graduate students), and the data were presented to them. The explanation that seemed clear to all the participants was that joint decisions indicate negotiations, and men are more successful than women in such situations; men choose this option more frequently because they are surer than women that they can influence the outcomes of the negotiations. Women, on the other hand, knowing that they will not be able to influence the outcomes of negotiations as strongly as men, prefer a clear, à-priori, and non-negotiable division of roles to ensure that they attain equality. Some participants even thought that "negotiation" provides men with flexibility to change the division whenever it suits them, whereas a clear-cut decision to embrace equality is more rigorous. Men, the group seemed to assume, are more prone to pressures at work and know that they may face situations at work in which their previous decisions concerning sharing domestic responsibilities will become irrelevant. Therefore, they wish to allow themselves a wider range of options. Women, on the other hand, attempt to pre-empt these work pressures by defining an equal division.

The focus group also reached a conclusion according to which if women today adopt more instrumental traits, and learn how to negotiate effectively, and if they have high-paying careers, they may succeed in getting their partners to take on a larger share of domestic responsibilities, especially if their partners have also changed and are among the men who adopt a wider range of expressive traits. Such men, more in tune with their feelings than men in previous generations, seeking a stronger bond with their partners and children, tend to grasp the benefits of such relationships and are more willing to share home responsibilities.

Of course, not all men and women are interested in sharing responsibilities. Some still prefer to adhere to the traditional division of roles. But what happens when one partner is traditional and the other is not? The focus groups concluded that when a traditional woman finds herself with a non-traditional partner, she tends to do all that she can to protect what she sees as her domain and make it harder for her partner to share the domestic benefits. (For example, women who choose intensive motherhood and/or prolonged breastfeeding tend to "push" their partners out of intense involvement at home, because one of them has to take care of the financial needs of the family). On the other hand, if a woman is more egalitarian and the man is more traditional, she will do her best to get her partner involved in family life while she shares the financial responsibilities and takes care of her career needs.

Hence, although "traditional" feminists tend to blame men for holding women back to prevent equality in the work sphere, women too should be held accountable for women's unequal treatment in workplaces. They are often as powerful in the domestic sphere as men are in the work sphere. To equally share the benefits of work life, they should also share the benefits of family life. Women seem as reluctant to give up the advantages they enjoy (e.g. the huge benefits of meaningful bonds with their children, being able to choose to not be burdened with breadwinning, having more flexibility in time allocation, and so forth), as men were reluctant to relinquish their advantages at work.

It is not surprising, therefore, that family structure is changing, and so are the family roles. With the growing desire of many women to share domestic responsibility (and their need to do so because of career pressures), and men's willingness to share more equally, many more women have become the major breadwinners for their families. According to Goldstein (2000), the proportion of couples in which the woman is chief breadwinner has been increasing so markedly that nearly one in three working wives nationwide now is paid more than her husband, compared with fewer than one in five in 1980. The trend is particularly pronounced among the most highly educated women, nearly half of whom have incomes higher than their spouses, according to the most recent Federal data. Still, in many cases these women still carry much of the domestic load, claims Goldstein (2000).

It seems logical to conclude, therefore, that families will continue to change: fewer people actually marry (more opt for cohabitation), and therefore the divorce rate will continue to decline, the age of parents will continue to grow, and there will be fewer children per family, thus reducing the burden but making each child more precious to the parents, thus still compelling them to invest in the upbringing of their children. In addition, as men become more in tune with their emotions, and women's earning potential increases, they will more happily change their roles, despite the traditional, age-old accord between husbands and wives.

Changing Organizations

Work organizations, as many social institutions, have already begun to accept these changes. In many work settings, the need to accommodate working parents led to creating solutions that are implemented with growing ease and tolerance. Hence, flexible working hours, job-sharing practices and work-from-home arrangements hinder workers' careers less than in past decades. The technological changes (like video conferences, broadband and high-speed internet access), and the proliferation of communications media that facilitate contacting home (while at work) or work (while at home) further enhance these trends.[8] Furthermore, changes in the structures of organizations create new flexibilities that work better for families. Virtual organizations (i.e., a new temporary organization created by several organizations to work on a project until the goal is accomplished), for example, tend to demand less long-term commitment, with less structured advancement opportunities, and are thus better suited to young individuals—especially women—who are not yet sure of their work-related preferences (Drago, Colbeck, Hollenshead, and Sullivan, 2008).

Another trend that is becoming more noticeable in recent years is that of addressing emotions in organizations. Questions like "Why does #affect matter in organizations?" (Barsade and Gibson, 2007, p. 36) were not asked in the past, when rationality was considered the only way to manage formal organizations, but are highly relevant today.[9]

When research on emotions began (in the 1990s), it focused mainly on how affect is inseparable from work processes: "As emotional arenas, organizations bond and divide their members. Workday frustrations and passions—boredom, envy, fear, love, anger, guilt, infatuation, embarrassment, nostalgia, anxiety—are deeply woven to the roles enacted and learned, power is exercised, trust is held, commitment formed and decisions made" (Fineman, 2006, p. 1).

Dealing with emotions and attempting to harness their energy to increase organizational effectiveness is becoming more widespread (Ashkanasy, Härtel, and Zerbe, 2000; Lewis and Simpson, 2007). As emotions (and emotional behaviors) are associated more strongly with women than with men, accepting the importance of emotions to organizational processes and governance enhances the understanding of women's contributions and increases the roles women can play in organizations (Domagalski, 1999).

Generational Changes:
The Added Complexity of Generation Y

As we have seen, both men and women are changing, and this leads to significant changes in both families and work organizations. But these changes are made more complex by cultural/generational changes that are apparent today. The generation born between the late 1980s and 2000—Generation Y (also referred to as millennials or nets)—are different from what we have come to know in society, in the corporate world, and in families.[10] Young adults of this generation see life as a journey in search of themselves and the fulfillment of their needs, rather than as a series of duties and obligations, of expectations, or of full-time employment. Agility and resilience typify them more than steadfastness and long-term loyalty. They are technologically savvy and enthusiastic about social responsibility, and prefer to work collaboratively (Ferri-Reed, 2010).

According to Childs, Gingrich and Piller (2010), 96% of the millennials belong to at least one social network, often joining a professional network as well. They use these networks to communicate electronically and share their experiences, update friends, and post pictures and videos of their activities. The information often turns into "viral communications" and serves to warn others away from uncooperative workplaces or unpleasant or overbearing bosses, and strengthens members' understanding of what they can or cannot demand or expect. This exposure, combined with millennials' lack of inbred respect for authority and their desire for clear and rapid mobility, makes them a very different type of workforce (Wagner, Docksai and Cohen, 2009).

In addition, the learning styles and expectations of this group are very different from those of earlier generations (Shaw and Fairhurst, 2008): they acquire knowledge quickly and independently (through technology-based information sources as well as social networks); they tend to change jobs— even occupations—rather easily, they get bored quickly and are less willing to accept what they consider unfair treatment or undue hindrance to their self-actualization; and they are bound to have several careers during their lifetimes, in several organizations (Dries, Pepermans, and De Kerpel, 2008), searching for jobs that will allow them to develop their skills and enjoy interesting and fulfilling social relations.

One of the possible consequences of these tendencies is lower stability in both their family and work life. Shifting balances between the two spheres may appear, so that at one period family is more important than work, and at another the wheel turns so that work becomes more central. Social planning as well as organizational forecasts may suffer because of these unpredictable shifts, and new assumptions concerning the relevance of work and constancy in individuals' lives must be made. For example, the notions concerning the suitable worker must change, as should the suppositions concerning how to create and maintain motivation, both of which rely on the assumption that a worker wants to keep on working in the organization, and that the existing rewards (mainly money, benefits, status and/or power) appeal to these workers (Cennamo and Gardner, 2008). But these factors seem less relevant to Generation Y workers. Organizations and social planners must define new ways to manage and motivate these individuals, although most of the planners belong to earlier generations (mostly the baby-boomers or Generation X), which had different needs and desires, and although the tools to develop the skills that generation Y individuals need, such as quick grasping of issues, resilience and adjustment to complexity and change, are not yet easily available (HaeJung, Knight, and Crutsinger, 2009).

The first to acknowledge the need to develop new lines of thinking about expanding skills and new methods for managing these individuals, with their diverse social and family needs, were human resources offices in organizations. Many of their management tools do not suit the needs of Generation Y workers, and they had to adapt to the new requirements of these workers. For example, evaluation of performance can no longer be homogeneous across the organization, as distinct divisions may have different organizational structures and processes, necessitating workers with diverse characteristics, who should be evaluated according to different procedures and measures. Hence, developing individuals in any organization and evaluating their performance entails department- or division-specific methods and measures. The same may be true for even smaller units within the organization (i.e., groups or teams).

Organizations today must relinquish linear thinking when it comes to both their growth and their workers. Though non-linear thinking may increase costs, it ensures the maintaining of high growth rates and the conservation of the most flexible and effective workers. (However, as most decision-makers in organizations belong to earlier generations, either Generation X or Baby-Boomers, they often fail to make the switch to a non-linear, even chaotic way of thinking. [Hurst and Goode, 2009]).

This kind of thinking is especially typical of high-tech organizations and occupations, but it is certainly not limited to them. The change may reach low-tech industries at a slower rate, but it is bound to become a necessity there too. Human resources should prepare for the eventuality, or risk becoming irrelevant: workers in low-tech, in public sector, and in non-profit organizations are bound to be as affected by the new trends, perceptions, attitudes and needs as workers in high-tech ones. Hence, human resources must change their perceptions and practices and help organizations to change. Although in most cases Generation Y workers have not yet reached their highest positions, they may decline managerial jobs if they will not suit their needs, and, therefore, organizations must "tailor" their changes to correspond with those of the potential future managers. The multi-generational organizations generate complexities that lead to the most innovative solutions to working patterns.

Moreover, in addition to dealing with the diverse preferences of distinct professional categories of workers (e.g., the requirements and needs of workers in R&D departments or workers in Sales or Project Management departments), organizations must address issues of multi-culturalism (especially in multi-national organizations, but also in organizations that operate in a single country that is composed of diverse cultural groups), as well as multi-generational issues. Questions of recruitment, developing human assets, organizational learning, talent management, promotion strategies and criteria, and so forth provide new challenges for organizations and their managers, who must now attempt to attract workers and engage them in order to maintain their long-term loyalty.

Because members of Generation Y view their lives as including family and careers, as well as leisure, the existence of flexibility in work options that allows for continued employment while raising a family will be highly valued, especially by women (Bosco and Bianco, 2005). The ability to offer family leave, telecommuting, job sharing, or other flexible work arrangements will be desirable selling points to these potential employees, because those options allow workers to balance their careers and homes. Employers who provide multiple options to these employees who are concerned with career and family balance will clearly have the advantage in attracting and retaining such workers.

Several trends may be found, and are expected to become more noticeable. Both men and women have several legitimate choices of lifestyles: they can choose to work in full- or part-time jobs, or they can choose not to work at all; they can choose whether to marry or stay single, whether to postpone getting married, and whether to have children or not; they can decide to postpone having children until their careers are well established, or choose to turn to part-time employment or quit their jobs until their children reach school age; or they can decide to postpone both marriage and work, and turn to higher education and/or enjoy the freedom available to younger individuals, especially those whose families are well-off and are willing to support them. Given the growing flexibility in many work places, combining these options is feasible in Western societies, and therefore choosing the right alternative for oneself is more confusing for young adults than it has been in the past.

Following Hooks (1998) and others, Bosco and Bianco, (2005) adapted Mash's (1978) Lifestyle Preference Instrument to include eight prevalent life styles, all assuming that young adults work full-time before they marry and/or have children: (a) full-time work, no marriage; (b) full-time work, marriage, no children; (c) full-time work, marriage, children, and continue to work with only minor interruptions for childbirth; (d) full-time work, marriage, children, stop working but return to full-time job before the youngest is in school; (e) full-time work, marriage, children, stop working but return to part-time job before the youngest is in school; (f) full-time work, marriage, children, stop working at least until the youngest is in school, then pursue full-time work; (g) full-time work, marriage, children, stop working until the youngest is in school, then pursue part-time work; and (h) full-time work, marriage, children, stop working. If we apply these optional life styles to both men and women, the number of possible combinations is immense (though not all combinations are viable: for example, a man who wants children and a spouse that does not work when the children are young will probably not choose a spouse who plans to have a full-time career; on the other hand, a woman who desires to apply "Intensive Motherhood" principles will not choose a spouse who wants to work part-time in order to actively participate in raising the children).

According to Bosco and Bianco (2005,) socialization processes will influence the selection of life styles for this generation. They claim that the choices made by Generation Y individuals (and their preferences for their spouses) reflect the lifestyle patterns they were exposed to in their homes. These would depend mostly on the extent of their mothers' employment. Those women whose mothers had worked full-time throughout their childhoods chose a similar lifestyle for themselves, which is indicative of the gender role they learned from their mothers. This, however, does not take into account all the different aspects found in the younger generation, their diverse needs and preferences. Hence, while the influence of the mothers may be noticeable, members of Generation Y require greater flexibility of choice. Even daughters of full-time working mothers may prefer to leave their jobs and become "Full-time Moms."

However, in Israel, these trends are only relevant among the young secular Jewish individuals, and they may not be the majority in their society in the near future. With religious Jews and Arabs propagating at a much higher rate, their proportion in the entire population may decline. The opposing trends—of conservative traditionalism—are strengthening in Israel as well as in other societies.

Conclusions and Extrapolations

All these trends and changes should be viewed in the context of Israeli society. Throughout the book, the focus has been on how the considerable changes in the social context of Israeli society influence individuals (agents), and how changes in the beliefs, perceptions and attitudes of social agents transform the social context (and its rules, traditions, institutions, resources, and moral codes), in accord with Giddens' Structuration Theory (see Chapter One). Moreover, the processes discussed in these chapters support Giddens' assumptions that social life is not the sum of all micro-level activity, and social activity cannot be completely explained from a macro perspective. Both levels must be examined simultaneously in order to understand structuration; the repetition of the acts of individual agents reproduces the structure; and social structures are neither indisputable nor permanent.

Giddens also claims that the significant distinction between cultures today is between traditional and modern (post-traditional) cultures. Traditional societies are those that prescribe social and cultural practices and define normative, sanctioned, and socially acceptable guidelines which social agents follow more or less closely. In contrast, post-traditional (modern) societies are societies in which a larger repertoire of behavioral options is available to social agents and socially legitimated. Members in such societies become more reflexive as they constantly make decisions and choices concerning all aspects of their behavior in a changing world. The shift from traditional to post-traditional societies is a gradual, often slow process. The structuration process that yields new practices encounters diverse constraints, and not all systems change at the same rate. Some of the systems are more resistant to change, and their power structures exercise their ability to block trends that will decrease their advantage.

However, examination of developments in Israeli society shows that it changes from a predominantly mobilized, enlisted, collectivistic, and socialist society to a multi-cultural society in which two main trends (with many variations in each) compete for dominance: (1) the liberal trend—toward a universalist, individualistic, pluralistic, open-to-outside-influences, flexible society, with weakening categorizations (of ethnic, gender, educational groups) and greater tolerance for competing ideologies and lifestyles; and (2) the conservative trend—toward a religion-oriented, traditionalist, particularistic society, attempting to avoid influences from competing ideologies and values to prevent normative changes.

Moreover, these processes have led to significant changes in the categorizations within Israeli society. Thus, some of the quasi-dichotomous distinctions have eroded (e.g. the ethnic distinction between Mizrahi and Ashkenazi), and were replaced by more pluralistic distinctions (which include the Ethiopian and Russian Jews as additional categories). Similar processes can be seen regarding the clear-cut Left-Socialist /Right-Capitalist distinction, which has become a continuum with most Israelis considering themselves "Center"; the education that has become available to all members of society, not only to the privileged Jews of Western origin; and the erosion of polarized gender roles, which has allowed women to share the benefits and burdens of employment, and so forth. Still, other distinctions have become more pronounced (e.g., the gap between rich and poor has grown, as did the one between center and periphery). The most distinct gap has grown between religious and secular, conservative and liberal, and between those whose world view emphasizes Israel as the Promised Land of the Jews and those whose world view sees Israel as one of the world's nations. The overlapping of these categories (the religious conservatives, who consider Israel the Promised Land, versus the secular liberals, who consider Israel part of the world) and their dichotomous (bi-polar) nature, seem to dictate distinct lifestyles and identities.

According to Giddens' approach, every agent chooses the lifestyle that best suits him or her, constrained by the social system. Because of the societal changes in Israel, some of the lifestyles that were considered mainstream or desirable in the past (like the tough, macho fighter who heavily relied on the military comrades who formed his social network) are no longer legitimated. Other lifestyles, more in tune with the societal changes in the twenty-first century with its technological changes and the globalization processes it enables, seem to have become more visible and legitimate (e.g., the metrosexual, the liberal male, the career woman), encouraging the development of suitable self-identities. The new lifestyles are the products of the complex multiplicity of practices that exists in Israeli society and reflects its varied structures.

The social forces that limit agents' choices and actions become apparent in those instances where agents attempt to disregard social rules. Thus, "straying" from the path is possible for those who follow the first (liberal) trend, but not for those who follow the second (conservative) one. Those who are part of the second trend, but attempt to resist conventions or breach the accepted codes of "normal" behavior, encounter categorical, even angry, negative reactions and sanctioning. Moreover, those adhering to the liberal trend have the option to choose a more conservative lifestyle without societal opposition, but not vice versa.

In modern and well-developed societies, self-identity becomes an inescapable issue, and all individuals have to decide who to be and how to act, and consequently about all spheres of their lives from relationships, beliefs and occupations to choice of clothes and life styles. In more traditional societies, the social orders are much less complex, change is slower, and structuration processes provide social agents with much greater stability and more clearly defined roles. In post-traditional societies, self-identity is more than a set of traits or observable characteristics: it makes sense of a person's life and his or her actions; it provides structure to his or her past experiences and creates continuity between these experiences and future expectations. The social context of diverse changes, some of which lead to a more liberal society while others lead other social agents in the opposite (conservative) direction, adds complexity to the choices of self-identities and lifestyles.

The antagonistic relationship between the two trends that compete for dominance in Israel, with the lifestyles they encourage and their related behaviors, is exacerbated by the three categories of structures in social systems:

Signification (which produces meaning through the use of language)— The liberal trends encourage multiple voices to co-exist, finding beauty and even social necessity in the varied interpretations of meanings. Thus, the new trends of the younger generation (discussed earlier in the chapter) are willingly accepted and legitimized. The conservative trend, on the other hand, demands uniformity. Though it is willing to accept some variations within the religious context, it is mostly unwilling to accept secular variations and consequently secular representations are expunged from the public sphere of the religious/conservative world (e.g., the ban on presenting any and all pictures of women in public places throughout Orthodox neighborhoods, the prohibition on owning television sets or watching television programs, and the avoidance of secular culture). The followers of the two trends usually have limited knowledge of each other and often misunderstand each other.

Legitimation (which produces a moral order by way of societal norms and values)—The liberal trends tolerate a multiplicity of value systems. It thus accepts diverse sexual preferences and varied social and political attitudes, even those that negate their own values of tolerance and acceptance of variety. The conservative trend, on the other hand, expects its value system to supersede all others. Seeing its morality as superior to all others, even perhaps the only way which is right for Jews, the trend and its adherents attempt to impose their normative system (the religious law) on the entire Israeli society (seculars and non-Jews included). The (secular) Israeli Supreme Court even ruled three years ago that it is legitimate to build whole neighborhoods defined "for religious Jews only," but building only for secular Jews is prohibited, because such a separation is legitimate according to the religious value system but it is not sanctioned by the secular one.

Domination (which produces [and makes use of] power through the control of resources)—Encouraging plurality, the liberal trend finds it difficult to mobilize individuals to participate in any specific cause. The conservative trend, on the other hand, has the ability to organize mass demonstrations or to activate massive crowds to attain their goals. When the rabbis decide on a cause, their followers hurry to obey. Their ability to marshal resources (both financial and human) is far superior to that of the opposing trend.

These analytical distinctions are interrelated, and they both mobilize and reinforce each other, according the upper hand to the conservative trend. If they continue in the same vein, the secular segments which now compose about half of the entire Jewish population will become the dominated class. The shift from traditional to post-traditional societies is a gradual, often slow process, claims Giddens (1998). The structuration process that yields new practices encounters diverse constraints. Some of the systems are more resistant to change, and their power structures exercise their ability to block trends that will decrease their advantage. As a result, attempts to enforce modernization often fail, as they deal with but a segment of the system that needs to be changed, not with its practices, norms and values. Similarly, when the fundamental institutions refuse to become modern, as in the Israeli case, and the leaders enforce traditions so that they do not change, the attempt to modernize society is likely to fail. Still, the growing availability of cellular phones, and the spreading of internet use (still banned in most Ultra-Orthodox homes), may open the younger generation of this group to the options existing in Western societies, suggest new possible identities, and make them aware of alternative, attractive lifestyles to choose from. Opposing their leaders is not easy, but some breaking away from strict Orthodoxy is noticeable even today, and responsiveness to religious authority among some adolescent men is eroding. If these young men will be allowed to join the Israeli army, and to perform their duty for three years like the secular and less Orthodox men, the hold of separatist Orthodox institutions over them may decline even further. It also remains to be seen whether the secular, highly educated, often better off will be able to unite to defend their beliefs.

ENDNOTES

1 For example, in the UK, Statutory Maternity Pay is six weeks with 90% pay and up to thirty-three further weeks with a flat rate of £123.06, or 90% pay, whichever is less; in Israel it is fourteen weeks with full pay and up to a year after which the employer must rehire the mother.

2 The term was coined by Mark Simpson in 1994 (in the Independent), but gained acceptance more rapidly in Simpson's 2002 salon.com publication: http://dir.salon.com/story/ent/feature/2002/07/22/metrosexual/index.html and David Coad's (2008) book by that name.

3 Moreover, men are not considered caregivers in many third-world countries (Coltrane, 2004; DeWolff and van Ijzendoorn, 1997). Many children in the world miss years with their fathers because of parental separation, migration of a parent to seek work, death of a parent, and other factors. Percent of childhood years spent with a mother only: Ecuador 7%; Mali 8%; Peru 9%; Brazil 9%; Colombia 13%; Dominican Republic 14%; Senegal 16%; Kenya 27%; Ghana 29%; Zimbabwe 30%; Botswana 36% (Barker, 2009; Howard, Dryden, and Johnson, 1999). Between 10% and 30% of developing country households are officially defined as female-headed. In countries with the highest rates of men's migration and/or low marriage rates, such as the Caribbean, the proportion can reach 50%.

4 Still, a review of studies of 156 societies found that only 20% promoted men's close relationships with infants, and only 5% with young children. Fewer countries provide prolonged leave or financial considerations for fathers upon the births of their children.

5 Other terms refer to similar practices are "Natural Parenting," "Instinctive Parenting," "Intuitive Parenting," and "Immersion Parenting."

6 The term was introduced by the U.S. Census Bureau to describe different family configurations.

7 From the earliest structuring of formal ("scientific") management, it was defined in terms of traits like precision, objectivity, impartiality, rationality and control, which were perceived as associated with masculinity, emphasizes Rutherford (2001). That was done to prevent irrational and unpredictable personalized control, based on feelings and emotions. Women were considered incapable of such masculine traits and behaviors.

8 This leads to new problems that stem from the blurring of family-work boundaries. However, dealing with these issues is beyond the scope of this book.

9 The first conference on emotions in organizations was held in 1998, before the meeting of the Academy of Management in San Diego,

10 Generation Z, who were born since then, are of less interest in this context as they have not reached work age yet, and little is known about them except that

they are highly technological with a short attention span and great multi-tasking capability, and tend to have a pampered and egocentric view of the world ("I am the center of my parents' universe and therefore I expect everybody else to see me the same way"). Very little research exists so far on this generation because of its youth.

REFERENCES

Abele, A. E. (2003). The dynamics of masculine-agentic and feminine-communal traits: Findings from a prospective study. *Journal of Personality and Social Psychology*, 85, 768–776.

Adler, M. A. (1997). Social change and declines in marriage and fertility in Eastern Germany. *Journal of Marriage and the Family*, 59, 37-49.

Adler, M. A. (2002). Working women and the dynamics of power at work. In B. Berberoglu (Ed.), *Labor and capital in the age of globalization: The labor process and the changing of work in the global economy*. Lanham, MD: Rowman and Littlefield.

Agassi, J. B. (1989). Theories of gender equality: Lessons from the Israeli Kibbutz. *Gender and society*, 3, 160-186.

Aiba, K., & Wharton, A. S. (2001). Job-level sex composition and the sex pay gap in a large Japanese firm. *Sociological Perspectives*, 44, 67-87.

Ajzenstadt, M., & Gal, J. (2001). Appearances can be deceptive: Gender in the Israeli welfare state. *Social Politics*, 8, 292-324.

Alderfer, C. P. (1972). *Existence, relatedness, and growth: Human needs in organizational settings*. New York: Free Press.

Al-Haj, M., & Leshem, E. (2000). *Immigrants from former Soviet Union in Israel: Ten years later: A research report*. Haifa: The Center for Multiculturalism and Educational Research, University of Haifa.

Altman, S. L., & Grossman, F. K. (1977). Women's career plans and maternal employment. *Psychology of Women Quarterly*, 1, 365-376.

Amato, P. R. (2000). The consequences of divorce for adults and children. *Journal of Marriage and the Family*, 62, 1269–1287.

Amir, D., & Benjamin, O. (1997). Defining encounters: Who are the women entitled to join the Israeli collective? *Women's Studies International Forum*, 20, 5-6.

Amsden, A. H. (Ed.). (1979). *The economics of women and work*. New York: Penguin Books, Readings in Economic Series.

Andersen, M. L. (1993). *Thinking about women: Sociological perspectives on sex and gender*. New York: Macmillan.

Anderson, B. S. (2000). *Joyous greetings: The first international women's rights movement, 1830-1860*. Oxford, UK: Oxford University Press.

Anderson, C. D., & Tomaskovic-Devey, D. (1995). Patriarchal pressures: An exploration of organizational processes that exacerbate and erode gender earnings inequality. *Work and Occupations*, 22, 328-356.

Anderson, E. (2005) Orthodox and inclusive masculinity: Competing masculinities among heterosexual men in a feminized terrain. *Sociological Perspectives*, 48, 337-355.

Antecol, H. (2001). Why is there interethnic variation in the gender wage gap? The role of cultural factors. *Journal of Human Resources*, 36, 119-143.

Antonucci, T. C. (2001). Social Relations: An examination of social networks, social support, and sense of control. In J. E. Birren, & K. Warner Schai (Eds.), *Handbook of the psychology of aging* (5th edition) (pp. 427-453). San Diego, CA: Academic Press.

Aquilino, W. S. (1996). The life course of children born to unmarried mothers: Childhood living arrangements and young adult outcomes. *Journal of Marriage and the Family*, 58, 293–310.

Arendell, T. (2000). Conceiving and investigating motherhood: The decade's scholarship. *Journal of Marriage and the Family*, 62, 1192-1207.

Ariel, M., & Giora, R. (1998). A self versus other point of view in language: Redefining femininity and masculinity. *International Journal of Sociology of Language*, 129, 59-86.

Arnolds, C. A., & Boshoff, C. (2002). Compensation, esteem valence and job performance: An empirical assessment of Alderfer's ERG theory. *International Journal of Human Resource Management,* 13, 697-719.

Ashforth, B. E., & Mael, F. (1989). Social identity theory and the organization. *Academy of Management Review,* 14, 20-39.

Ashkanasy, N. M., Härtel, C. E. J., & Zerbe, W. J. (Eds). (2000). *Emotions in the workplace: Research, theory, and practice.* Westport, CT: Greenwood Publishing.

Ashmore, R. D., Del Boca, F. K., & Wohlers, A. J. (1986). Gender stereotypes. In R. D. Ashmore & F. K. Del Boca (Eds.), *The social psychology of female-male relations.* Orlando, FL: Academic Press.

August, R. A., & Quintero, V. C. (2001). The role of opportunity structures in older women workers' careers. *Journal of Employment Counseling,* 38, 62-81.

Auster, D. (1978). Occupational values of male and female nursing students. *Sociology of Work and Occupations,* 5, 209-233.

Auster, E. R. (2001). Professional women's midcareer satisfaction: Toward an explanatory framework. *Sex Roles: A Journal of Research,* 44, 719-750.

Avishai, O. (2008). Halakhic niddah consultants and the orthodox women's movement in Israel: Evaluating the story of enlightened progress. *Journal of Modern Jewish Studies,* 7, 195-216.

Ayalon, H. (2000). Differences between men and women in the choice of academics fields of study. *Israeli Sociology,* 8, 523-544.

Baloush-Kleinman, V., & Sharlin, S. A. (2004). Social, economic, and attitudinal characteristics of cohabitation in Israel. *Journal of Family and Economic Issues,* 25, 255-269.

Baltes, B. B., & Heydens-Gahir, H. A. (2003). Reduction of work-family conflict through the use of selection, optimization, and compensation behaviors. *Journal of Applied Psychology,* 88, 1005-1014.

Barak-Erez, Yanisky-Dvir, D., S., Biton, Y., & Fugach, D. (2007). *Studies of law, gender and feminism.* Qiriat Ono: Nevo Publications. (Hebrew).

Barker, G. (2009). Capacity-building for mainstreaming a gender perspective into national policies and programmes to support the equal sharing of responsibilities between women and men, including care-giving in the context of HIVC/AIDS. *United Nations.* Retrieved from *http://www.un.org/womenwatch/daw/csw/csw53/panels/capacity-buidling/barker.pdf*

Barker, G. (2009). *Engaging men and boys in Caregiving: Reflections from research, practice and policy Advocacy.* Presented at the United Nations, Commission on the Status of Women, Fifty-third session, New York (March 2—13, 2009).

Barnett, R. C., Gareis, K. C., & Brennan, R. T. (1999). Fit as a mediator of the relationships between work hours and burnout. *Journal of Occupational Health Psychology*, 4, 307-317.

Barnett, R. Barsade, S., & Gibson, D. E. (2007). Why does affect matter in organizations? *Academy of Management Perspectives*, 21, 36-59.

Bartol, K. M. (1978). The sex structuring of organizations: A search for possible causes. *Academy of Management Review*, 3, 805-815.

Baum, D. (2006). Women in black and men in pink: Protesting against the Israeli occupation. *Social Identities,* 12, 563-574.

Baum, N., Rahav, G., & Sharon, D. (2005). Changes in the self-concepts of divorced women. *Journal of Divorce and Remarriage*, 43, 47-68.

Baumgardner, J., & Richards, A. (2000). *ManifestA: Young women, feminism, and the future.* New York: Farrar, Straus and Giroux.

Baumgardner, J., & Richards, A. (2004). Feminism and femininity: Or how we learned to stop worrying and love the thong. In A. Harris (Ed.), *All about the girl: Power, culture and identity (pp. 59-68).* New York: Routledge.

Baumgardner, J., & Richards, A. (2005). *Grassroots: A field guide for feminist activism.* New York: Farrar, Straus and Giroux Paperbacks.

Baumond, D. (1972). From each according to her ability. *School Review,* 80, 1961-1990.

Beck, D., & Davis, E. (2005). EEO in senior management: Women executives in Westpac. *Asia Pacific Journal of Human Resources,* 43, 273-288.

Beck, E. M., Horan, P. M., & Tolbert, C. M. (1980). Industrial segmentation and labor market discrimination. *Social Problems,* 28, 113-130.

Beck, U., Giddens, A. & Lash, S. (1994). *Reflexive modernization. Politics, tradition and aesthetics in the modern social order.* Cambridge: Polity Press

Becker, G. S. (1964). *Human capital.* New York: National Bureau of Economic Research.

Becker, G. S. (1971). *The economics of discrimination.* Chicago: University of Chicago Press.

Becker, G. S. (1993). *Human capital* (3rd edition). Chicago: University of Chicago Press.

Beller, A. H. (1984). Trends in occupational segregation by sex and race: 1960-1981. In B. F. Reskin (Ed.), *Sex segregation in the workplace: Trends, explanations, remedies.* Washington, D.C.: National Academy Press.

Bem, S. L. (1974). The measurement of psychological androgyny. *Journal of Consulting and Clinical Psychology,* **42,** 155–162.

Bem, S. L. (1981). Gender schema theory: A cognitive account of sex typing. *Psychological Review,* 88, 354-364.

Bem, S. L. (1987). Masculinity and femininity exist only in the mind of the perceiver. In J. Machover, L. A. Rosenblum, & S. A. Sanders (Eds.). *Masculinity/femininity, basic perspectives.* New York: Oxford University Press.

Bem, S. L. (1993). *The lenses of gender: Transforming the debate on sexual inequality.* New Haven: Yale University Press.

Ben-Ari, E., Rosenhek, Z. & Maman, D. (2001).The military, state and society in Israel: An introductory essay". In D. Maman, E. Ben-Ari & Z. Rosenhek (Eds.). *The military, state and society in Israel: Theoretical and comparative perspectives* (pp. 1-39). New Brunswick, NJ: Transaction Publishers.

Ben David, J. (1963). Professions in the class system of present-day societies. *Current Sociology,* 12, 247-298.

Ben Rafael. E., Olshtein, E., & Geijst E. (1998). Identity and Language: The social insertion of Soviet Jews in Israel. In E. Leshem, & J. T. Shuval (Eds.), *Immigration to Israel: Sociological Perspectives.* NY: Transaction Publishers.

Benbow, C. P. (1988). Sex differences in mathematical reasoning ability in intellectually talented preadolescents: Their nature, effects, and possible causes. *The Behavioral and Brain Sciences*, 11, 169-183.

Ben-David, A. (1996). The narrative of life: Immigrant women in single-parent families. *Journal of Feminist Family Therapy*, 8, 29-45.

Benjamin, O., & Barash, T. (2004). 'He thought I would be like my mother': The silencing of Mizrachi women in Israeli inter- and intra-marriages. *Ethnic and Racial Studies*, 27, 266-289.

Benjamin, O., & Ha'elyon, H. (2004). Silenced reality: Power relations between marital blueprints in Israeli marriages. *Symbolic Interaction*, 27, 461-483.

Ben-Zur, H., & Zeidner, M. (1988). Sex differences in anxiety, curiosity, and anger: A cross-cultural study. *Sex Roles: A Journal of Research*, 19, 335-347.

Berger, J., Cohen, B. P., & Zelditch, M. (1973). Status characteristics and social interaction. In R. Ofshe (Ed.), *Interpersonal behavior in small groups.* Englewood Cliffs, New Jersey: Prentice Hall.

Berger, J., Wagner, D. G., & Zelditch, M., Jr. (1985). Expectations state theory: review and assessment. In J. Berger, & M. Zelditch (Eds.), *Status rewards and influence: How expectations organize behavior.* San Francisco: Jossey-Bass.

Bergman, B. R. (1974). Occupational segregation, wages and profits when employers discriminate by race or sex. *Eastern Economic Journal*, 1, 103-110

Bergman, B. R. (1986). *The economic emergence of American women.* New York: Basic Books.

Berkeley, K. C. (1999). *The women's liberation movement in America.* Westport, Connecticut: Greenwood Press.

Berkowitz, S. J. (2003). Can we stand with you? Lessons from women in black for global feminist activism. *Women and Language, 26,* 94-99.

Bernstein, A., & Galily, Y. (2008). Games and sets: Women, media and sport in Israel. *Nashim: A Journal of Jewish Women's Studies and Gender Issues,* 15, 175-196. (Hebrew).

Bernstein, D. S. (1983). Economic growth and female labour: The case of Israel. *The Sociological Review,* 31, 263-292.

Bernstein, D. S. (1992). Introduction. In D. S. Bernstein, (Ed.) *Pioneers and homemakers: Jewish women in pre-state Israel* (pp. 1-20). New York: SUNY, Series in Israeli Studies.

Bernstein, D. S., & Swirski, S. (1982). The rapid economic development of Israel and the emergence of the ethnic division of labour. *The British Journal of Sociology,* 23, 64-86.

Bianchi, S. M., Robinson, J. R., & Milkie, M. A. (2006). *Changing rhythms of American family life.* New York: Russell Sage.

Bianchi, S. M., & Robinson, J. R. (2010). *National survey of parents, 2000-2001.* Retrieved on February 6, 2010, from *http://www.icpsr. umich.edu/icpsrweb/ICPSR/studies/4247* .

Bibb, R., & Form, W. H. (1977). The effects of industrial, occupational and sex stratification on wages in blue collar markets. *Social Forces,* 55, 974-997.

Bielby, D. (1992). Commitment to work and family. *Annual Review of Sociology,* 18, 281-302.

Bielby, D., & Bielby, W. T. (1984). Work commitment, sex- role attitudes, and women's employment. *American Sociological Review,* 49, 234-247.

Bielby, W. T., & Baron, J. N. (1984). A woman's place is with other women: Sex segregation in the workplace. In B. Reskin (Ed.), *Sex segregation in the workplace: Trends, explanations, remedies.* Washington, D.C.: National Academy Press.

Blackmore, J. (1997). Level playing field? Feminist observations on global/local articulations of the re-gendering and restructuring of educational work. *International Review of Education / Internationale Zeitschrift fur Erziehungswissenschaft / Revue Internationale de Pedagogie,* 43, 439-461.

Blau, F., & Jusenius, C. (1976). Economists' approaches to sex segregation in the labor market: An appraisal. In M. Blaxall, & B. Reagan (Eds.), *Women and the work place.* Chicago: University of Chicago Press.

Blau, F. D. (1977). *Equal pay in the office.* Lexington, MA: Lexington Books.

Blau, F. D., & Ferber, M. A. (1986). *The economics of women, men and work.* Englewood Cliffs, NJ: Prentice Hall.

Blau, F. D., & Ferber, M. A. (1987). Occupations and earnings of women workers. In K. S. Koziara, M. H. Moskow, & L. D. Tanner (Eds.), *Working women: Past, present, future* (pp. 37-68). Washington, DC: Bureau of National Affairs, Inc.

Blossfeld, H. P., & Huinink, J. (1991). Human capital investments or norms of role transition? How women's schooling and career affect the process of family formation. *The American Journal of Sociology,* 97, 143-168.

Blumberg, R. L. (1979). A paradigm for predicting the position of women: Policy implications and problems. In J. Lipman Blumen, & J. Bernard (Eds.), *Sex roles and social policy.* Beverly Hills, Calif.: Sage Publications.

Blumen, O. (2002). Criss-crossing boundaries: Ultraorthodox Jewish women go to work. *Gender, Place and Culture,* 9, 133-151.

Bogoch, B. (1997). Gendered lawyering: Difference and dominance in lawyer-client interaction. *Law and Society Review*, 31, 677-712.

Bogoch, B. (1999). Courtroom discourse and the gendered construction of professional identity. *Law and Society*, 24, 329-375.

Borman, C. A., & Guido DiBrito, F. (1986). The career development of women: Helping Cinderella lose her complex. *Journal of Career Development*, 12, 250-261.

Bosco, S. M., & Bianco, C. A. (2005). Influence of maternal work patterns and socioeconomic status on Gen Y lifestyle choice. *Journal of Career Development*, 32, 165-182.

Botting, E. H. (2006). Mary Wollstonecraft's enlightened legacy: The modern social imaginary of the egalitarian family. *The American Behavioral Scientist*, 49, 687-702.

Botting, E. H., & Carey, C. (2004). Wollstonecraft's philosophical impact on nineteenth-century American women's rights advocates. *American Journal of Political Science*, 48, 707-722.

Bowen. D. D. (1985). Were men meant to mentor women? *Training and Development Journal*, 39, 31-34.

Bowes, A. (1978). Women in the Kibbutz movement. *The Sociological Review*, 26, 237-262.

Brainerd, E. (2000). Women in transition: Changes in gender wage differentials in Eastern Europe and the former Soviet Union. *Industrial and Labor Relations Review*, 54, 138-162.

Brandow, S. K. (1980). Ideology, myth, and reality: Sex equality in Israel. *Sex Roles: A Journal of Research*, 6, 403-419.

Braver, S. L., & O'Connell, E. (1998). *Divorced dads: Shattering the myths*. New York: Tarcher, Putnam.

Bridges, W. P. (1980). Industrial marginality and female employment: a new appraisal. *American Sociological Review*, 45, 58-75.

Broverman, I. K., Broverman, D. M., Clarkson, F. E., Rosenkrantz, P.S., & Vogel, S.R. (1970). Sex-role stereotypes and clinical judgments of mental health. *Journal of Counseling and Clinical Psychology*, 34, 1–7.

Bryant, C. G. A., & Jary, D. (2001). *The contemporary Giddens: Social theory in a globalizing age.* Palgrave: Macmillan.

Budig, M. J. (2002). Male advantage and the gender composition of jobs: Who rides the glass escalator? *Social Problems*, 49, 258-277.

Budig, M. J., & England, P. (2001). The wage penalty for motherhood. *American Sociological Review*, 66, 204-225.

Burke, E. (1986). *Reflections on the revolution in France.* New York: Penguin Books.

Burke, R. J. (1984). Mentors in organizations. *Group and Organization Studies*, 9, 353-372.

Burke, R. J., & McKeen, C. A. (1996). Gender effects in mentoring relationships. Journal of Social Behavior and Personality, 11, 91-104.

Bushardt, S. C., & Allen, B. (1988). Role ambiguity in the male/female protégé relationship. Equal Opportunity International, 7, 5-8.

Butler, J. (1986). Sex and gender in Simone de Beauvoir's 'Second Sex'. *Yale French Studies*, 72, 35-49.

Caine, B. (1997). *English feminism, 1780-1980.* New York: Oxford University Press.

Calandra, B. (2002). Teaching to learn: Scientists who balance teaching and research enjoy rewards and recharging. *The Scientist*, 17, 51.

Canter, R. J. (1979). Achievement - related expectations and aspirations in college women. *Sex Roles: A Journal of Research*, 5, 453-469.

Cappelli, P., Constantine, J., & Chadwick, C. (2000). It pays to value family: Work and family tradeoffs reconsidered. *Industrial Relations*, 39, 175-198.

Carlson, D. S., & Kacmar, K. M. (2000). Work–family conflict in the organization: Do life role values make a difference? *Journal of Management, 26, 5.*

Casad, B. J. (2008). Issues and trends in work–family integration. In A. Marcus-Newhall, D. F. Halpern, & S. J. Tan (Eds.), *The changing realities of work and family* (pp. 277-292). New York: Wiley-Blackwell.

Catter, L. A., Scott, A. F., & Martyna, W. (1977). *Women and men: Changing roles, relationships, and perceptions.* New York: Praeger Publishers.

Cennamo, L., & Gardner, D. (2008). Generational differences in work values, outcomes and person-organisation values fit. *Journal of Managerial Psychology, 23,* 891-906.

Central Bureau of Statistics. (1955). *The yearbook,* Vol. 18. p. 21.

Central Bureau of Statistics. (1956). *Registration of population (Part B).* Special Publications Series, 53. Jerusalem, Israel.

Central Bureau of Statistics. (1957). *Labor force survey, 1954* (Table 42, p.70). Special Publications Series, 56. Jerusalem, Israel.

Central Bureau of Statistics. (1968). *Labor force survey, 1964-1966.* Special Publications Series, 243. Jerusalem, Israel.

Central Bureau of Statistics. (1970). *Statistical abstract of Israel* (pp. 274, 292). Jerusalem, Israel.

Central Bureau of Statistics. (2007). *The statistical yearbook* (Figure 4.4). Jerusalem, Israel.

Central Israel Bureau of Statistics (2008a). *Social Indicators survey, 2002-2004.* Press Release 74/2006, April 9, 2006. Jerusalem, Israel. (Retrieved from *http//:www1.cbs.gov.il/reader/*)

Central Israel Bureau of Statistics (2008b). *Society in Israel.* Report No. 1: *Social Indicators survey.* Jerusalem, Israel.

Central Bureau of Statistics (2008c). *Labor force survey, 1996-2006.* Special Publication Series. Jerusalem, Israel. *http://www.cbs.gov.il/www/statistical/population.htm*

Chafetz, J. S. (1988). *Feminist sociology: An overview of contemporary theories.* New York: Cengage Learning.

Chafetz, J. S. (1990). *Gender equity: An integrated theory of stability and change.* New York: Sage.

Chafetz, J. S., & Dworkin, A. G. (1986). *Female revolt: Women's movements in world and historical perspective.* New York: Rowman and Littlefield.

Chafetz, J. S., Lorence, J., & Larosa, C. (1993). Gender depictions of the professionally employed: A content analysis of trade publications, 1960-1990. *Sociological Perspectives,* 36, 63-82.

Charles, M. (1992). Cross-national variations in occupational sex segregation. *American Sociological Review,* 57, 483-502.

Chasmir, L. H. (1982). Job commitment and the organizational women. *Academy of Management Review,* 7, 595-602.

Chassin, L., Zeiss, K., Cooper, K., & Reaven, J. (1985). Role perceptions, self-role congruence and marital satisfaction in dual career couples with pre-school children, *Social Psychology Quarterly,* 48, 301-311.

Cinamon, R. G. (2006). Anticipated work-family conflict: Effects of gender, self-efficacy, and family background. *Career Development Quarterly,* 54, 202-215.

Cinamon, R. G., & Rich, Y. (2002a). Gender differences in the importance of work and family roles: Implications for work-family conflict. *Sex Roles: A Journal of Research,* 47, 531-541.

Cinamon, R. G., & Rich, Y. (2002b). Profiles of attribution of importance to life roles and their implications for the work-family conflict. *Journal of Counseling Psychology,* 49, 212-220.

Cinamon, R. G., & Rich, Y. (2005). Work-family conflict among female teachers. *Teaching and Teacher Education,* 21, 365-378.

Clarke-Stewart, K. A., Vandell, D. L., McCartney, K., Owen, M. T., & Booth, C. (2000). Effects of parental separation and divorce on very young children. *Journal of Family Psychology,* 13, 304–326.

Clawson, J. G., & Kram, K. E. (1984). Managing cross-gender mentoring. *Business Horizons, 27,* 22-32.

Cleveland, J., Stockdale, N. M., & Murphy, K. R. (2000). *Women and men in organizations: Sex and gender issues at work.* Mahwah, NJ, US: Lawrence Erlbaum Associates.

Cleveland, J. N. (2008). Age, work, and family: Balancing unique challenges for the twenty-first century. In A. Marcus-Newhall, D. F. Halpern, & S. J. Tan (Eds.), *The changing realities of work and family* (pp. 108-139). New York: Wiley-Blackwell.

Coad, D. (2008). The metrosexual: Gender, sexuality, and sport. New York: SUNY Press.

Cockburn, C. (1991). *In the way of women: Men's resistance to sex equality in organizations.* Basingstoke: Macmillan.

Cockburn, C. (1991). *Brothers: Male dominance and technological change.* London: Pluto Press

Code, L. (2000). *Encyclopedia of feminist theories.* London: Routledge/ Taylor and Francis Group.

Cohen, I. J. (1987). Structuration Theory and Social Praxis. In A. Giddens, & J. Turner (Eds.), *Social theory today* (pp. 273-308). Stanford: Stanford University Press.

Cohen, L. D. (1991). Sex differences in the course of personality development: A meta-analysis. *Psychological Bulletin,* 109, 252-266.

Cohen, Y., & Pfeffer, J. (1984). Employment practices in the dual economy. *Industrial relations,* 23, 58-72.

Cohen, Y., & Stier, H. (2006). The rise in involuntary part-time employment in Israel. *Research in Social Stratification and Mobility,* 24, 41-54.

Coltrane, S. (2004). Fathering: Paradoxes, contradictions, and dilemmas. In M. Coleman, & L. Ganong (Eds.), *Handbook of contemporary families: Considering the past, contemplating the future* (pp. 224-243). Thousand Oaks, CA: Sage.

Connell, R. W. (1993). Men and the women's movement. *Social Policy*, 23, 72-78.

Cook, R. J. (1994). *Human rights of women: National and international perspectives*. Philadelphia, PA: University of Pennsylvania Press.

Cooke, R., & Rousseau, D. (1984). Stress and strain from family roles and work role expectations. *Journal of Applied Psychology*, 69, 252-260.

Coolsen, P. (1990). Work and family: Times have changed. *Families in Society*, 71, 323-376.

Coser, R. L., & Rokoff, G. (1971). Women in the occupational world: Social disruption and conflict. *Social Problems*, 18, 535-554.

Cowan, R. S. (1983). *More work for mother*. NY: Basic Books.

Crary, D. (2009, May 6). Obama's presidency puts fatherhood in a new focus. *The Philadelphia Inquirer*. Retrieved from *http://www.philly.com/inquirer /world_us/20090506 _Obama_s_presidency_puts_fatherhood_in_a_new_focus.html*

Crites, J. O., & Fitzgerald, L. F. (1978). The competent male. *Counseling Psychologist*, 7, 10-14.

Crompton, R., & Harris, F. (1998). Explaining women's employment patterns: 'Orientations to work' revisited. *British Journal of Sociology*, 49, 118–136.

Crosby, F. J. (1987). Introduction. In F. J. Crosby (Ed.), *Spouse, parent, worker: On gender and multiple roles*. New Haven: Yale University Press.

Crosby, F. J. (1991). *Juggling: The unexpected advantages of balancing career and home for women and their families*. New York: Free Press.

Crosby, F. J., & Jaskar, K. L. (1993). Women and men at home and at work: Realities and illusions. In S. Oskamp, & M. Costanzo (Eds.), *Gender issues in contemporary society* (pp. 143-171). Thousand Oaks, CA, US: Sage Publications.

Crosby, F. J., & Ropp, S. A. (2002). Awakening to discrimination. In M. Ross, & D. T. Miller (Eds.), *The justice motive in everyday life* (pp. 382-396). N.Y.: Cambridge University Press.

Crosby, F. J., Williams, J. C., & Biernat, M. (2004). The maternal wall. *Journal of Social Issues*, 60, 675-682.

Crouter, A. C. (1984). Spillover from family to work: The neglected side of the work-family interface. *Human Relations*, 37, 425-442.

Cuddy, A. J. C., Fiske, S. T., & Glick, P. (2004). When professionals become mothers, warmth doesn't cut the ice. *Journal of Social Issues*, 60, 701-718.

Dahan-Kalev, H. (1997). Oppression of women by other women, *ISSR - Israeli Social Science Research*, 12, 31-44.

Dahan-Kalev, H. (2001). Tensions in Israeli feminism: The Mizrahi Ashkenazi rift. *Women's Studies International Forum*, 24, 669-684.

Dahan-Kalev, H. (2002). Feminism as part of the fight against oppression. *Mifneh*, 18, 17-22. (Hebrew).

Dahan-Kalev, H. (2006). Mizrahi feminism, post-colonialism, and globalization. *Democratic Culture*, 10, Bar Ilan University. (Hebrew).

Daley, C., & Nolan, M. (1994). International feminist perspectives on suffrage: An introduction. In C. Daley, & M. Nolan (Eds.), *Suffrage and beyond: International feminist perspectives* (pp. 1-22). New York: New York University Press.

Dancer, S. L., & Gilbert, L. A. (1993). Spouses' family work participation and its relation to wives' occupational level. *Sex Roles: A Journal of Research*, 28, 127-145.

Darley, S. A. (1976). Big time careers for the little women: A dual role dilemma. *Journal of Social Issues*, 32, 85-94.

Datta, A. (2005). MacDonaldization of gender in urban India: A tentative exploration. *Gender, Technology and Development*, 9, 125-135.

Davies Netzley, S. A. (2002). Gender stereotypic images of occupations correspond to the sex segregation of employment. In Hunter, A. E., & Forden, C. (Eds.), *Readings in the psychology of gender: Exploring our differences and commonalities.* (pp. 281-299). Needham Heights, MA: Allyn and Bacon.

Davis, K. & Moore, W. (1945). Some principles of stratification. *American Sociological Review*, 10, 242-249.

de Beauvoir, S. (1973). *The Second Sex.* New York: Vintage Books.

Deaux, K. (1984). Blue collar barriers. *American Behavioral Scientist*, 27, 287-300.

Deklyen, M., Brooks-Gunn, J., Mclanahan, S., & Knab, J (2006). The mental health of married, cohabiting, and non-coresident parents with infants. *American Journal of Public Health*, 96, 1836-1841.

Desrochers, S., Andreassi, J., & Thompson, C. (2002). *Identity theory, a Sloan work and family encyclopedia.* Chestnut Hill, MA: Boston College.

Dettwyler, K. A. (1995). Beauty and the breast: The cultural context of breastfeeding in the United States. In K. A. Dettwyler, & P. Stuart-Macadam (Eds.), *Breastfeeding: Biocultural perspectives* (pp. 167-215). New York: Adline de Gruyter.

Dew, J. (2009). Has the marital time cost of parenting changed over time? *Social Forces*, 88, 519-541.

DeWolff, M. S., & van IJzendoorn, M. H. (1997). Sensitivity and attachment: A meta-analysis on parental antecedents of infant attachment. *Child Development*, 68, 571–591.

Diekman, A. B., & Murnen, S. K. (2004). Learning to be little women and little men: The inequitable gender equality of nonsexist children's literature. *Sex Roles: A Journal of Research*, 50, 373-385.

Doherty, W. J. (1998). Responsible fathering: An overview and conceptual framework. *Journal of Marriage and the Family, 60,* 277–292.

Domagalski, T. A. (1999). Emotion in organizations: Main currents. *Human Relations, 52,* 833-852.

Dor, R. B., & Lieberfeld, D. (2008). Mission accomplished?: Israel' s "Four Mothers" and the legacies of successful antiwar movements. *International Journal of Peace Studies*, 13, 85-97.

Douglas, S. J., & Michaels, M. W. (2004). *The mommy myth*. New York: The Free Press.

Douvan, E. (1976). The role of models in women's professional development. *Psychology of Women Quarterly*, 1, 5-21.

Drago, R., Colbeck, C., Hollenshead C., & Sullivan, B. (2008). Work–family policies and the avoidance of bias against caregiving. In A. Marcus-Newhall, D. F. Halpern, & S. J. Tan (Eds.), *The changing realities of work and family* (pp. 43-66). New York: Wiley-Blackwell.

Dries, N., Pepermans, R., & De Kerpel, E. (2008). Exploring four generations' beliefs about career: Is "satisfied" the new "successful?" *Journal of Managerial Psychology*, 23, 907-928

Dryden, H. S. J. & Johnson, B. (1999). Childhood resilience: Review and critique of literature. *Oxford Review of Education*, 25, 307-323.

Echols, A. (2002). *Shaky ground: The '60s and its aftershocks*. New York: Columbia University Press.

Eckes, T. (2002). Paternalistic and envious gender stereotypes: Testing predictions from the stereotype content model. *Sex Roles: A Journal of Research*, 47, 99-114.

Eden, D. (2000). Israel's gender equality policy in education: Revolution or containment? *Urban Education*, 35(4), 473-495.

Effroni, L. (1980). *Advancement and pay in the Israeli government service - are women discriminated?* The Hebrew University, Jerusalem: The Institute for Labor and Welfare Research.

Ehrensaft, M. K. (2005). Interpersonal relationships and sex differences in the development of conduct problems. *Clinical Child and Family Psychology Review*, 8, 39-63.

Eichler, M. (1975). Power and sexual fear in primitive societies. *Journal of Marriage and Family*, 37, 917-926.

Eisenstadt, S. N. (1967). *Israeli society: Background, development and problems.* Jerusalem: Magnes Press, the Hebrew University.

Eisenstadt, S. N. (1985). *The transformation of Israeli society.* Boulder, Colorado: Westview Press.

Eisenstadt, S. N., & Lissak, M. (1984). Preface. In Y. Nahon (Ed.), *Trends in the occupational status - the ethnic dimension.* Jerusalem, Israel: The Jerusalem Institute for Israel Studies. (Hebrew)

Eisenstein, H. (1983). *Contemporary feminist thought.* Boston, MA: G.K. Hall

Elboim-Dror, R. (1994). Gender and utopianism: The Zionist case. *History Workshop Journal, 37,* 99–116.

Elizur, D. (1994). Gender and work values: A comparative analysis. *Journal of Social Psychology, 134,* 201-212.

Ellemers, N., van den Heuvel, H., de Gilder, D., Maass, A., Bonvini, A., & Fischlmayr, I. C. (2002). Female self perception as barrier to international careers? *International Journal of Human Resource Management, 13,* 773-783.

El-Or, T. (1993). You cannot see Iceland from Shilo: The Rehelin event. *Alpayim, 7,* 59-81. (Hebrew).

El-Or, T. (1994). Are they like their grandmothers? A paradox of literacy in the life of Ultraorthodox Jewish women. *Anthropology and Education Quarterly, 24,* 61-81.

Engels, F. (1884) (translated and edited by Eleanor B. Leacock, 1972). *The origin of the family private property and the state.* New York: International Publishers Co®.England, P. (1981). Assessing trends in occupational sex segregation: 1900-1976. In I. Berg (Ed.), *Sociological perspectives on labor market.* New York: Academic Press.

Engle, P. (1997). The role of men in families: achieving gender equity and supporting children. In C. Sweetman (Ed.), *Men and masculinity* (pp. 31-40). Oxford: Oxfam, UK.

Epstein, C. F. (1971). Encountering the male establishment: sex-status limits on women's careers in the professions. In A. Theodore (Ed.),

The professional woman. Cambridge, MA: Schenkman Publishing Company.

Epstein, C. F. (1988). *Deceptive distinctions: Sex, gender, and the social order.* New Haven: Yale University Press.

Erickson, R. J. (1993). Reconceptualizing family work: The effect of emotion work on perceptions of marital quality. *Journal of Marriage and the Family*, 55, 888-900.

Eriksen, J. A., & Klein, G. (1981). Women's employment and changes in family structure. *Sociology of Work and Occupations*, 8, 5-24.

Eskeles Gottfried A., & Gottfried, A. W. (2008). The upside of maternal and dual-earner employment: A focus on positive family adaptations, home environments, and child development in the Fullerton longitudinal study. In A. Marcus-Newhall, D. F. Halpern, & S. J. Tan (Eds.), *The changing realities of work and family* (pp. 25-42). New York: Wiley-Blackwell.

Etzion, D., Nicolaou-Smokoviti, L., & Bailyn, L. (1993). A cross-cultural comparison of American, Israeli and Greek women pursuing technical and scientific careers. *Revue Internationale de Sociologie / International Review of Sociology*, 1-2, 76-94.

Exum, W. H., Menges, R. J., Watkins, B., & Berglund, P. (1984). Making it to the top: Women and minority faculty in the academic labor market. *American Behavioral Scientist*, 27, 301-325.

Fagenson, E. A. (1989). The mentor advantage: Perceived career/job experiences of protégé vs. nonprotégé, *Journal of Organizational Behavior*, 10, 309-320.

Faircloth, C. (2009). Mothering as identity-work: Long-term breastfeeding and intensive motherhood. *Anthropology News*, 50, 15–17.

Faludi, S. (1993). *Backlash: The undeclared war against women.* London: Vintage.

Fatherhood Institute (2005). Worldwide study heralds global increase in father involvement. *Fatherhood Institute: The UK's Fatherhood Think Tank.* Retrieved from *http://www.fatherhoodinstitute. org/2005/worldwide-study-heralds-global-increase-in-father-involvement-and-reveals-why-men-have-nipples/*

Fatherhood Institute (2005). Flexibility is key. *Fatherhood Institute: The UK's Fatherhood Think Tank.* Retrieved from *http://www. fatherhoodinstitute.org/index.php?id=14andcID=256.*

Featherman, D. L., & Hauser, R. M. (1976). Sexual inequalities and socioeconomic achievement in the U.S., 1962-1973. *American Sociological Review, 41,*462-484.

Fenster, T. (2005). Identity issues and local governance: Women's everyday life in the city. *Social Identities,* 11, 21-36.

Ferree, M. M. (1991). The gender division of labor in two-earner marriages: Dimensions of variability and change. *Journal of Family Issues,* 12, 158-180.

Ferri-Reed, J. (2010). The keys to engaging millennials. *Journal for Quality and Participation,* 33, 31-33.

Ferris, A. L. (1971). *Indicators of trends in the status of American women.* New York: Russell Sage Foundation.

Fineman, S. (2006). Emotional arenas revisited. In S. Fineman (Ed.), Emotion in organizations (pp. 1-24). Thousand Oaks, CA: Sage.

Fiorino, S. J. (1994). Nontraditional occupational aspirations and attainment of potential female recruits. *Feminist Issues,* 14, 73-90.

First, A. (1995). Nothing new under the sun? A comparison of images of women in Israeli advertisements in 1979 and 1994. *Sex Roles: A Journal of Research,* 38, 11-12.

Fischlmayr, I. C. (2002). Female self-perception as barrier to international careers? *The International Journal of Human Resource Management,* 13, 773–783.

Fisher, C. D., & Ashkanasy, N. M. (2000). The emerging role of emotions in work life: an introduction. *Journal of Organizational Behavior,* 21, 123-129.

Fisher, H. (1999). *The first sex: The natural talents of women and how they are changing the world.* New York: Random House.

Fitt. L. W., & Newton. D. A. (1981). When the mentor is a man and the protégé is a woman. *Harvard Business Review*, 59, 56-60.

Fitzgerald, L. F., Crites, J. O. (1980). Toward a career psychology of women: What do we know? What do we need to know? *Journal of Counseling Psychology*, 27, 44-62.

Floge, L., & Merrill, D. N. (1986). Tokenism reconsidered: Male nurses and female physicians in a hospital setting. *Social Forces*, 64, 925-947.

Fogiel—Bijaoui, S. (1992). On the way to equality? The struggle for women's suffrage in the Jewish *Yishuv*, 1917—1926. In D. S. Bernstein (Ed.), *Pioneers and homemakers: Jewish women in pre-state Israel* (pp. 261—282). New York: SUNY, Series in Israeli Studies.

Fox, K. D., & Nickols, S. Y. (1983). The time crunch: Wife's employment and family life. *Journal of Family Issues*, 4, 61-82.

Fowlkes, M. R. (1987). Role combinations and role conflict: Introductory perspective. In F. J. Crosby (Ed.), *Spouse, parent, worker.* New Haven: Yale University Press.

Freedman, E. B. (2003). *No turning back: The history of feminism and the future of women.* London: Ballantine Books.

Friedan, B. (1963). *The feminine mystique.* New York: Laurel.

Friedman, A., Tzukerman, Y., Wienberg, H., & Todd, J. (1992). The shift in power with age: Changes in perception of the power of women and men over the life cycle. *Psychology of Women Quarterly*, 16, 513-525.

Fuchs, V. R. (1989). Women's quest of economic equality. *Journal of Economic Perspectives.* 3, 25-41.

Fuller, M. (1941). Woman in the nineteenth century. In M. Wade (Ed.), *The writings of Margaret Fuller* (pp. 110-218). New York: Viking Press.

Gabriel, A. H. (1992). Grief and rage: Collective emotions in the politics of peace and the politics of gender in Israel. *Culture, Medicine and Psychiatry,* 16, 311-335.

Gackenbach, J. I., & Auerbach, S. M. (1975). Empirical evidence for the phenomenon of the "well-meaning liberal male". *Journal of Clinical Psychology,* 31, 632-635.

Gal, I. (2009). *Ministry of Health: New regulations for babies' nutrition.* Retrieved from *http://www.ynet.co.il/ articles/ 0,7340,L-3714668,00.html*

Gal-Ezer, M. (2006). Vicki Knaffo: Body, habitus, nationality and protest. *Gadish,* 10, 290-292. (Hebrew).

Garcia Martin, T. (2001). *Social class, household strategies and inequalities among Spanish women in the dilemma between family and work.* Paper presented at the 5th ESA Conference of Sociology, Helsinki, 2001.

Gauntlett, D. (2002). *Media gender and identity.* New York: Routledge.

Gaynor, A. (2006). Neither shall they train for war anymore: Reflections on Zionism, militarism, and conscientious objection. *NWSA Journal,* 18, 181-190.

Gelbard, M. (2009, January 1). Evading military duty—destroying common resources. *Haaretz,* p. 7.

Gerson, K. (1985). *Hard choices: How women decide about work, career and motherhood.* Berkeley: University of California Press.

Gerson, K. (2004). Understanding work and family through a gender lens. *Community, Work and Family,* 7, 163-178.

Gibson, D. E., & Cordova, D. I. (1999). Women's and men's role models: The importance of exemplars. In A. J. Murress, F. J. Crosby, & R. J. Ely (Eds.), *Mentoring dilemmas* (pp. 121–142). Mahwah, NJ: Erlbaum.

Giddens, A. (1979). *Central problems in social theory: action, structure and contradiction in social analysis.* London: Macmillan.

Giddens, A. (1981). *The class structure of the advanced societies*: London: Hutchinson.

Giddens, A. (1984). *The constitution of society: Outline of the Theory of Structuration*. Cambridge: Polity Press.

Giddens, A. (1990). *The consequences of modernity*: Cambridge: Polity Press.

Giddens, A. (1991). *Modernity and self-identity: Self and society in the late Modern Age*. Cambridge: Polity Press.

Giddens, A. (1994). *Beyond Left and Right — the future of radical politics*. Cambridge: Polity Press.

Giddens, A. (1995). *Politics, Sociology and social theory: Encounters with classical and contemporary social thought*. Cambridge: Polity Press.

Giddens, A. (1998). *The Third Way: The renewal of social democracy*. Cambridge: Polity Press.

Giddens, A. (1999). *Runaway world: How globalization is reshaping our lives*. London: Profile.

Giddens, A. (2000a). *Runaway world*. London: Routledge.

Giddens, A. (2000b). *The Third Way and its critics*. Cambridge: Polity Press.

Giddens, A. (2002). *Where now for new labour?* Cambridge: Polity Press.

Giddens, A. (Ed.). (2005). *The new Egalitarianism*. Cambridge: Polity Press

Giddens, A., & Pierson, C. (1999). *Conversations with Anthony Giddens*. Stanford: Stanford University Press.

Gilbert, L. A. (1994). Reclaiming and returning gender to context: Examples from studies of heterosexual dual-earner families. *Psychology of Women Quarterly*, 18, 539-558.

Gilligan, C. (1977). In a different voice: Women's conceptions of self and morality. *Harvard Education Review*, 47, 481–517.

Gilligan, C. (1982). *In a different voice: Psychological theory and women's development.* Cambridge, MA: Harvard University Press.

Gillis, S., Howie, G., & Munford, R. (2007). Third wave feminism: A critical exploration. London: Palgrave.

Glassman, I., & Eisikovits, R. A. (2006). Intergenerational transmission of motherhood patterns: Three generations of immigrant mothers of Moroccan descent in Israel. *Journal of Comparative Family Studies, 37*, 461-477.

Glick, P., & Fiske, S. T. (2001). An ambivalent alliance: Hostile and benevolent sexism as complementary justifications for gender inequality. *American Psychologist, 56*, 109-118.

Goh, S. C. (1991). Sex differences in perceptions of interpersonal work style, career emphasis, supervisory monitoring behavior, and job satisfaction. *Sex Roles: A Journal of Research, 24*, 701-711.

Goh, S. C., & Mealiea, L. W. (1984). Fear of success and its relationship to the job performance, tenure, and desired job outcomes of women. *Canadian Journal of Behavioural Science, 16*, 65-75.

Golan, G. (1997). Militarization and gender: The Israeli experience. *Women's Studies International Forum, 20*, 5-6.

Goldberg, P. A. (1968). Are women prejudiced against women? *Transaction, 5*, 28-30.

Goldshmidt, O. T., & Weller, L. (2000). Talking emotions: Gender differences in a variety of conversational contexts. *Symbolic Interaction, 23*, 117-134.

Goldstein, A. (2000, February 27). Breadwinning wives alter marriage equation. *Washington Post.* Retrieved on May 10, 2009, from *http://pqasb.pqarchiver.com/washingtonpost/access/50337805.html*

Goldstein, O., & Spielman, V. (2005). Only one mother? Following Yaross-Hakak vs. the Legal Advisor to the Government 10280/01. *Heaarat Din, 2*, 92. (Hebrew).

Good wife's guide. (1955, May 13). *Housekeeping Weekly.*

Goode, W. J. (1960). A theory of role strain. *American Sociological Review*, 25, 483-496.

Gornick, V., & Moran, B. K. (1971). *Woman in sexist society: Studies in power and powerlessness*. New York: Basic Books.

Gottfredson, D. C. (1981). Black-white differences in the educational attainment process. *American Sociological Review*, 46, 542-57.

Gottfried Eskeles, A., Gottfried, A. W., Bathurst, K., & Killian, C. (1999). Maternal and dual earner employment: Family environment, adaptations, and the developmental impingement perspective. In M. E. Lamb (Ed.), *Parenting and child development in "nontraditional" families* (pp. 15-37). Mahwah, NJ, US: Lawrence Erlbaum Associates.

Gray, D. J. (1983). The married professional woman: An examination of her role conflicts and coping strategies. *Psychology of Women Quarterly*, 7, 235-243.

Gray, J. (1992). *Men are from Mars, women are from Venus*. New York: HarperCollins.

Greenberg, H. (2009). Female officers agree: A revolution is the status of women in the Israeli Army. (Hebrew). Retrieved on March 10, 2009 from *http://www.ynet.co.il/articles/0,7340,L-3682838,00.html*

Greenbers, J. (1996, January 3). Ruling expands women's roles in the Israeli military. *New York Times*. Retrieved from *http://query. nytimes.com/gst/fullpage.html?res=9F01EFDF1239F930A35752C0 A960958260andsec=andspon=andpagewanted=all*

Greenhaus, J. H., & Parasuraman, S. (1999). Research on work, family, and gender: Current status and future directions. In G. N. Powell (Ed.), *Handbook of gender and work* (pp. 391-412). Newbury Park, CA: Sage.

Greenstein, T. N. (1986). Social-psychological factors in perinatal labor-force participation. *Journal of Marriage and the Family*, 48, 565-571.

Griffin, C. (2004). Good girls, bad girls: Anglocentrism and diversity in the constitution of contemporary girlhood. In A. Harris (Ed.),

All about the girl: Power, culture and identity (pp. 29-44). New York: Routledge.

Griswold, R. L. (1997). Generative fathering: A historical perspective. In A. J. Hawkins, & D. C. Dollahite (Eds.), *Generative fathering: Beyond deficit perspectives* (pp. 71-86). New York: Sage.

Grzywacz, J. G., Butler, A. B., & Almeida, D. M. (2008). Work, family, and health: Work–family balance as a protective factor against stresses of daily life. In A. Marcus-Newhall, D. F. Halpern, & S. J. Tan (Eds.), *The changing realities of work and family* (pp. 194-215). New York: Wiley-Blackwell.

Gurin, P. (1981). Labor market experiences and expectations. *Sex Roles: A Journal of Research*, 7, 1079-1093.

Gustavsson, E. (2005). Virtual servants: Stereotyping female front office employees on the internet. *Gender, Work and Organization*, 12, 400-419.

Gutek, B. A. (2001). Women and paid work. *Psychology of Women Quarterly*, 25, 379-393.

Haas, L., & Hwang, C.P. (2008). The impact of taking parental leave on fathers' participation in childcare and relationships with children: Lessons from Sweden. *Community, Work and Family*, 11, 85-104.

Haberfeld, Y., & Cohen, Y. (1998). Earnings gaps between Israel's native-born men and women: 1982-1993. *Sex Roles: A Journal of Research*, 39, 11-12.

Haberfeld, Y., & Cohen, Y. (2007). Gender, ethnic, and national earnings gaps in Israel: The role of rising inequality. *Social Science Research*, 36, 654-672.

Habermas, J. (1999). *The structural transformation of the public sphere: An inquiry into a category of bourgeois society* (T. Burger & F. Lawrence, Trans.). Cambridge, MA: MIT Press.

Hacker, D. (2001). Single and married women in the law of Israel—A feminist perspective. *Feminist Legal Studies*, 9, 29-56.

Hacker, D. (2005). Motherhood, fatherhood and law: Child custody and visitation in Israel. *Social and Legal Studies*, 14, 409-431.

Haddad, Y. Y. (1985). Islam, women and revolution in twentieth century Arab thought. In Y. Y. Haddad & E. B. Findly (Eds.), *Women, religion and social change* (pp. 107-126). Albany: SUNY

HaeJung, K., Knight, D. K., & Crutsinger, C. (2009). Generation Y employees' retail work experience: The mediating effect of job characteristics. *Journal of Business Research*, 62, 548-556.

Haelyon, H. (2006). Longing for a child: Perceptions of motherhood among Israeli-Jewish women undergoing in vitro fertilization. *Nashim: A Journal of Jewish Women's Studies and Gender Issues*, 12, 177-202. (Hebrew).

Hakim, C. (2002). Lifestyle preferences as determinants of women's differentiated labor market careers. *Work and Occupations*, 29, 428-459.

Halevi, N., & Klinov-Malul, R. (1967). *The economic development of Israel*. Jerusalem: Academon Press. (Hebrew). See also Central Bureau of Statistics. (1957). *Labor force survey, 1954*. Special Publications Series, 56 (Table 25 p. 50-51). Jerusalem, Israel.

Halevi, S., & Blumen, O. (2005). 'I carry out small wars': The impact of women's studies on Palestinian and Jewish students in Israel. *Journal of Gender Studies*, 14, 233-249.

Hall, D. T. (1977). A model of coping with role conflict: The role behavior of college educated women. *Administrative Science Quarterly*, 62, 471-487.

Halpern, D. F., Tan, S. J., & Carsten, M. (2008). California paid family leave: Is it working for caregivers? In A. Marcus-Newhall, D. F. Halpern, & S. J. Tan (Eds.), *The changing realities of work and family* (pp. 159-174). New York: Wiley-Blackwell.

Halpin, D. (2003). *Hope and education: The role of the utopian imagination*. New York: Routledge.

Harlan, C. L., & Jansen, M. A. (1987). The psychological and physical well being of women in sex stereotyped occupations. *Journal of Employment Counseling*, 24, 31-39.

Harlan, S. L., & O'Farrel, B. (1982). After the pioneers: Prospects for women in nontraditional blue-collar jobs. *Work and Occupations*. 9, 363-386.

Harpaz, I. (1992). *The meaning of work in Israel*. New York: Praeger.

Harpaz, I., & Snir, R. (2003). Workaholism: Its definition and nature. *Human Relations*, 56, 291-319.

Hattery, A. (2001) *Women, work, and family*. London: Sage Publications.

Hawk, S. R. (1990). Effect of locus of control on perceptions of participative decision-making. *Psychological Reports*, 67, 1307-1313.

Hayes, J., Allinson, C. W., & Armstrong, S. J. (2004). Intuition, women managers and gendered stereotypes. *Personnel Review*, 33, 403-417.

Hays, S. (1996). *The cultural contradictions of motherhood*. New Haven, CT: Yale University Press.

Hays, S. (1998). The fallacious assumptions and unrealistic prescriptions of Attachment Theory: A comment on "parents' socioemotional investment in children". *Journal of Marriage and the Family*, 60, 782-790.

Hays, W. L. (1966). *Statistics for psychologists*. N.Y.: Holt, Rinehart and Winston.

Hearn, J., & Collinson, D. L. (1994). Theorizing unities and differences between men and between masculinities. In H. Brod & M. Kaufman. *Theorizing masculinities*. Thousand Oaks: Sage Publications.

Heath, A., & Britten, N. (1984). Women's jobs do make a difference: a reply to Goldthorpe. *Sociology*, 18, 475-490.

Heilman, M. E. (1995). Sex stereotypes and their effects in the workplace: What we know and what we don't know. *Journal of Social Behavior and Personality*, 10, 3-26.

Held, D., & Thompson, J. B. (1989). *Social theory of modern societies: Anthony Giddens and his critics*. Cambridge: Cambridge University Press.

Helman, S., & Rapoport, T. (1997). Women in black: Challenging Israel's gender and socio-political orders. *The British Journal of Sociology*, 48, 681-700.

Henry, A. (2004). *Not my mother's sister: Generational conflict and third-wave feminism*. Bloomington: Indiana University Press.

Herbert, M. S. (1994). Feminism, militarism and attitudes toward the role of women in the military. *Feminist Issues*, 14, 25-48.

Herzog, H. (1992). The fringes of the margin: Women's organizations in the civic sector of the *Yishuv*. In D. S. Bernstein, (Ed.), *Pioneers and homemakers: Jewish women in pre-state Israel* (pp. 283—304). New York: SUNY, Series in Israeli Studies.

Herzog, H. (1994). *Realistic women: women in local politics in Israel*. Jerusalem: Jerusalem Institution for the Study of Israel, Research Publications No. 51. (Hebrew).

Herzog, H. (1999). *Gendering politics: Women in Israel*. Ann Arbor: University of Michigan Press.

Herzog, H. (2006). Trisection of forces: Gender, religion and the state—The case of state-run religious schools in Israel. *British Journal of Sociology*, 57, 241-262.

Herzog, S. (2007). Public perceptions of sexual harassment: An empirical analysis in Israel from consensus and feminist theoretical perspectives. *Sex Roles: A Journal of Research*, 57, 7-8.

Hetherington, E. M. (2003). Social support and the adjustment of children in divorces and remarried families. *Childhood*, 10, 217-36.

Hetherington, E. M., & Kelly, J. (2002). *For better or for worse: Divorce reconsidered*. New York: Norton.

Hetherington, E. M., & Stanley-Hagan, M. M. (1997). The effects of divorce on fathers and their children. In M. E. Lamb (Ed.), *The role of the father in child development* (3rd edition, pp. 191–211). New York: Wiley.

Hewlett S. A. (2002). *Creating a life: Professional women and the quest for children.* New York: Talk Miramax Books.

Heywood, L., & Drake, J. (Eds.,) (1997). *Third wave agenda: Being feminist, doing feminism.* Twin Cities, MI: University of Minnesota Press.

Hill, E. J. (2005). Work-family facilitation and conflict, working fathers and mothers, work-family stressors and support. *Journal of Family Issues, 26,* 793-819.

Hill. S. E. K., Bahniuk, M. H., & Dobos, J. (1989). The impact of mentoring and collegial support on faculty success: An analysis of support behavior, information adequacy, and communication apprehension. *Communication Education, 38,* 15-33.

Himen-Reish, N. (2008). Women and civil society. *Parliament,* 57. Retrieved on April 16, 2009, from *http://www.idi.org.il/ Parliament/2008/Pages/57_2008/E_57/ Parliament_Issue_57_D. aspx*

Hochschild, A. (1997). *Time bind: When work becomes home and home becomes work.* New York: Metropolitan Books.

Hoff Sommers, C. (1995) *Who stole feminism? How women have betrayed women.* New York: Touchstone/Simon and Schuster.

Hoffman, C., & Reed, J. S. (1981). Sex discrimination?—The XYZ affair. *The Public Interest.* 62, 21-39.

Holahan, C. K. (1979). Stress experienced by women doctoral students, need for support and occupational sex typing: An interactional view. *Sex Roles: A Journal of Research, 5,* 425-436.

Hong, S. M., & Giannakopoulos, E. (1994). The relationship of satisfaction with life to personality characteristics. *The Journal of Psychology, 128,* 547-558.

Hooks, B. (2000). *Feminism is for everybody: Passionate politics.* London: Pluto Press.

Horan, P. M. (1978). Is status attainment research atheoretical? *American Sociological Review*, 43, 334-341.

Horner, M. (1972). Achievement-related conflicts in women. *Journal of Social Issues*, 28, 157-175.

Hornig, L. S. (1984). Women in science and engineering: Why so few? *Technology Review*, (Nov.), 30-41.

Horowitz, A. V. (1982). Sex Role Expectations, Power, and Psychological Distress. *Sex Roles: A Journal of Research*, 8, 607-623.

Horowitz, D., & M. Lissak. (1978). *The origins of the Israeli polity.* Chicago: The University of Chicago Press.

Horowitz, D., & Lissak, M. (1989) *Trouble in Utopia: The overburdened polity of Israel.* New York: State University of New York Press.

Hovav, M., & Amir, M. (1979). Israeli Police: History and analysis. *Police Studies*, 18, 25-13.

Hunsberger, B. (1995). Religion and prejudice: The role of religious fundamentalism, quest and right wing authoritarianism. *Journal of Social Issues*, 51, 113-127.

Hunt, D. M., & Michael, C. (1983). Mentorship: A career training and development tool. *Academy of Management Review*, 8, 475-485.

Hunt, J. W., & Saul, P. N. (1975). The relationship of age, tenure and job satisfaction in males and females. *Academy of Management Journal*, 18, 690-702.

Hunt, P. (1980). *Gender and class consciousness.* NY: Holmes and Meier.

Hurst, J. L., & Good, L. K. (2009). Generation Y and career choice: The impact of retail career perceptions, expectations and entitlement perceptions. *The Career Development International*, 14, 570-593.

Ichilov, O. (1994). Israeli adolescents' perceptions of the costs of the transition to an egalitarian gender role allocation. *Gender and Education*, 6, 307-318.

Inglehart, R. (1990). *Culture shift in advances industrial society.* Princeton, NJ: Princeton University Press.

Inglehart, R., & Abramson, P. R. (1994). Economic security and value change. *American Political Science Review,* 88, 336-354.

Isaacs, M. B. (1981). Sex role stereotyping and the evaluation of the performance of women: Changing Trends. *Psychology of Women Quarterly,* 6, 187-195.

Israeli Police. (1995). *Annual Report.* Jerusalem, Israel: Police Headquarters.

Izraeli, D. N. (1979). Sex structure of occupations - the Israeli experience. *Sociology of Work and Occupations,* 6, 404-429.

Izraeli, D. N. (1981). The Zionist women's movement in Palestine, 1911-1927: A sociological analysis. *Signs,* 7, 87-114.

Izraeli, D. N. (1983). Sex effects or structural effects: an empirical examination of Kanter's theory of proportions. *Social Forces,* 61, 153-165.

Izraeli, D. N. (1990). Sex structure of occupations: The Israeli experience. *Work and Occupations,* 6, 404-429.

Izraeli, D. N. (1991). Women and work: From collective to career. In B. Swirski, and M. Safir (Eds.), *Calling the equality bluff* (pp. 165–178). New York: Pergamon.

Izraeli, D. N. (1992a). Culture, policy and women in dual-earner families in Israel. In S. Lewis, D. N. Izraeli, & H. Hootsmans (Eds.), *The dual earner family in comparative perspective.* London: Sage.

Izraeli, D. N. (1992b). The women workers' movement: First wave feminism in pre-state Israel. In D. S. Bernstein (Ed.), *Pioneers and homemakers: Jewish women in pre-state Israel* (pp. 183—209). New York: SUNY, Series in Israeli Studies.

Izraeli, D. N. (1993). Work/family conflict among women and men managers in dual-career couples in Israel. *Journal of Social Behavior and Personality,* 8, 371-388.

Izraeli, D. N. (2003). Gender politics in Israel: The case of affirmative action for women directors. *Women's Studies International Forum*, 26, 109-128.

Izraeli, D. N., & Adler, N. J. (1993). Competitive frontiers: Women managers in a global economy. In N. J. Adler, & D. N. Izraeli (Eds.), *Competitive frontiers: Women managers in a global economy*. Cambridge, MA: Blackwell Publishers.

Jackson, L. A., Hodge, C. N., & Ingram, J. M. (1994). Gender self concept: Differences and the role of gender attitudes. *Sex Roles: A Journal of Research*, 30, 615-630.

Jacobs, J. (1989). *Revolving doors: Sex segregation and women's careers.* Stanford, CA: Stanford University Press.

Jacobs, J. A., & Gerson, K. (2004). *The time divide: Work, family, and gender inequality.* Cambridge, MA: Harvard University Press.

Jacobson, J. P. (1994). Trends in work force segregation 1960-1990. *Social Science Quarterly*, 61, 161-171.

James, L. (1990). *Men, women and Margaret Fuller.* New York: Golden Heritage Press.

Janman, K. (1989). One step behind: Current stereotypes of women, achievement, and work. *Sex Roles: A Journal of Research*, 21, 209-230.

Jenkins, R. (1996). *Social identity.* London: Routledge.

Jervis, L., & Zeisler, A. (Eds.). (2006). *Bitchfest.* New York: Farrar, Straus, and Giroux.

Johnson, W. B., & Huwe, J. M. (2003). Designing the mentor relationship. In W. B. Johnson, & J. M. Huwe (Eds.), *Getting mentored in graduate school* (pp. 97-112). Washington, DC: American Psychological Association.

Jones, A. (1994). Postfeminism, feminist pleasures, and embodied theories of art. In J. Frueh, C. L. Langer, & A. Raven (Eds.), *New feminist criticism: Art, identity, action* (pp. 16–41). New York: HarperCollins.

Jones, B. H., & McNamara, K. (1991). Attitudes toward women and their work roles: Effects of intrinsic and extrinsic religious orientations. *Sex Roles: A Journal of Research*, 24, 21-29.

Jones, S. (1986). *Police women and equality*. London: Macmillan.

Joyner, K. (2009). Justice and the fate of married and cohabiting couples. *Social Psychology Quarterly*, 72, 61-76.

Kahn, S. E. (1979). Psychological barriers to the occupational success of mature women. *Canadian Counselor*, 13, 211-214.

Kalachek, E., & Pains, F. (1976). The structure of wage differentials among mature male workers. *Journal of Human Resources*, 35, 484-506.

Kalekin-Fishman, D. (2003). Traditionalist education and modern political power in Israel: The case of 'the front of Biblical education'. *International Journal of Contemporary Sociology*, 40, 33-54.

Kamir, O. (2002). *Feminism, rights and Law*. Tel Aviv: Ministry of Defense Publications, Broadcasted University Series. (Hebrew).

Kampf, R. (1996). The media in search of breaches in the wall: The interaction between women's protest groups and Israel society. *Patuach*, 3, 4-26. (Hebrew).

Kanter, R. M. (1977a). *Men and women of the corporation*. N.Y.: Basic Books.

Kanter, R. M. (1977b). Some effects of proportion on group life: Skewed sex ratios and responses to token women. *American Journal of Sociology*, 82, 965-990.

Karaian, L., Bryn Rundel, L., & Mitchell, A. (Eds.). (2001). *Turbo chicks: Talking young feminisms*. Toronto, Canada: Sumach Press.

Karniol, R., Grosz, E., & Schorr, I. (2003). Caring, gender role orientation, and volunteering. *Sex Roles: A Journal of Research*, 49, 1-2.

Katz, D., & Kahn, R. L. (1978). *The social psychology of organizations*. New York: Wiley.

Katz, R. (1982). The immigrant woman: Double cost or relative improvement. *International Migration Review,* 16, 661-677.

Katz, R. (1989). Strain and enrichment in the role of employed mothers in Israel. *Marriage and Family Review,* 14, 1-2.

Kaufman, D. R. (1992). Professional women: How real are the recent gains? In J. A. Kouraney, J. P. Sterba, & R. Tong (Eds.), *Feminist philosophies.* Englewood Cliffs, NJ: Prentice Hall.

Kaufman, D. R. (1994). Paradoxical politics: Gender politics among newly Orthodox Jewish women in the United States. In V. M. Moghadam (Ed.), *Identity politics and women: Cultural reassertions and feminisms in international perspective* (pp. 349-366). Boulder, CO: Westview.

Kaufman, I. (2008). Resisting occupation or institutionalizing control? Israeli women and protest in West Bank checkpoints. *International Journal of Peace Studies,* 13, 43-62.

Keller, E. F. (1984). Women in basic research: Respecting the unexpected. *Technology Review.* Nov., 44-7.

Kelly, J. B. (2000). Children's adjustment in conflicted marriage and divorce: A decade review of research. *Journal of the America Academy of Child and Adolescent Psychiatry,* 39, 963–973

Kelley J., & Evans, M. D. R. (1993). The legitimation of inequality: Occupational earnings in nine nations. *American Journal of Sociology,* 99, 75-125.

Kelly, J. B., & Lamb, M. E. (2003). Developmental issues in relocation cases involving young children: When, whether, and how? *Journal of Family Psychology,* 17, 193–205.

Keohane, N. O., & Gelpi, B. C. (1982). Forward. In N. O. Keohane, B. C. Gelpi, & M. Z. Rosaldo (Eds.), *Feminist theory: A critique of ideology* (pp. vii-xii). Chicago: University of Chicago Press.

Kessler-Harris, A. (1990). *A woman's wage: Historical meanings and social consequences.* Lexington, Kentucky: The University Press of Kentucky.

Kiesler, S. B. (1975). Actuarial prejudice toward women and its implications. *Journal of Applied Social Psychology*, 5, 201-216.

Kimmerling, B. (1993). State building, state autonomy, and the identity of society: The case of the Israeli state. *Journal of Historical Sociology*, 6, 397-429.

Kinser, A. (2004). Negotiating space for/through Third-Wave Feminism. NWSA Journal 16, 124–153.

Kirchmeyer, C. (1992). Nonwork participation and work attitudes: A test of scarcity vs. expansion models. *Human Relations*, 45, 775-795.

Klein, D. (2008). Business impact of flexibility: An imperative for working families. In A. Marcus-Newhall, D. F. Halpern, & S. J. Tan (Eds.), *The changing realities of work and family* (pp. 232-244). New York: Wiley-Blackwell.

Klein, U. (1997). The gendering of national discourses and the Israeli-Palestinian conflict. *European Journal of Women's Studies*, 4, 341-351.

Klein, U. (2002). The gender perspective of civil-military relations in Israeli society. *Current Sociology / La Sociologie Contemporaine*, 50, 669-686.

Kram, K. E. (1985a). *Mentoring at work*. Glenview, IL: Scott, Foresman.

Kram, K E. (1985b). Improving the mentoring process. *Training and Development Journal*, 39, 40-43.

Kraus, V., & Yonay, Y. P. (2000). The effect of occupational sex composition on the gender gap in workplace authority. *Social Science Research*, 29, 583-605.

Kouraney, J. A., Sterba, J. P., & Tong, R. (Eds.). (1992). *Feminist philosophies*. Englewood Cliffs, NJ: Prentice-Hall.

Krefting, L. A. (2003). Intertwined discourses of merit and gender: Evidence from academic employment in the USA. *Gender, Work and Organization*, 10, 260-278.

Kulik, L. (1996). Contemporary perceptions of work and occupations among Israeli students: Are there gender differences? *Journal of Psychology and Judaism*, 20, 233-245.

Kulik, L. (1999). Gendered personality disposition and gender role attitudes among Israeli students. *Journal of Social Psychology*, 139, 736-747.

Kulik, L. (2000a). Intrafamiliar congruence in gender-role ideology: Husband-wife versus parents-offspring. *Journal of Comparative Family Studies*, 31, 91-106.

Kulik, L. (2000b). The impact of gender and age on attitudes and reactions to unemployment: The Israeli case. Sex Roles: A Journal of Research, 43, 1-2.

Kulik, L. (2002). Equality in marriage, marital satisfaction, and life satisfaction: A comparative analysis of preretired and retired men and women in Israel. *Families in Society*, 83, 197-207.

Kulik, L. (2003). Morning passages from home to work among managers in Israel: Intergender differences. *Sex Roles: A Journal of Research*, 48, 205-215.

Kulik, L. (2004a). Perceived equality in spousal relations, martial quality, and life satisfaction: A comparison of elderly wives and husbands. *Families in Society* 85, 243-250.

Kulik, L. (2004b). Strategies for managing home-work conflict and psychological well-being among Jews and Arabs in Israel: The impact of sex and sociocultural context. *Families in Society*, 85, 139-147.

Kulik, L. (2004c). Predicting gender-role attitudes among mothers and their adolescent daughters in Israel. *Affilia*, 19, 437-449.

Kulik, L. (2007). Equality in the division of household labor: A comparative study of Jewish women and Arab Muslim women in Israel. *The Journal of Social Psychology*, 147, 423-440.

Kulik, L., & Rayyan, F. (2003a). Spousal relations and well-being: A comparative analysis of Jewish and Arab dual-earner families in Israel. *Journal of Community Psychology*, 31, 57-73.

Kulik, L., & Rayyan, F. (2003b). Wage-earning patterns, perceived division of domestic labor, and social support: A comparative analysis of educated Jewish and Arab-Muslim Israelis. *Sex Roles: A Journal of Research*, 48, 53-66.

Kulik, L., & Rayyan, F. (2005). Spousal relations: Strategies for coping with home-work conflict and well-being—A comparative analysis of Jewish and Arab women. *Megamot*, 43, 633-658. (Hebrew)

Kulman, A. (1986). Working mothers and the family context: Predicting positive coping. *Journal of Vocational Behavior*, 28, 241-253.

Labi, N., & McDowell, J. (2009). Girl power. Time, 151(25). Retrieved on February 3, 2009, from http://www.time.com/time/magazine / article/0,9171,988643,00.html,

Lahav, P. (1977). Raising the status of women through law: The case of Israel. *Signs*, 3, 193-209.

Lamb, M. E. (1999). Non-custodial fathers and their impact on the children of divorce. In R. A. Thompson & P. R. Amato (Eds.), *The post-divorce family: Research and policy issues* (pp. 105–125). Thousand Oaks, CA: Sage.

Lamb, M. E. (2002a). Infant-father attachments and their impact on child development. In C. S. Tamis-LeMonda, & N. Cabrera (Eds.), *Handbook of father involvement: Multidisciplinary perspectives* (pp. 93–117). Mahwah, NJ: Erlbaum.

Lamb, M. E. (2002b). Noncustodial fathers and their children. In C. S. Tamis-LeMonda, & N. Cabrera (Eds.), *Handbook of father involvement: Multidisciplinary perspectives* (pp. 169–184). Mahwah, NJ: Erlbaum.

Lavee, Y., & Katz, R. (2002). Division of labor, perceived fairness, and marital quality: The effect of gender ideology. *Journal of Marriage and Family* 64, 27-39.

Laws, J. L. (1975). The psychology of Tokenism: an analysis. *Sex Roles: A Journal of Research*, 1, 51-67.

Lee, E. (2008). Living with risk in the age of 'intensive motherhood': Maternal identity and infant feeding. *Health, Risk and Society*, 10, 467-477.

Lefcourt, H. M. (1981). *Locus of control: Current trends in theory and research*. Hillsdale, NJ: Erlbaum.

Lefcourt, H. M. (1983). *Research with the locus of control construct* (Vol.1). New York: Academic Press.

Lefcourt, H. M., & Davidson-Katz, K. (1991). Locus of control and health. In C. R. Snyder, & D. R. Forsyth (Eds.), *Handbook of social and clinical psychology: The health perspective* (pp. 246-66). New York: Pergamon Press.

Lefkowitz, J. (1994). Sex-related differences in job attitudes and dispositional variables: Now you see them..... *Academy of Management Journal*, 37, 323-349.

Lehrer, E. L., & Stokes, H. (1985). Determinants of the female occupational distribution: A Log-Linear Probability analysis'. *Review of Economics and Statistics*, 67, 395-404.

LeMaster, J., Marcus-Newhall, A., Casad, B. J., & Silverman, N. (2005). Life experiences of working and Stay at Home Mothers. In J. L. Chin, (Ed). *The psychology of prejudice and discrimination: Bias based on gender and sexual orientation* (Vol. 3) (pp. 61-91). Westport, CT: Praeger Publishers/Greenwood Publishing Group, Inc.

Lemish, D. (2000). The whore and the other: Israeli images of female immigrants from the former USSR. *Gender and Society*, 14, 333-349.

Lemish, D., & Barzel, I. (2000). Four Mothers: The womb in the public sphere. *European Journal of Communication*, 15, 147–169.

Lengua, L. J., & Stormshak, E. A. (2000). Gender, gender roles and personality: Gender differences in the prediction of coping and psychological symptoms. *Sex Roles: A Journal of Research*, 43, 787-820

Lentin, R. (1996). Israeli and Palestinian women working for peace. *Peace Review*, 8, 385-390.

Lentin, R. (2004). 'No woman's law will rot this state': The Israeli racial state and feminist resistance. *Sociological Research Online*, 9(3). Retrieved on May 5, 2009, from *http://ideas.repec.org/a/sro/srosro/2004-22-2.html*

Leung, C., & Moore, S. (2003). Individual and cultural gender roles: A comparison of Anglo-Australians and Chinese in Australia. *Current Research in Social Psychology*, 8, 21-24.

Levant, R. F., & Kopecky, G. (1995). *Masculinity reconstructed: Changing the rules of manhood: At work, in relationships and in family life.* New York: Dutton.

Levy S., Levinsohn, H., & Katz, E. (1993). *Beliefs, observances and social interaction among Israeli Jews.* Jerusalem: The Louis Guttman Israel Institute of Applied Social Research.

Levy, S., Levinsohn, H., & Katz, E. (2004). The many faces of Jewishness in Israel. In: U. Rebhun, & C. I. Waxman (Eds.), *Jews in Israel: contemporary social and cultural patterns* (pp. 265-284). Hanover: Brandeis University Press.

Lewis, P., & Simpson, R. (Eds.). (2007). *Gendering emotions in organizations.* Gordonsville, VA: Palgrave Macmillan.

Lewis, S. K., Ross, C. E., & Mirowsky, J. (1999). Establishing a sense of personal control in the transition to adulthood. *Social Forces*, 77, 1573-1599.

Lieblich, A. (2002). Women and the changing Israeli Kibbutz: A preliminary three-stage theory. *The Journal of Israeli History*, 21, 63-84.

Liedloff, J. (1977). *The Continuum Concept.* New York: Addison-Wesley.

Liedloff, J. (1998). *The Continuum Concept: In search of happiness lost.* Reading, MA: Perseus Books.

Liedloff, J. (2009). Who's in control? The unhappy consequences of being child-centered. Retrieved on July 25, 2009, from *http://www. continuum-concept.org/reading/whosInControl.html*

Lind, A., & Farmelo, M. (1996). Gender and urban social movements, women's community responses to restructuring and urban poverty. *UNRISD Discussion Paper*, no. 76. Retrieved on June 8, 2009, from *http://www.unrisd.org/unrisd/website/document.nsf/0 / c59d935ec5987d6180256b65004ff007/$FILE/dp76e.pdf*

Lindsay, J. (1999). Diversity but not equality: Domestic labour in cohabiting relationships. *Australian Journal of Social Issues*, 34, 267-283.

Linehan, M. (2002). Senior female international managers: Empirical evidence from Western Europe. *International Journal of Human Resource Management*, 13, 802-814.

Linton R. (1936). *The study of men.* New York: Appleton-Century.

Liron, Y. (1973). *Deprivation and the socio-economic gap in Israel.* Jerusalem: Israel Economist.

Liss, L. (1975). Why academic women do not revolt: Implications for affirmative action. *Sex Roles: A Journal of Research*, 1, 209-223.

Lissak, M. (1969). Images of class and society in the Yeshuv and Israeli society. In S. N. Eisenstadt, H. Adler, R. Bar-Yosef, & R. Kahana (Eds.), *The social structure of Israel.* Jerusalem: Academon Press. (Hebrew)

Lixia, Q., Weston, R., & de Vaus, D. (2009). Cohabitation and beyond: The contribution of each partner's relationship satisfaction and fertility aspirations to pathways of cohabiting couples. *Journal of Comparative Family Studies*, 40, 587-601.

Lobel, T. E., Mashraki-Pedhatzur, S., Mantzur, A., & Libby, S. (2000). Gender discrimination as a function of stereotypic and counterstereotypic behavior: A cross-cultural study. *Sex Roles: A Journal of Research*, 43, 5-6.

Lobel, T. E., Slone, M., & Winch, G. (1997). Masculinity, popularity, and self-esteem among Israeli preadolescent girls. *Sex Roles: A Journal of Research*, 36, 5-6.

Lomsky-Feder, E., & Rapoport, T. (2003). Juggling models of masculinity: Russian-Jewish immigrants in the Israeli army. *Sociological Inquiry*, 73, 114-137.

Long, V. O., & Goldfarb, K. P. (2002). Masculinity and self-esteem in Israeli Jewish professional women. *Journal of Applied Social Psychology*, 32, 2598-2610.

Loo, R. (2001). Motivational orientations toward work: An evaluation of the Work Preference Inventory. *Measurement and Evaluation in Counseling and Development*, 33, 222-233.

Luzzato, D., & Gvion, L. (2007). The coming of the young and sexy lesbian: The Israeli urban scenario. *Social Semiotics*, 17, 21-41.

Lyness, K. S., & Terrazas, J. M. B. (2006). Women in management: An update on their progress and persistent challenges. In J. K. Ford, & G. P. Hodgkinson (Eds.), *International review of industrial and organizational psychology*: Vol. 21 (pp. 267-294). Hoboken, NJ: Wiley Publishing.

Maccoby, E. E., & Jacklin, C. N. (1974). *The psychology of sex differentiation*. Stanford: Stanford University Press.

MacKinnon, C. (1989). *Toward a feminist theory of the state.* Cambridge: Harvard University Press.

Mandel, H., & Semyonov, M. (2005). Family policies, wage structures, and gender gaps: Sources of earnings inequality in 20 countries. *American Sociological Review*, 70, 949-967.

Mannheim, B. (1993). Gender and the effects of demographics, status, and work values on work centrality. *Work and Occupations*, 20, 3-22.

Mannheim, B., & Seger, T. (1993). Mothers' occupational characteristics, family position, and sex role orientation as related to work values of children. *Youth and Society*, 24 276-299.

Marcus-Newhall, A., Casad, B. J., LeMaster, J., Peraza, J., & Silverman, N. (2008). Mothers' work-life experiences: The role of cultural factors. In A. Marcus-Newhall, D. F. Halpern, & S. J. Tan (Eds.), *The changing realities of work and family* (pp. 85-107). New York: Wiley-Blackwell.

Marini, M. M., & Brinton, M. C. (1984). Sex stereotyping in occupational socialization. In B. Reskin (Ed.), *Sex segregation in the work place: Trends, explanations and remedies*. Washington, DC: National Academy Press.

Marini, M. M., & Greenberger, E. (1978). Sex differences in occupational aspirations and expectations. *Sociology of Work and Occupations*, 5, 147-179.

Marks, S. R. (1977). Multiple roles and role strain. *American Sociological Review*, 42, 921-936.

Marks, S. R., & MacDermid, S. M. (1996). Multiple roles and the self: A theory of role balance. *Journal of Marriage and the Family*, 58, 417-432.

Marsh, K., Darity W.A., Jr., Cohen, P.N., Casper, L.M., & Salters, D. (2007). The emerging black middle class: Single and living alone. *Social Forces*, 86, 735-762,

Marso, L. J. (2003). A feminist search for love: Emma Goldman on the politics of marriage, love, sexuality and feminism. *Feminist Theory*, 4, 305-320.

Martin, S. (1990). *Women on the move*. Washington, DC: Police Foundation.

Marwit, S. J. (1981). Assessment of sex-role stereotyping among male and female psychologist practitioners. *Journal of Personality Assessment*, 45, 593-599.

Matras, J. (1965). *Social change in Israel*. Chicago: Aldine.

Matthews, L., Conger, R. D., & Wickerama, K .A. S. (1996). Work-family conflict and marital quality: Mediating processes. *Social Psychology Quarterly*, 59, 62-79.

McCall, L. (2000). Gender and the new inequality: Explaining the college/non-college wage gap. *American Sociological Review*, 65, 234-255.

McDonald, P. K., Bradley, L. M., & Guthrie, D. (2005). Good mothers, bad mothers: Exploring the relationship between attitudes towards nonmaternal childcare and mother's labour force participation. *Journal of Family Studies*, 11, 62-82.

McElhinny, B. (1994). An economy of affect: Objectivity, masculinity and the gendering of police work. In A. Cornwon, & N. Leindisfome (Eds.), *Dislocative masculinity*. NY: Routledge.

McKenzie, I. K. (1993). Equal opportunities in policing: A comparative examination of anti-discrimination policy and practice in British police. *International Journal of the Sociology of Law*, 21, 159-174.

McRobbie, A. (1999). *In the culture society: Art, fashion and popular music*. New York: Routledge.

McRobbie, A. (2004). Notes on postfeminism and popular culture: Bridget Jones and the new gender regime. In A. Harris (Ed.), *All about the girl: power, culture and identity (pp. 3-14)*. New York: Routledge.

McRobbie, A. (2008) *The aftermath of feminism: Gender, culture and social change*. New York: Sage.

Mellor, A. (2002). Mary Wollstonecraft's vindication of the rights of woman and the woman writers of her day. In C. Johnson (Ed.), *The Cambridge companion to Mary Wollstonecraft* (pp. 141-159). Cambridge, UK: Cambridge University Press.

Mernissi, F. (1987). *Beyond the veil: Male-female dynamics in a modern Muslim society*. Bloomington: University of Indiana Press.

Merton, R. K. (1957). *Social Theory and Social Structure*. Glencoe, IL: Free Press.

Mestrovic, S. (1998). *Anthony Giddens: The last Modernist*, New York: Routledge.

Meyer, M. (2004). Organizational identity, political contexts, and SMO action: Explaining the tactical choices made by peace organizations in Israel, Northern Ireland, and South Africa. *Social Movement Studies,* 3, 167-197.

Milkie, M. A., Mattingly, M. J., Nomaguchi, K. M., Bianchi, S. M., & Robinson, J. P. (2004). The Time-Squeeze: Parental statuses and feelings about time with children. *Journal of Marriage and Family,* 66, 739-761.

Milkie, M. A., Raley, S. B., & Bianchi, S. M. (2009). Taking on the second shift: Time allocations and time pressures of U.S. parents with preschoolers. *Social Forces,* 88, 487-517.

Millett, K. (1970). *Sexual politics.* New York: Doubleday.

Millward, L. J., & Freeman, H. (2002). Role expectations as constraints to innovation: The case of female managers. *Creativity Research Journal,* 14, 93-109.

Ministry of Immigration Absorption. (1999). *Immigration to Israel.* Jerusalem. (Hebrew).

Mirowsky, J., Ross, C. E., & van Willigen, M. (1996). Instrumentalism in the land of opportunity. *Social Psychology Quarterly,* 59, 322–37.

Moen, P., & Wethington, E. (1992). The concept of family adaptive strategies. *Annual Review of Sociology,* 18, 233-251.

Moghadam, V. M. (1992). Patriarchy and the politics of gender in modernizing societies: Iran, Pakistan and Afghanistan. *International Sociology,* 7, 35-54.

Molina, V. S. (2008). Setting the stage: Do women want it all? In A. Marcus-Newhall, D. F. Halpern, & S. J. Tan (Eds.), *The changing realities of work and family* (pp. 245-254). New York: Wiley-Blackwell.

Molm, L. D. (1978). Sex role attitudes and the employment of married women: The direction of causality. *Sociological Quarterly,* 19, 522-533.

Moore, D. (1991). Entitlement and justice evaluations: Who should get what and why? *Social Psychology Quarterly,* 54, 208-223.

Moore, D. (1992). *Labor market segmentation and its implications: Social justice, relative deprivation and entitlement.* New York: Garland Publishing.

Moore, D. (1994). Entitlement as an epistemic problem: Do women think like men? *Journal of Social Behavior and Personality,* 9, 665-684.

Moore, D. (1995a). Attitude (in)congruence: Sociopolitical orientation and the gendered division of labor. *Sociological Imagination,* 32, 143-163.

Moore, D. (1995b). Feminism and sex segregation. *International Journal of Sociology of the Family,* 25, 99-125.

Moore, D. (1995c). Gender role attitudes and division of labor: Sex or occupation (an Israeli example). *Journal of Social Behavior and Personality,* 10, 215-234.

Moore, D. (1998a). Gender identities and social action: Arab and Jewish women in Israel. *The Journal of Applied Behavioral Science,* 34, 5-29.

Moore, D. (1998b). No longer complacent? Why Israeli women did not rebel. *Journal for the Theory of Social Behaviour,* 28, 169-192.

Moore D. (1999). Gender traits and identities in a "masculine" organization: The case of Israeli police. *Journal of Social Psychology,* 139, 49-68.

Moore, D. (2000). Gender identity, nationalism, and social action among Jewish and Arab women in Israel: Redefining the social order? *Gender Issues,* 18, 3-28.

Moore, D. (2003). Perceptions of sense of control, relative deprivation, and expectations of young Jews and Palestinians in Israel. *Journal of Social Psychology,* 143, 521-541.

Moore, D. (2004). Gender identities and social action: Arab and Jewish women in Israel. *The Journal of Applied Behavioral Science,* 40, 182-207.

Moore, D. (2007). Self perceptions and social misconceptions: The implications of gender traits for locus of control and life satisfaction. *Sex Roles: A Journal of Research*, 56, 767-780.

Moore, D. (2008). Towards a more just world: What makes people participate in social action? In K. Hegtvedt & J. Clay-Warner (Eds.), *Advances in Group Processes*, vol. 25: *Justice* (pp.213-240). Series edited by E. Lawler & S. R. Thye.

Moore, D. (2009). Job concessions, role conflict and work satisfaction in gender-typical and -atypical occupation: The case of Israel. *Gender Issues*, 26, 42-64.

Moore, D., & Aweiss, S. (2004). *Bridges over troubled water: Political, economic and social attitudes (Cross-cultural comparisons of Palestinians and Israelis)*. Westport, CT: Praeger.

Moore, D., & Gai A. (2006). Combining family and work: Implications for perceived well being of working women. *Social Issues in Israel*, 2, 45-73. (Hebrew).

Moore, D., & Gobi, A. (1995). Role conflict and perceptions of gender roles: The case of Israel. *Sex Roles: A Journal of Research*, 32, 251-272.

Moore, D., & Toren, N. (1998). Thresholds, ceilings or hurdles?: Career patterns of women in academia. *Sociological Imagination*, 35, 96-118.

Morgan, D. H. (1994). Theater of war: Combat, the military and masculinities. In H. Brod, & M. Kaufman. *Theorizing masculinities*. Thousand Oaks: Sage Publications.

Moriel, L. (1998). Diva in the Promised Land: A blueprint for newspeak? *World Englishes*, 17, 225-237.

Morrison, A. M., & White, R. P. (1987). Women with promise. *Working Woman*, 12, 79-85.

Morrow, P. C. (1993). *The theory and measurement of work commitment*. London: JAI Press.

Motzafi-Haller, P. (2001a). Research on women in rural Israel: The gender gap. *Journal of Rural Cooperation*, 29, 3-23.

Motzafi-Haller, P. (2001b). Scholarship, identity, and power: Mizrahi women in Israel. *Signs*, 26, 697-734.

Mueller, C. W., & Wallace, J. E. (1992). Employee commitment: Resolving some issues. *Work and Occupations*, 19, 211-236.

Mueller, K. A., & Yoder, J. D. (1997). Gendered norms for family size, employment, and occupation: Are there personal costs for violating them? *Sex Roles: A Journal of Research*, 36, 207-220.

Muhlbauer, V. (2001). Israeli women and the peace movements. *Peace Review*, 13, 287-293.

Muhlbauer, V., Rabin, C., & Hollander, N. (1986). The definition of social problems: Differing perceptions of Israeli social workers and women. *Journal of Sociology and Social Welfare*, 13, 701-720.

Musico, I. (2002). *Cunt: A declaration of independence*. California: Seal Press.

Natanson, R., Tzameret, H., & Cohen, A. (2004). *Encouraging employers to employ women: A comparative study*. Tel Aviv, Israel: Naamat. (Hebrew). Retrieved on December 21, 2008, from *http:// www.macro.org.il/lib/5879939.pdf*.

Netz, J. S., & Haveman, J. D. (1999). All in the family: Family, income, and labor force attachment. *Feminist Economics*, 5, 85-106.

Niemi, I. (1995). A general view of time use by gender. In I. Niemy (Ed.), *Time use of women in Europe and North America*. U.N. Economic Commission for Europe.

Noe, R. A. (1988). An investigation of the determinants of successful assigned mentoring relationships. *Personnel Psychology*, 41, 457-479.

Noonan, M. C. (2001). The impact of domestic work on men's and women's wages. *Journal of Marriage and the Family*, 63, 1134-1145.

Noonan, M. C., Corcoran, M. E., & Courant, P. N. (2005). Pay differences among the highly trained: Cohort differences in the sex gap in lawyers' earnings. *Social Forces*, 84, 853-872.

Novarra, V. (1980). *Women's work, men's work: The ambivalence of equality*. London: Marion Boyars.

Oakley, R. (1993). A specialist support unit for community and race relations training for the British police. *Police Studies*, 16, 129-137.

Obama, B. (2009). Retrieved from *http://www.duncanfisher.com/index.php/2009/01/24/barack-obama-launches -new-fatherhood-programme/*

Okin Moller, S. (1979). *Women in Western political thought*. Princeton: Princeton University Press.

Ollenburger J. C., & Moore, H. A. (1992). *A sociology of women: The intersection of patriarchy, capitalism and colonization*. Englewood Cliffs, NJ: Prentice Hall.

Olmsted, J. C. (2002). Assessing the impact of religion on gender status. *Feminist Economics*, 8, 99-111.

Oppenheimer, V. (1970). *The female labor force in the U.S.* Population Monograph Series, No. 5. Berkeley: University of California Press.

Orlofsky, J. L., & Stake, J. E., (1981). Psychological masculinity and femininity: Relationship to striving and self-concept in the achievement and interpersonal domains. *Psychology of Women Quarterly*, 6, 218-233.

Orlofsky, J. L., & Windle, M. T. (1978). Sex role orientation, behavioral adaptability, and personal adjustment. *Sex Roles: A Journal of Research*, 4, 801-811.

Orr, E., & Dinur, B. (1995). Social setting effects on gender differences in self-esteem: Kibbutz and urban adolescents. *Journal of Youth and Adolescence*, 24, 3-27.

Owen, C. L., Scherer, R. F., Sincoff, M. Z., & Cordano, M. (2003). Perceptions of women as managers in Chile and the United States. *Mid American Journal of Business*, 18, 43-50.

Padan, D. (1968). Inter-generational occupational mobility of women: Status mobility as a two-stage process of social change. In S. N. Eisenstadt, R. Bar-Yosef, R. Kahana, & I. Shelach (Eds.), *Social Strata in Israel*. Jerusalem: Academon Press. (Hebrew)

Padan-Eisenstark, D. D. (1973). Are Israeli women really equal? Trends and patterns of Israeli women's labor force participation: A comparative analysis. *Journal of Marriage and the Family*, 35, 538-545.

Palgi, M. (1994). Women in the changing Kibbutz economy. *Economic and Industrial Democracy*, 15, 55-73.

Parke, R. (1996). *Fatherhood*. Cambridge, MA: Harvard University Press.

Parker, S. K. (2000). From passive to proactive motivation: The importance of flexible role orientations and role breadth self-efficacy. *Applied Psychology: An International Review*, 49, 447-469.

Pazy, A. (1992). Sex-linked bias in promotion decisions: The role of candidate's career relevance and respondent's prior experience. *Psychology of Women Quarterly*, 16, 209-228.

Pazy, A., & Oron, I. (2001). Sex proportion and performance evaluation among high-ranking military officers. *Journal of Organizational Behavior*, 22, 689-702.

Pelham, B. W., Hetts, J. J., & Stratton, L. S. (2001).Underworked and overpaid: Elevated entitlement in men's self-pay. Why does more house-work lower women's wages? Testing hypotheses involving job effort and hours flexibility. *Journal of Experimental Social Psychology*, 37, 93-103.

Peres, Y., & Meivar, H. (1986). Self-presentation during courtship: A content analysis of classified advertisements in Israel. *Journal of Comparative Family Studies*, 17, 19-31.

Pessetta-Schubert, A. (1999). *Private sphere and public sphere: The case study of Jewish student mothers in Israel*. Unpublished Ph.D. dissertation, The Hebrew University of Jerusalem. (Hebrew).

Pfau-Effinger, B. (1999). The modernization of family and motherhood in Western Europe. In R. Crompton (Ed.), *Restructuring gender relations and employment*. Oxford: Oxford University Press.

Pines, A. M., Dahan-Kalev, H., & Ronen, S. (2001). The influence of feminist self-definition on the democratic attitudes of managers. *Social Behavior and Personality*, 29, 607-615.

Pitman, J. F., & Orthner, D. K. (1988). Gender differences in prediction of job commitment. *Journal of Social Behavior and Personality*, 3, 227-248.

Pleck, E. J., & Pleck, J. H. (1996). Fatherhood ideals in the United States: Historical dimensions. In M. E. Lamb (Ed.), *The Role of the Father in Child Development* (pp. 33-48). New York: Wiley.

Pleck, J. H. (1977). The work-family role system. *Social Problems*, 24, 417-427.

Pleck, J., & Masciadrelli, B. (2004). Paternal involvement by U. S. residential fathers: Levels, sources and consequences. In M. E. Lamb (Ed.), *The role of the father in child development* (4th ed.), (pp. 222–270). New York: Wiley.

Plesner, Y. (1994). *The political economy of Israel: From ideology to stagnation*. Albany: State University of New York Press.

Polachek, S. (1985). Occupational segregation: A defense of human capital predictions. Reply to England. *Journal of Human Resources*, 20, 437-440, 444

Poloma, M. M., & Pendleton, B. F. (1990). Religious domains and general well-being. *Social Indicators Research*, 22, 255-276.

Potuchek, J. L. (1992). Employed wives' orientations to bread-winning: A gender theory analysis. *Journal of Marriage and the Family*, 54, 548-558.

Powell, G. N. (1988) *Women and men in management*. Thousand Oaks, CA: Sage.

Powell, G. N., Butterfield, D. A., & Parent, J. D. (2002). Gender and managerial stereotypes: Have the times changed? *Journal of Management*, 28, 177-193.

Prince-Gibson, E., & Schwartz, S. H. (1998). Value Priorities and Gender. *Social Psychology Quarterly*, 61, 49-67.

Putnam, L. L., & Mumby, D. K. (1993). Organizations, emotion and the myth of rationality. Emotion in organizations. *In* Fineman, S. (Ed), *Emotion in organizations* (pp.138-167). New York: Sage

Rabin, C., & Lahav, T. (2001). Sephardi women in Israel: Identity, family and change. *Journal of Feminist Family Therapy*, 13, 33-46.

Ragins, B. R. (1999). Gender and mentoring relationships: A review and research agenda for the next decade. In G. N. Powell (Ed), *Handbook of gender and work* (pp. 347-370). Thousand Oaks, CA: Sage Publications.

Ragins, B. R. & Cotton, J. L. (1991). Easier said than done: Gender differences in perceived barriers to gaining a mentor. *Academy of Management Journal*, 34, 939-951.

Ragins, B. R., & Cotton, J. L. (1993). Gender and willingness to mentor in organizations. *Journal of Management*, 19, 97-111.

Ragins, B. R., & Cotton, J. L. (1999). Mentor functions and outcomes: A comparison of men and women in formal and informal mentoring relationships. *Journal of Applied Psychology*, 84, 529-550.

Ragins, B. R., & McFarlin, D. B. (1990). Perceptions of mentor roles in cross-gender mentoring relationships. *Journal of Vocational Behavior*, 37, 321-339.

Ramazanoglu, C. (1989). *Feminism and the contradictions of oppression*. London: Routledge

Rapoport, T., & El-Or, T. (1997). Cultures of womanhood in Israel: Social agencies and gender production. *Women's Studies International Forum*, 20, 5-6.

Rapoport, T., & Garb, Y. (1998). The experience of religious fortification: The coming of age of religious Zionist young women. *Gender and Education*, 10, 5-20.

Rediger, G. L. (1979). The feminine mystique and the ministry, *Christian Century*, July 11, p. 699. Retrieved on September 13, 2006, from *http://www.religion-online.org/showarticle.asp?title=1244*

Reece, H. (2006). From parental responsibility to parenting responsibility. In: M. Freeman (Ed.), *Law and sociology: current legal issues* (pp. 459-483). Oxford, MA: Oxford University Press.

Reich, M. H. (1985). Executive views from both sides of mentoring. *Personnel,* 62, 42-46.

Reinharz, S. (1984). Toward a model of female political action: The case of Manya Shohat, founder of the first Kibbutz. *Women's Studies International Forum,* 7, 275-287.

Remennick, L. I. (1999a). Women of the "Sandwich" generation and multiple roles: The case of Russian immigrants of the 1990s in Israel. *Sex Roles: A Journal of Research,* 40, 347-378.

Remennick, L. I. (1999b). 'Women with a Russian accent' in Israel: On the gender aspects of immigration. *European Journal of Women's Studies,* 6, 441-461.

Remennick, L. (2005a). Cross-cultural dating patterns on an Israeli campus: Why are Russian immigrant women more popular than men? *Journal of Social and Personal Relationships,* 22, 435-454.

Remennick, L. (2005b). Immigration, gender, and psychosocial adjustment: A study of 150 immigrant couples in Israel. *Sex Roles: A Journal of Research,* 53, 847-863.

Reskin, B. F. (1988). Bringing the men back in: Sex differentiation and the devaluation of women's work. *Gender and Society,* 2, 58-81.

Reynolds, J., & Aletraris, L. (2007). Work-Family conflict, children, and hour mismatches in Australia. *Journal of Family Issues.* 28, 749-772.

Richmond-Abbott, M. (1992). Women wage earners. In J. A. Kouraney, J. P. Sterba, & R. Tong (Eds.), *Feminist philosophies.* Englewood Cliffs, NJ: Prentice-Hall.

Ridgeway C. L. (1993). Gender, status, and the social psychology of expectations. In P. England (Ed.), *Theory on gender, feminism on theory.* New York: Aldine de Gruyter.

Riordan, J. (2005). *Breastfeeding and human lactation*. Sudbury, Mass.: Jones and Bartlett.

Ritzer, G. (1995). *The McDonaldization of society*. London: Pine Forge Press.

Ritzer, G. (Ed.). (2003). *The Blackwell companion to major contemporary social theorists*. New York: Blackwell Publishing.

Robbins, J., & Ben-Eliezer, U. (2000). New roles or 'new times'? Gender inequality and militarism in Israel's nation-in-arms. *Social Politics*, 7, 309-342.

Romanov, D., Tur-Sinai, A., & Eizman, G. (2008). *Overeducation, job mobility, and earnings mobility among holders of first degrees in Israel*. Working Paper Series #39. Jerusalem: The Council for Higher Education. (Hebrew). Retrieved on January 26, 2009, from *http://www.cbs.gov.il/www/publications/pw39.pdf*

Romem, P., & Anson, O. (2005). Israeli men in nursing: Social and personal motives. *Journal of Nursing Management*, 13, 173-178.

Roos, P. A. (1985). *Gender and work: A comparative analysis of industrial societies*. NY: State University of New York Press.

Rosen, R. (2000). *The world split open: How the modern women's movement changed America*. New York: Viking.

Rosenberg, J., & Gitana G., (1998). Riot Grrrl: Revolutions from within. *Signs*, 23, 809-841.

Rosenberg-Friedman, L. (2006). The complex identity of religious-Zionist women in pre-state Israel, 1921-1948. *Israel Studies*, 11, 83-107.

Rosenfeld, H., & Carmi, S. (1976). The privatization of public means, the state-made middle class and the realization of family value in Israel. In J. C. Persitiany (Ed.), *Kinship and modernization in the Mediterranean society*. The Center for Mediterranean Studies, American Field Staff, Italy.

Ross, C., Mirowsky, J., & Huber, J. (1983). Dividing work, sharing work, and in between: Marriage patterns and depression. *American Sociological Review*, 48, 809-823.

Rothausen, T. J. (1994). Job satisfaction and the parent worker: The role flexibility and rewards. *Journal of Vocational Behavior*, 44, 317-336.

Rothbard, N. P. (2001). Enriching or depleting? The dynamics of engagement in work. *Administrative Science Quarterly*, 46, 655-686.

Rotter, J. B. (1966). Generalized expectancies for internal vs. external control of reinforcement. *Psychological Monographs*, 80, 1-28.

Rowe, R., & Snizek, W. E. (1995). Gender differences in work values: Perpetuating the myth. *Work and Occupations*, 22, 215-229.

Rowe-Finkbeiner, K. (2004). *The F-word*. Avalon Publishing Group.

Roxburgh, S. (1996). Gender differences in work and well-being: Effects of exposure and vulnerability. *Journal of Health and Social Behavior*, 37, 265-277.

Roxburgh, S. (2006). I wish we had more time to spend together...: The distribution and predictors of perceived family time pressures among married men and women in the paid labor force. *Journal of Family Issues*, 27, 529-553.

Rozin, T. (2005). *What's feminism, anyway?* Tel Aviv, Israel: Zmora Bitan. (Hebrew).

Rubinstein, G. (1995). Right-wing authoritarianism, political affiliation, religiosity, and their relation to Psychological Androgyny. *Sex Roles: A Journal of Research*, 33, 569-586.

Ruble, T. L., Cohen, R., & Ruble, D. N. (1984). Sex stereotypes: Occupational barriers for women. *American Behavioral Scientist*, 27, 339-356.

Ruderman, M. N., Ohlcott, P. J., Panzer, K., & King, S. N. (2002). Benefits of multiple roles for managerial women. *Academy of Management Journal*, 45, 369-386.

Rutherford, S. (2001). Any difference? An analysis of gender and divisional management styles in a large airline. *Gender, Work and Organization*, 8, 326-345.

Safir, M. P., Flaisher-Kellner, S., & Rosenmann, A. (2005). When gender differences surpass cultural differences in personal satisfaction with body shape in Israeli college students. *Sex Roles: A Journal of Research*, 52, 369-378.

Safran, H. (2005). Alliance and denial: Lesbian protest in women in black. In C. Frankfort-Nachmias, & E. Shadmi (Eds.), *Sappho in the Holy Land* (pp. (191-209). Albany, NY: SUNY Press (SUNY series in Israeli studies).

Safran, H. (2006). *Don't want to be nice: the fight for the right to vote and the beginning of new feminism in Israel.* Haifa, Israel: Pardes. (Hebrew).

Samocha, S. (2003). Implication of the move toward peace on Israeli society. In M. Al-Haj, & U. Ben-Eliezer (Eds.), *In the Name of Security: Sociology of Peace and War in an Era of Change* (pp. 455-488). Haifa: Haifa University Press. (Hebrew).

Sands, R. G., & Roer-Strier, D. (2004a). Divided families: Impact of religious difference and geographic distance on intergenerational family continuity. *Family Relations*, 53, 102-110.

Sands, R. G., & Roer-Strier, D. (2004b). The contexts of religious intensification among American-Israeli women who have become Orthodox. *Social Work Forum*, 37, 63-84.

Sasson-Levy, O. (2003). Feminism and military gender practices: Israeli women soldiers in "masculine" roles. *Sociological Inquiry*, 73, 440-465.

Sasson-Levy, O., & Amram-Katz, S. (2007). Gender integration in Israeli officer training: Degendering and regendering the military. *Signs*, 33, 105-133.

Sasson-Levy, O., & Rapoport, T. (2003). Body, gender, and knowledge in protest movements: The Israeli case. *Gender and Society*, 17, 379-403.

Scandura, T. (1998). Dysfunctional mentoring relationships and outcomes. *Journal of Management*, 24, 449-467.

Schachter, S. (2005). Lesbians in the women's peace movement. In C. Frankfort-Nachmias, & E. Shadmi (Eds.), *Sappho in the Holy Land* (pp. 175-189). Albany, NY: SUNY Press (SUNY series in Israeli studies).

Schein, V. E. (1978). Sex role stereotyping, ability and performance: Prior research and new directions. *Personnel Psychology*, 31, 259-268.

Schein, V. E. (1994) Managerial sex typing: A persistent and pervasive barrier to women's opportunities. In M. Davidson, & R. Burke (Eds.), *Women in Management, Current Research Issues* (pp. 94–113). London: Routledge.

Schilt, K. (2003). A little too ironic: The appropriation and packaging of Riot Grrrl politics by mainstream female musicians. *Popular Music and Society*, 26, 5-16

Scott, R. D. (1956). Notes on the body image and schema. *Journal of Analytical Psychology*, 1, 145-160.

Sears W., Sears, M., & Pantley, E. (1995). *Discipline book: How to have a better-behaved child from birth to age ten*. Boston, MA: Little, Brown and Company.

Sears W., Sears, M., & Pantley, E. (2002). *The successful child: What parents can do to help their kids turn out well*. Boston, MA: Little, Brown and Company.

Segal-Engelchin, D., & Wozner, Y. (2005). Quality of life of single mothers by choice in Israel: A comparison to divorced mothers and married mothers. *Marriage and family review*, 37, 7-28.

Sekaquaptewa, D., & Thompson, M. (2003). Solo status, stereotype threat, and performance expectancies: Their effects on women's performance. *Journal of Experimental Social Psychology*, 39, 68-74.

Semyonov, M., & Scott, R. I. (1983). Industrial shifts, female employment and occupational differentiation: a dynamic model for American cities, 1960-1970. *Demography*, 20, 163-176.

Senecal, C., Vallerand, R. J., & Guay, F. (2001). Antecedents and outcomes of work-family conflict: Toward a motivational model. *Personality and Social Psychology Bulletin, 27,* 176-186.

Sered, S. (1997). Women and religious change in Israel: Rebellion or revolution. *Sociology of Religion, 58,* 1-24.

Sewell, W. F. (1992). A theory of Structure: Duality, Agency, and Transformation. *The American Journal of Sociology, 98,* 1-29.

Shadmi, E. (1993). Female police officers in Israel: Patterns of integration and discrimination. *Feminist Issues, 13,* 23-45.

Shadmi, E. (2000). Between resistance and compliance, feminism and nationalism: Women in Black in Israel. *Women's Studies International Forum, 23,* 23-34.

Shadmi, E. (2005). The construction of lesbianism as nonissue in Israel. In C. Frankfort-Nachmias, & E. Shadmi (Eds.), *Sappho in the Holy Land* (pp. 251-267). Albany, NY: SUNY Press (SUNY series in Israeli studies).

Shadmi, E. (2007). *Think woman: Women and feminism in a masculine society.* Mevaseret Zion: Tzivonim Publications.

Shafir, G., & Peled, Y. (Eds.). (2000). *The new Israel: Peacemaking and liberalization.* Boulder, CO: Westview Press.

Shainess, N. (1980). The working wife and mother: A 'new' woman? *American Journal of Psychotherapy, 34,* 374-387.

Shalom, H. (2005). The story of ClaF: The community of lesbian feminists. In C. Frankfort-Nachmias, & E. Shadmi (Eds.), *Sappho in the Holy Land* (pp. 39-64). Albany, NY: SUNY Press (SUNY series in Israeli studies).

Shapira Berman, O. (2004). Why do married mothers choose to do all house tasks? Re-examining feminist agenda and its implications for therapy. *Journal of Feminist Family Therapy, 16,* 51-70.

Shapira, R., Etzioni-Halevy, E., & Chopp-Tibou, S. (1978). Occupational choice among female academicians: The Israeli case. *Journal of Comparative Family Studies, 9,* 69-82.

Sharpe, M. J, Heppner, P. P, & Dixon, W. A. (1995). Gender role conflict, instrumentality, expressiveness, and well-being in adult men. *Sex Roles: A Journal of Research.* 33, 1-18.

Shaw, S., & Fairhurst, D. (2008). Engaging a new generation of graduates. *Education and Training*, 50, 366-378.

Shenhav, Y. A., & Haberfeld, Y. (1988). Scientists in organizations: Discrimination processes in an internal labor market. *The Sociological Quarterly*, 29, 451-462.

Shilo, M. (1996). The transformation of the role of women in the first *Aliyah*, 1882-1903. *Jewish Social Studies*, 2, 64-86.

Shiran, V. (2002). To decipher power, to create a new world. (Hebrew). Retrieved from *http://www.itu.org.il/Index.asp?ArticleID=1415and CategoryID=521andPage=1*

Shtarkshall, R. A. (1987). Motherhood as a dominant feature in the self-image of female adolescents of low socioeconomic status. *Adolescence*, 22, 565-570.

Sieber, S. D. (1974). Toward a theory of role accumulation. *American Sociological Review*, 39, 567-578.

Sikron, M. (1957). *The immigration to Israel: 1948-1953.* Jerusalem, Falk Center. (Hebrew).

Sikron, M. (2004). *Demography: The demography of Israel— characteristics and trends.* Carmel: Jerusalem (Hebrew).

Silver, H., & Goldscheider, F. (1994). Flexible work and house work: Work and family constraints in women's domestic labor. *Social Forces*, 72, 1103-1119.

Simpson, M. (2003, June 22). Metrosexual? That rings a bell.... *Independent on Sunday. Retrieved from http://www.marksimpson. com/pages/journalism/metrosexual_ios.html*

Singleton, A., & Maher, J. (2004). The "New Man" is in the house: Young men, social change, and housework. *Journal of Men's Studies*, 12, 227-240.

Skinner, E. A. (1996). A guide to constructs of control. *Journal of Personality and Social Psychology, 71*, 549-570.

Smith, S. C., Ellis, J. B., & Benson, T. A. (2001). Gender, gender roles, and attitudes toward violence: Are viewpoints changing? *Social Behavior and Personality, 29*, 43-47.

Snir, R., & Harpaz, I. (2005). Test-retest reliability of the relative work centrality measure. *Psychological Reports, 97*, 559-562.

Snoek, D. J. (1966). Role strain in diversified role sets. *American Journal of Sociology, 4*, 363-372.

Spade, J. Z. (1994). Wives' and husbands' perceptions of why women work. *Gender and Society, 8*, 170-188.

Spence, J. T., & Helmreich, R. L. (1978). *Masculinity and femininity: Their psychological dimensions, correlates and antecedents.* Austin: University of Texas Press.

Spenser, A., & Podmore, D. (Eds.). (1987). *In a man's world: Essays on women in male-dominated professions.* London: Tavistock.

Stafford, I. P. (1984). Relation of attitudes toward women's roles and occupational behavior to women's self esteem. *Journal of Counseling Psychology, 31*, 332-338.

Staines, G., Tavris, C., & Jayaratne, T. E. (1974). The queen bee syndrome. *Psychology Today, 7*, 55–60.

Stanton. E. C., Anthony, S. B., & Gage, M. J. (1889). *History of woman suffrage:* Vol. I. *1848-1861.* Rochester, NY: Charles Mann.

Stearns, P. N. (2003). *Anxious parents: A history of modern childrearing in America.* New York: New York University Press.

Steers, R., & Porter, L. (1991). *Motivation and work behavior.* New York: McGraw Hill.

Stier, H. (1996). Continuity and change in women's occupations following first childbirth. *Social Science Quarterly, 77*, 60-75.

Stier, H., & Lewin Epstein, N. (2000). Women's part-time employment and gender inequality in the family. *Journal of Family Issues, 21*, 390-410.

Stier, H., & Lewin Epstein, N. (2003). Time to work: A comparative analysis of preferences for working hours. *Work and Occupations*, 30, 302-326.

Still, L.V. (1994). Where to from here? Women in management: the cultural dilemma. *Women in Management Review*, 9, 3-10.

Storey A. E., Walsh, C. J., Quinton, R. L., & Wynne-Edwards, K. E. (2000). Hormonal correlates of paternal responsiveness in new and expectant fathers. *Evolution and Human Behavior*, 21, 79–95.

Strading, S. G., Crowe, G., & Touhy, A. P. (1993). Changes in self-concept during occupational socialization of new recruits to the police. *Journal of Community and Applied Social Psychology*, 3, 131-147.

Strum, P. (1989). Women and the politics of religion in Israel. *Human Rights Quarterly*, 11, 483-503.

Stryker, S., & Serpe, R. (1982). Commitment, identity salience and role behavior: Theory and research example. In W. Ickes, & E. S. Knowles (Eds.), *Personality, roles, and social behavior*. New York: Springer-Verlag.

Students of the World (2005). Countries of the world: Gross national product (GNP) per capita-2005 (Wealth levels around the world). Retrieved from *http://www.studentsoftheworld.info/infopays/rank/PNBH2.html*

Svirsky, G. (2004). Local coalitions, global partners: The women's peace movement in Israel and beyond. *Signs*, 29, 543-549.

Swift, C. F., Bond, M. A., & Serrano Garcia, I. (2000). Women's empowerment: A review of community psychology's first 25 years. In J. Rappaport, & E. Seidman (Eds), *Handbook of community psychology* (pp. 857-895). Dordrecht, Netherlands: Kluwer Academic Publishers.

Tamis-LeMonda, C. S., & Cabrera, N. (Eds.). (2002). *Handbook of father involvement: Multidisciplinary perspectives* (pp. 93–117). Mahwah, NJ: Erlbaum.

Tan, S. J. (2008). The myths and realities of maternal employment. In A. Marcus-Newhall, D. F. Halpern, & S. J. Tan (Eds.), *The changing realities of work and family* (pp. 9-24). New York: Wiley-Blackwell.

Taylor, C. (2004). *Modern social imaginaries.* Durham, NC: Duke University Press.

Thoits, P. A. (1987). Negotiating Roles. In F. J. Crosby (Ed.), *Spouse, parent, worker: On gender and multiple roles.* New Haven: Yale University Press.

Thompson, J. A., & Bunderson, J. S. (2001). Work-non-work conflict and the phenomenology of time: Beyond the balance metaphor. *Work and Occupations, 28,* 17-39.

Thompson, S. C., Sobolew-Shubin, A., Galbraith, M. E., Schwankovsky, L., & Cruzen, D. (1993). Maintaining perceptions of control: Finding perceived control in low-control circumstances. *Journal of Personality and Social Psychology, 64,* 293-304.

Thompson, W. (1983). *Appeal of one half the human race, women, against the pretensions of the other half, men, to retain them in political, and thence in civil and domestic slavery.* London: Virago.

Thomson, K. (1998). *Emotional capital: Capturing hearts and minds to create lasting business success.* Oxford: Capstone.

Tiedge, L. B., Wortman, C. B., Downey, G., Emmons, C., Biernat, M., & Lang E. (1990). Women with multiple roles: Role –compatibility perceptions, satisfaction, and mental health. *Journal of Marriage and the Family, 52,* 63-72.

Toch, H. (1991). *Police as problem solvers.* New York: Plenum Press.

Tomkiewicz, J., Frankel, R., Adeyemi-Bello, T., & Sagan, M. (2004). A comparative analysis of the attitudes toward women managers in the US and Poland. *Cross Cultural Management,* 11, 58-70.

Toren, N. (1988). Women at the top: Female full professors in higher education in Israel. *Higher Education,* 17, 525-544.

Toren, N. (2000). *Hurdles in the halls of science: The Israeli case.* Lanham, Lexington Books.

Toren, N. (2001). Women in academe: The Israeli case. *The International Journal of Sociology and Social Policy*, 21, 1-2.

Toren, N. (2003). Tradition and transition: Family change in Israel. *Gender Issues*, 21, 60-76.

Toren, N., & Moore, D. (1997). The academic hurdle race: A case study. *Higher Education*, 6, 1-17.

Truss, C., Goffee, R., & Jones, G. (1995). Segregated occupations and gender stereotyping: A study of secretarial work in Europe. *Human Relations*, 48, 1331-1354.

Twenge, J. M. (1999). Mapping gender: The multifactorial approach and the organization of gender-related attributes. *Psychology of Women Quarterly*, 23, 485-502.

UNDP (1999). *Human development report 1999*. New York: Oxford University Press.

UNDP (2008). *Human development report - a statistical update 2008*. Retrieved from *http://hdr.undp.org/en/statistics/*

Valentine, S. (1998). Self esteem and men's negative stereotypes of women who work. *Psychological Reports*, 83, 920-922.

Valentine, S. (1999). Locus of control as a dispositional determinant of men's traditional sex role attitudes. *Psychological Reports*, 85, 1041-1044.

Voydanoff, P., & Kelly, R. K. (1984). Determinants of work-related family problems among employed parents. *Journal of Marriage and the Family*, 46, 881-892

Waddington, P. A. J. (1994). Coercion and accommodation: Policing order after the Public Order Act. *The British Journal of Sociology*, 45, 367-386.

Wahl, A., & Holgersson, C. (2003). Male managers´ reactions to gender diversity activities in organizations. In M. Davidson, & S. Fielden (Eds.), *Individual diversity and psychology in organizations*. Chichester: Wiley.

Wajcman, J. (1998) *Managing like a man: Women and men in corporate management.* Cambridge: Polity Press.

Wajcman, J., & Martin, B. (2002). Narratives of identity in modern management: The corrosion of gender difference? *Sociology,* 36, 985-1002.

Walker, R. (1995). *To be real:Ttelling the truth and changing the face of feminism.* New York: Anchor/Random House.

Walstedt, J. J. (1977). The altruistic other orientation: An exploration of female powerlessness. *Psychology of Women Quarterly.* 2, 162-176.

Warner, J. (2005). *Perfect madness: Motherhood in the Age of Anxiety.* New York: Riverhead Books.

Waters, L. (2004). Protégé-mentor agreement about the provision of psychosocial support: The mentoring relationship, personality, and workload. *Journal of Vocational Behavior,* 65, 519-532.

Weinbaum, B. (2001). The radicalizing impact of children on mothers' activism: Insight from oral histories with some Jewish Israeli mothers, Summer 1999. *Journal of Feminist Family Therapy,* 13, 23-40.

Weiss, R. S. (1987). Men and their wives' work. In F. Crosby (Ed.), *Spouse, parent, worker: On gender and multiple roles.* New Haven, CT: Yale University Press.

Weiss, S., & Yishai, Y. (1980). Women's representation in Israeli political elites. *Jewish Social Studies,* 42, 165-176.

Weitzman, L J. (1984). Sex role socialization: A focus on women. In J. Freeman (Ed.), *Women: A feminist perspective.* Palo Alto: Mayfield.

West, C., & Fenstermaker, S. B. (1993). Power, inequality and the accomplishment of gender. In P. England (Ed.), *Theory on gender / Feminism on theory.* New York: Aldyne Gruyter.

West, C., & Zimmerman, D. H. (1987). Doing Gender. *Gender and Society,* 1, 125-151.

Westman, M., & Etzion, D. L. (2005). The crossover of work-family conflict from one spouse to the other. *Journal of Applied Social Psychology*, 35, 1936-1957.

Whitely, W., Dougherty, T. W., & Dreher, G. F. (1992). Correlates of career-oriented mentoring for early career managers and professionals. *Journal of Organizational Behavior*. 13, 141-154.

Whittier, N. (1995). *Feminist generations: The persistence of the radical women's movement.* Philadelphia. PA: Temple University Press.

Wiley, M. G. (1991). Gender, work and stress: The potential impact of role identity salience and commitment. *The Sociological Quarterly*, 32, 495-510.

Williams, C. L. (1995). *Still a man's world: Men who do women's work.* Berkeley, CA: University of California Press.

Williams, J. (2000). *Unbending gender: Why family and work conflict and what to do about it.* Oxford: Oxford University Press.

Wilson, O. E. (1975). *Sociobiology: The new synthesis.* Cambridge, MA: Harvard University Press.

Wilson, R. F. (2006). *Reconceiving the Family: Critique on the American law institute's principles of the law of family dissolution.* Cambridge, MA: Cambridge University Press.

Windle, J. (2000). *Mary Wollstonecraft Godwin, 1759-1797: A bibliography of the first and early editions.* New Castle, DE: Oak Knoll Press.

Wolf, J. B. (2007). Breast really best? Risk and total motherhood in the National Breastfeeding Awareness Campaign. *Journal of Health Politics, Policy and Law.* 32, 595-636

Wolf, W. C., & Rosenfeld, R. (1978). Sex structure of occupations and job mobility. *Social Forces*, 56, 823-845.

Wollstonecraft, M. (1995). A vindication of the rights of woman. In S. Tomaselli (Ed.), *A vindication of the rights of men and a vindication of the rights of woman* (pp. 65-294). Cambridge, UK: Cambridge University Press.

Women's Lobby. (2004). *Women in Israel—Data and information.* Jerusalem: The Women's Lobby. Retrieved from *http://www.iwn. org.il/SiteFiles/File/book2004.pdf.*

Woodhill, B. M., & Samuels, C. A. (2003). Positive and negative androgyny and their relationship with psychological health and well-being. *Sex-Roles: A Journal of Research,* 48, 555-565.

World Bank. (2000). *World development indicators 2000.* Washington, DC: World Bank.

World Health Organization. (2003a). *Global strategy for infant and young child feeding.* Retrieved on September 20, 2009, from *http://whqlibdoc.who.int/publications/2003/ 9241562218.pdf.*

World Health Organization. (2003b). *The world health report 2003: Shaping the future.* Retrieved from *http://www.who.int/whr/2003/ en/Annex1-en.pdf*

Wright, E. O., Baxter, J., & Birkelund, G. E. (1995). The gender gap in workplace authority in seven nations. *American Sociological Review,* 60, 407-435.

Wurtzel, E. (1999). *Bitch: In praise of difficult women.* Anchor Publishing.

Wuthrow R., & Lehrman, W. (1990). Religion: Inhibitor or facilitator of political involvement among women? In L. Tilly, & P. Gurin (Eds.), *Women, politics and change* (pp. 300-322). New York: Russell Sage.

Yadgar, Y. (2006). Gender, religion, and Feminism: The case of Jewish Israeli traditionalists. *Journal for the Scientific Study of Religion,* 45, 353-370.

Yaish, M., & Kraus, V. (2003). The consequences of economic restructuring for the gender earnings gap in Israel, 1972-1995. *Work, Employment and Society,* 17, 5-28.

Yanay, N., & Rapoport, T. (1997). Ritual impurity and religious discourse on women and nationality. *Women's Studies International Forum,* 20, 651-663.

Yankelovitch, D. (1985). *The world at work*. New York: Octagon Books, Inc.

Yoder, J. D. (1994). Looking beyond numbers: The effects of gender status, job prestige, and occupational gender typing on tokenism processes. *Social Psychology Quarterly*, 57, 150-159.

Yoder, J. D., & Sinnett, L. M. (1985). Is it all in the numbers? A case study of tokenism. *Psychology of Women Quarterly*, 9, 413-418.

Youssef, N. H., & Hartly, S. F. (1979). Demographic indicators of the status of women in various societies. In J. Lipman-Blumen, & J. Bernard (Eds.), *Sex roles and social policy: A complex social science equation* (pp. 83-112). Beverly Hills, CA: Sage Publications.

Yuval-Davis, N. (1980). The bearers of the collective: Women and religious legislation in Israel. *Feminist Review*, 4, 15-27.

Yuval-Davis, N. (1985). Front and rear: The sexual division of labor in the Israeli army. *Feminist Studies,* 11, 649-675.

Yuval-Davis, N. (1987). Woman/Nation/State: The demographic race and national reproduction in Israel. *Radical America*, 21, 37-59.

Zarhi, S. (1973). The public sector's contribution to economic growth in Israel. Review of public and co-operative economy in Israel. Annals of Public and Co-Operative Economy, 45, 56-79.

Zelditch, M. Jr. (1964a). Cross-cultural analyses of family structure In H. Christensen (Ed.), *Handbook of marriage and the family* (pp. 462-500). Rand McNally.

Zelditch, M. Jr. (1964b). Family, Marriage and Kinship. In R. E. L. Faris (Ed.), *Handbook of modern sociology* (pp. 680-733). Rand McNally.

Zemach, T., & Cohen, A.A. (1986). Perception of Gender Equality on Television and in Social Reality. Journal of Broadcasting and Electronic Media, 30, 427-444.

Zey, M. G. (1984). *The mentor connection*. Homewood, IL: Dow Jones-Irwin.

WEBSITES REFERENCED

Coalition of Women for Peace:

http://coalitionofwomen.org/

The New Man: Beyond the Macho Jerk and the New Age Wimp:

http://personallifemedia.com/podcasts/238-the-new-man

Fatherhood Institute: The UK's Fatherhood Think Tank:

http://www.fatherhoodinstitute.org

Haaretz Online:

http://www.haaretz.co.il/hasite/pages/ShArtPE.jhtml?itemNo=889 060andcontrassID=2andsubContrassID=6andsbSubContrassID=9 (Hebrew).

Religion-Online.org:

http://www.religion-online.org/showarticle.asp?title=1244/ newhodaot/hodaa_template.html?hodaa=200619074

Shatil: New Israel Fund:

http://www.shatil.org.il/data/tamar_herman_research.doc.

Women in Green: For Israel's Tomorrow:

http://www.womeningreen.org/

INDEX

www.ingramcontent.com/pod-product-compliance
Lightning Source LLC
Chambersburg PA
CBHW071732270326
41928CB00013B/2645